IRAQ

Christine Moss Helms

IRAQ

EASTERN FLANK OF
THE ARAB WORLD

THE BROOKINGS INSTITUTION
Washington, D.C.

Copyright © 1984 by
THE BROOKINGS INSTITUTION
1775 Massachusetts Avenue, N.W., Washington, D.C. 20036

Library of Congress Cataloging in Publication data:

Helms, Christine Moss.
Iraq, eastern flank of the Arab world.
Includes index.
1. Iraq—Politics and government. I. Title.
DS79.65.H45 1984   956.7'043   84-14934
ISBN 0-8157-3556-1
ISBN 0-8157-3555-3 (pbk.)

1 2 3 4 5 6 7 8 9

Foreword

THE concentration of oil resources in the Arabian Gulf and the political turmoil that affects the region have created major policy problems for Western countries over the past decade. Public understanding has been poorly prepared for these events. The countries of the region are not well known. Their history, their culture, and the character of their policy have been the preserve of a very few specialists, and have been little studied or discussed by government officials and voting publics forced to confront immediate issues of Western policy. Iraq in particular has not received the attention that its importance in the region warrants.

In this study Christine Moss Helms examines the fundamental determinants of Iraqi policy, influences that lie deep in the cultural history, recent political developments, and geographic configurations of the country. These influences will predictably endure and will shape Iraq's actions in response to immediate events.

Helms was fortunate to travel extensively in Iraq on two separate occasions and to interview a number of Iraqis who freely offered their time and hospitality. This study would not have been possible without their cooperation and interest. Only a few can be mentioned here; many others are identified in the text, while still others wish to remain anonymous. Four members of the Revolutionary Command Council of the Ba'th party, Saddam Husain, Taha Yasin Ramadhan, Tariq 'Aziz, and Naim Haddad, were responsible for granting the author access to the country and for providing important insights into their party and its control of Iraq. Nada Shawki al-Bakr served as a valued friend and guide during both trips. Two Iraqi ambassadors, Ismat Kittani and Riyadh al-Qaysi, offered useful suggestions. The Iraqi Interests Section in Washington, D.C., under the direction first of Zuhair al-Omar and then Nizar Hamdoon, provided essential support. Their staff—especially Muwaffiq al-'Ani, Kamal Issa, Ghannam al-Shibli, and Saad al-'Ani—facilitated

vii

preparations for the author's travel. Sahar Hamdoon, Nidal Issa, and Ahlam al-Shibli also extended their friendship to her.

The author wishes to thank Hanna Batatu, John Devlin, and Harold H. Saunders for their reviews of the manuscript. Among the many other persons who offered constructive counsel or assistance are Odeh Aburdene, Mumtaz Ahmad, Samir Anabtawi, Ijaz Azim, Amazia Baram, Hashim Behbehani, Joseph B. Berger, Richard K. Betts, Martin Binkin, Ursula Braun, William Campbell, John K. Cooley, Anthony Cordesman, William Eagleton, Murray Gart, Carney Gavin, Edmund Ghareeb, Stephen R. Grummon, Albert Hourani, Ibrahim Ibrahim, Kumait Jawdat, Namir Jawdat, Maxwell Orme Johnson, Majid Khadduri, Wilfrid Knapp, Gebran Majdalany, Cord Meyer, William Monroe, Max King Morris, Lucian Pugliaresi, William B. Quandt, Francis J. Ricciardone, John Rossant, Eric Rouleau, Kim Savit, Talcott Seelye, Talib Shabib, Tayyab Siddiqui, Dimitri Simes, James W. Spain, Wayne White, John C. Wilkinson, Stephen R. Woodall, and Joseph A. Yager. Others who have been especially supportive throughout this project are Margarett and Carl Helms, Alice and Mick Johnson, and Sandra Panem.

The author also thanks Nancy Brauer for providing administrative support; James F. Hitselberger and Steven M. Riskin for valuable research assistance; James D. Farrell for editing the manuscript; and Nancy A. Ameen and Alan G. Hoden for verifying its factual content. Antoinette G. Buena and Ann M. Ziegler were the project secretaries.

The book uses a consistent and simplified form of transliterating Arabic words, chosen for the general reader rather than for specialists. The transliteration may occasionally deviate from this form for one of two reasons. Some Arabic words have variant spellings, in which case the author followed available Arabic texts or colloquial preferences. Other Arabic words have become so common that standard English usage is maintained.

The research for this study was made possible by the Rockefeller Foundation and the U.S. Department of Energy. The views expressed are those of the author and should not be ascribed to any of the persons or institutions whose assistance has been acknowledged here or to the trustees, officers, or staff members of the Brookings Institution.

BRUCE K. MAC LAURY
President

June 1984
Washington, D.C.

Contents

FIGURES

*For Mabelle Kalmbach
and Thelma and James D. Haynes*

The Middle East

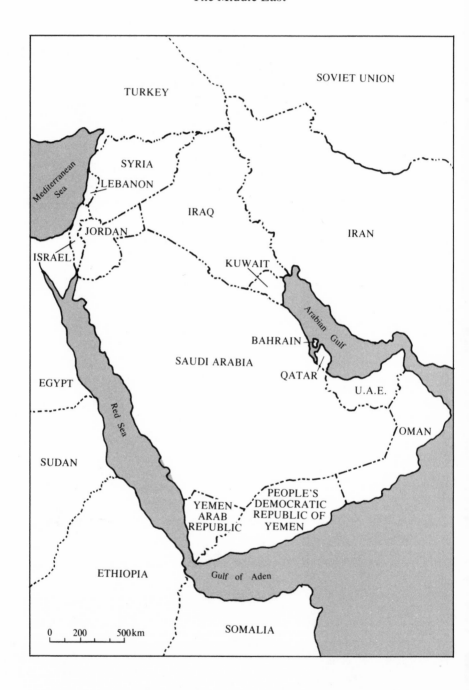

Iraq

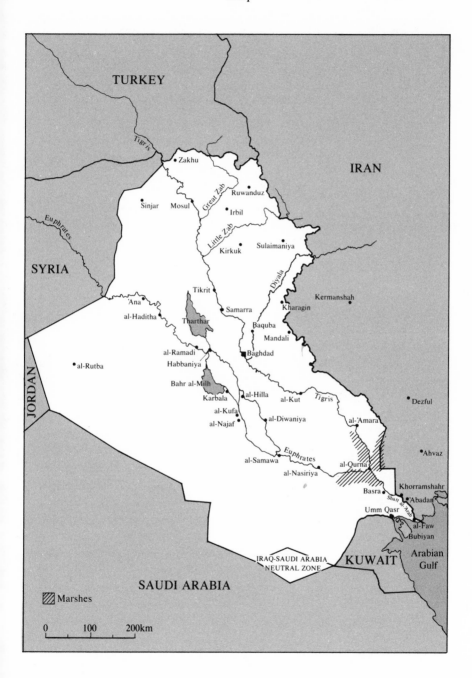

TURKEY

Tigris

Zakhu

Great Zab

Ruwanduz

Sinjar   Mosul

Irbil

Euphrates

Little Zab

IRAN

Kirkuk   Sulaimaniya

SYRIA

Diyala

Tikrit

'Ana

Kermanshah

al-Haditha   Tharthar   Samarra   Kharagin

Baquba

Mandali

al-Ramadi

JORDAN

al-Rutba   Habbaniya   Baghdad

Bahr al-Milh

al-Hilla   al-Kut   *Tigris*   Dezful

Karbala

al-Kufa   al-Diwaniya   al-'Amara   •Ahvaz

al-Najaf

al-Samawa   *Euphrates*   al-Qurna

al-Nasiriya   Khorramshahr

Basra   *Shatt al Arab*   •Abadan

Umm Qasr

al-Faw

Bubiyan

IRAQ-SAUDI ARABIA
NEUTRAL ZONE   KUWAIT   Arabian
Gulf

SAUDI ARABIA

Marshes

0   100   200km

Introduction

SINCE September 1980 the state of Iraq has been engaged in a war with the Islamic Republic of Iran, the course and outcome of which will affect the energy economy of the West and the prospects for political stability in the Arabian Gulf. Expansion of the war could place in jeopardy the world's largest known oil reserves, those of Saudi Arabia, and the oilfields of Iraq itself. Of immediate concern is the possibility that an escalation of hostilities between Iraq and Iran might lead other Arab Gulf states to intervene militarily and test the United States' commitment to keep the Strait of Hormuz open to world commerce. Every evidence suggests that the U.S. government would take the steps necessary to fulfill that commitment. Although less dramatic, this war will have a subtle but equally important impact on the content of political discussion in the Middle East generally and on its relations with the Western world.

In a situation of such import to Western policymakers, it is ironic that Iraq, a key player in the drama unfolding in the Gulf, receded from the attention of senior officials in Washington after the overthrow of the last openly pro-Western government in Baghdad in 1958. Diplomatic relations were formally broken nine years later, further restricting first-hand knowledge of Iraq and of the successive regimes that have governed it. If nothing else, the war and the stakes it involves have brought home the need to enlarge our understanding of Iraq, of its people, and of the concerns that motivate its leaders.

As in other Middle Eastern countries, the Iraqi leaders find themselves both motivated and constrained by popular aspirations. Those aspirations are shaped by a history of foreign intervention in domestic affairs; by traditions that are, in the main, Arab and Islamic; by evolving and sometimes contradictory perceptions of nationalism; by expectations of rising living standards; by tensions among ethnic, religious, and linguistic

1

groups; by the evolution of competing political philosophies; by increasingly educated and articulate populations; and by perceptions of Western biases against Arabs and Islam.

The decisions that the governments of Iraq and other Middle Eastern states must make in the next two decades are made more difficult by the pressures they labor under. Having emerged from a colonial heritage to independence within this century, some only within the decade of the 1970s, these countries face enormous tasks of internal political consolidation and socioeconomic development. The fact that in some states more than half the people are under the age of twenty-five, and that they pursue with increasing determination their right to participate in the political life of their countries, adds to the burden on governments. Such pressures cannot but influence the atmosphere in which these governments determine their priorities and choose among alternatives in domestic and foreign policy.

The following study, which some may find unconventional, explores the forces that influence policy formulation in Iraq. The selection of factors that are pertinent to such an analysis is obviously subjective and limited by time and the availability of resources. Certain issues are not treated fully or have been omitted altogether. In some cases, information was either impossible to obtain or was suspect. Moreover, rather than selecting issues of particular importance to other countries, the study seeks to evoke the perspective from which the Iraqi government itself views its problems and chooses its priorities. Iraqi relations with the United States and the Soviet Union, for example, are not examined in great detail but are discussed within the broader context of Iraqi interests.

The study is in three parts, the first of which explores factors that have shaped Iraq's evolution into the present Iraqi state. The subject is neither remote nor academic, for much of current Iraqi political behavior is conditioned not only by the country's political history but also by its geography, climate, and the availability of water. These factors have also influenced patterns of human settlement, the use of resources, including oil, and the emergence of diverse regional economies within the Iraqi state. Nor is it surprising that in a country as old as Iraq, whose antecedents reach back some four thousand years, the same factors have given rise to problems that have recurred throughout Iraqi history and exert a powerful influence on Iraqi domestic and foreign policy today. These themes will continue to recur and bedevil future Iraqi governments, whatever their base of support within the country or the means by which they justify their authority.

A new source of trouble arose when the present boundaries of Iraq were drawn in the twentieth century, primarily in response to European political and economic interests and with little regard for demographic patterns. The legacy has been continual tension between the Iraqi state, representing the central authority governing within defined boundaries, and the Iraqi nation, consisting of a number of smaller autonomous social groups. So pervasive is the tension between state and nation that it affects socioeconomic development, internal political consolidation, the legitimacy of the central government, and relations with neighboring countries. Those who seek an explanation for the war with Iran will find the beginning of it here.

Part 2 discusses the Arab Ba'th Socialist party, which has dominated the political life of Iraq since 1968. Let it be said at the outset that the Ba'th party is highly controversial, both within and outside Iraq. Yet, regardless of Western conceptions of this party, its history reflects the evolution and perhaps the maturation of political forces that have gathered momentum in the Middle East during the latter part of the twentieth century. The purpose of this study is neither to condemn nor to praise the party and its current leader, President Saddam Husain, but rather to explain wherever possible why they have adopted the positions and taken the actions that have characterized their tenure of power.

Although the Iraqi Ba'thists confront challenges similar to those faced by earlier Iraqi governments, they have applied their own view of the world in attempting to solve them, and in doing so have departed from the highly formalized ideology developed by the original Ba'thists. Their actions bespeak a pragmatism not bound by ideology. Far from being monolithic, the Iraqi Ba'th and its leaders have shown resilience in meeting the challenge both of domestic affairs and of the Iran-Iraq war. The return of peace, however, will not dispel critical domestic problems or necessarily confer upon the Ba'thist government two rewards that have eluded all Iraqi governments: acceptance of legitimacy by the population as a whole and good relations with neighboring countries.

The war between Iraq and Iran, the most costly and dangerous conflict that has occurred among third world countries, is the subject of part 3. This is neither a chronological account nor a military assessment of the war, but rather an analysis of the sources of conflict and of the decisions the Ba'thist government has made in the light of its presumed objectives and its assumptions about Iranian domestic affairs.

As the evidence suggests, and as Iraqis themselves maintain, it is not simply "a war over borders." While Iraqi claims concerning the Shatt al-'Arab waterway were a prominent grievance, the deeper cause of the war was a perceived threat to the Iraqi Ba'thists and to the Iraqi state arising from revolutionary Iran. On an ideological level, the opposing positions have been expressed in the extreme brand of Islamic conservatism espoused by Ayatullah Khomeini of Iran and in the Arab nationalism of the Ba'thists. The two are essentially irreconcilable, for the Iranian doctrine recognizes no political or geographic bounds to expansion of the revolution, and the Ba'thists reject the domination of religious elements in the administration of the state. In going to war, the Ba'thists sought to discredit or encourage the overthrow of the Islamic revolutionaries in Iran and thus lessen the threat. A closely related objective was to deliver a blow sufficient to dissuade Iran from inciting dissidence among Iraqi social groups, notably the large Shi'i population, among whom there are many of Persian descent.

Whatever their merits, the attainment of these objectives depended upon the accuracy of Iraqi assumptions about Iran's ability to conduct a war and the motivations of the Iranian leadership. The Ba'thist government expected a short war, but it miscalculated. It is now enmeshed in a war of attrition from which it has found no acceptable exit.

Unless the war ends in catastrophe for Iraq, the country will remain an important actor in the Middle East and could be of growing significance not only to the region but also to the United States, Western Europe, and Japan. The concluding chapter points out that the size of Iraq's oil reserves, its potential for diversifying its oil-based economy because of resources such as water, and its geographic and historical position should assure its influence within the regional and world economies. As Iraq's fluctuating relations with neighboring countries and with the superpowers have made clear, however, the Ba'thist government is acutely sensitive to the vulnerabilities arising from Iraq's pluralistic society and from its exposed position on the eastern flank of the Arab world. Although the West can improve its relations with Baghdad—by developing a common interest in maintaining the territorial integrity of nations and by abjuring interference in their domestic affairs, among other things—it is unlikely that Iraq in the near or long term will choose to open itself toward the West except within the framework of nonalignment.

PART ONE

The Iraqi Nation
versus the Iraqi State

CHAPTER ONE

Land and Peoples

POLITICAL behavior in Iraq, like that in any other country, is shaped by geography, by the availability of natural resources, and by human adaptation to the environment. In Iraq these factors have influenced the interaction between rural and urban society, the ability of a central government to extend its control, and the territorial aspirations of ruling elites relative to regional political forces and the strategic position of the state.

These factors have also produced a number of themes or conditions that have recurred throughout Iraqi history. Not only do they continue to influence domestic Iraqi politics, but Iraqis themselves view major foreign policy issues—such as the Iran-Iraq conflict, regional alliance patterns, and the vulnerability of their resources—in terms of the state's unique geographic and historical setting. While this study makes no attempt to be comprehensive, six themes that are pertinent to Iraqi politics can be usefully summarized.

—Modern Iraq, like its ancient counterparts, has had to develop extensive, complicated networks of trade with Europe and North Africa and through the Arabian Gulf to India in order to obtain raw materials. Iraq lacks, for example, the basic resources of stone, metallic ore, and timber. Great stone cities of the kind found at ancient and modern sites in Syria, Lebanon, and Jordan are absent in most parts of Iraq, where clay and baked brick have been the primary building materials. A striking sight in southern Iraq today is the hundreds of enormous brick kilns that rise out of the desert. Except in the mountainous northeastern region of Iraq, the absence of stone has hindered the development of roads and is one reason why many parts of southern Iraq, except for areas near a major city such as Basra, have not been easily accessible until recently.

—Geography and the availability of water have exerted powerful

7

influences on social structure, economic organization, and political jurisdiction in Iraq as in other Middle Eastern states. In the particular case of Iraq, the unique characteristics of the Tigris and Euphrates rivers set fundamental conditions that have affected patterns of settlement and communication, giving rise to distinctive regional economies within the state.

—The regional economies reflect cultural and ethnic divisions that persist despite the economic transformation of Iraq by the oil industry since the early 1950s.

—Since the second millennium B.C., leaders in Mesopotamia have shared a common aspiration—the union of the northern and southern sectors of the Tigris-Euphrates basin that meet in a zone of transition north of Baghdad, and political integration across this regional divide. The success and failure of these attempts comprise the history of ancient Iraq and are a focal point in modern Iraqi politics.

—The territory included within the present state of Iraq historically has been a frontier in the sense that Mesopotamia's unique geographic features and location have attracted a succession of invaders. The invading forces have contributed to the cultural diversity now found in Iraq and, as some Iraqis themselves have argued, shaped the regional perspective shared by many Iraqis. External influence is heightened by Iraq's position on the eastern flank of the Arab world adjoining two large non-Arab regions, the modern states of Iran and Turkey, with whom Iraq shares related population groups. Geographic propinquity has led over the years to a sense of vulnerability. Iraqi President Saddam Husain, for example, stated in a speech that obviously was intended to unify Iraqis in the early stages of the Iran-Iraq war that "Turkey once imposed on us the Turkish language and culture. . . . They used to take turns on Iraq. Turkey goes and Iran comes; Iran goes and Turkey comes. All this under the guise of Islam. Enough. . . . We are Iraqis and are part of the Arab homeland and the Arab nation. Iraq belongs to us."[1] The same sense of vulnerability has led Iraqi governments to take both defensive and offensive measures against neighboring countries.

—Finally, the creation of the modern Iraqi nation-state, whose borders remained undefined until 1926, has only intensified the interactions among geography, history, and politics. That the state structure was

1. Foreign Broadcast Information Service, *Daily Report: Middle East and Africa,* November 5, 1980, p. E4. (Hereafter FBIS, *Daily Report: MEA.*)

imposed by foreign powers after World War I has increased the difficulty of consolidating effective political control by Iraqi leaders and of establishing the legitimacy of a central government. There is continuing tension between the state as a political authority, exercising control within a prescribed territorial unit, and the nation, composed of smaller autonomous and competing social units. Unlike Egypt, for example, which has had a national identity for centuries, the Iraqi nation is an entity that is still evolving. As Faisal, the first Hashimite king of Iraq, remarked in the early 1930s, "I say in my heart full of sadness that there is not yet in Iraq an Iraqi people."[2]

The following discussion explores the influence of these factors on the origins of twentieth century Iraq and on the government's perceptions of Iraq's current strategic interests. It focuses on the most sensitive internal priorities of any Iraqi government, whatever its ideology or base of political support, as it seeks continuity and stability both internally and in its foreign relations. Although the Arab Ba'th Socialist party has had a pervasive influence on Iraq's domestic and foreign policy throughout the 1970s and into the 1980s, even this party's doctrine and membership have been responsive to the above-mentioned factors and to the recurrent problems they have produced.

Land Use and Patterns of Settlement

Although the introduction of twentieth century technology and the exploitation of oil reserves have altered priorities in the use and allocation of Iraq's wealth, geography and the accessibility of water still exert major influences on political and economic decisions in Iraq. They have led to the development of different regional economies and distinct cultural and ethnic divisions within the country. It is important to understand these fundamental conditions because they are intimately related to the domestic and foreign policy decisions of recent Iraqi governments, even if their solutions to specific problems have diverged.

Unlike oil, water is a renewable resource except when it exists as fossil water in underground aquifers. Its scarcity in the Middle East, heightened by urbanization and industrialization in the twentieth cen-

2. Edmund Ghareeb, *The Kurdish Question in Iraq* (Syracuse University Press, 1981), p. 2.

tury, has made it a commodity as highly valued as oil. Lack of rainfall precludes intensive agriculture or heavy industry in most Middle Eastern countries, and groundwater supplies, such as fossil water in central Arabia, are being rapidly depleted. Rivers are the only dependable and renewable source of water in this arid region. Iraq and Egypt are thereby distinguished from other countries in the Middle East.

The Tigris and Euphrates rivers in Iraq provide water for irrigation and land reclamation as well as for hydroelectric power, transportation, and communication. Before oil revenues began to play a significant role in Iraq's economy in the early 1950s, the country relied primarily on agriculture and livestock raising, which in turn depended on the effective use of water and grazing land. The fact that Iraq's agricultural potential is estimated to be greater than that of any other country in the Middle East, excluding perhaps that of Sudan, is particularly relevant to Iraq in light of its present dependence on oil. The additional fact that the oil industry in Iraq can employ only an extremely small percentage of the total population ensures that agricultural productivity will continue to be of central concern to future Iraqi governments.

Were it not for the two rivers, the whole of southern Iraq would be an extension of the great southern and western desert, which annually receives only 100 to 150 millimeters (mm) of precipitation (figure 1-1), about the same amount as Las Vegas, Nevada, which receives almost 100mm of annual precipitation, and Bakersfield, California, which receives approximately 160mm. Of Iraq's 44 million hectares (or 438,446 square kilometers), only about 3.2 million hectares, approximately 7.3 percent of the total land area, are suitable for rainfed agriculture. This land is concentrated in the extreme northeastern region, where rainfall nevertheless is nonexistent in summer and early fall. Another 4 million hectares, approximately 9.1 percent of the total, can be cultivated, but only because of a complex system of canals, reservoirs, and sluice gates linked to the rivers.[3] In short, more than 50 percent of Iraqi land under cultivation must be irrigated.

The use of water from Iraq's rivers entails difficulties that have imposed heavy burdens on government authorities. Unlike the Nile in Egypt, where the annual flood and the growing season correspond, the

3. W. B. Fisher, whose book *The Middle East: A Physical, Social and Regional Geography* (London: Methuen, 1978) provides one of the best geographic studies of the region, estimates even more striking figures (p. 210). He states that only 12 percent of Iraq's total land area can be cultivated and of that 77.6 percent must be irrigated.

Figure 1-1. *Water and Urban Settlement*

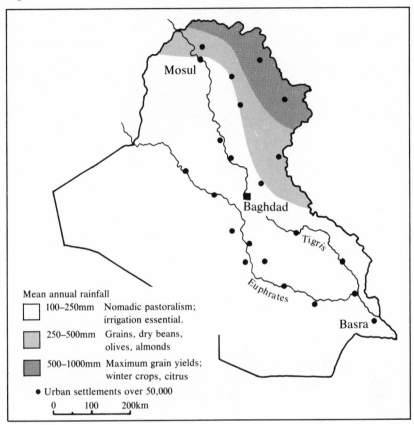

Mosul

Baghdad

Tigris

Euphrates

Mean annual rainfall

☐ 100–250mm   Nomadic pastoralism;
                        irrigation essential.
▨ 250–500mm   Grains, dry beans,
                        olives, almonds
■ 500–1000mm Maximum grain yields;
                        winter crops, citrus

• Urban settlements over 50,000

0   100   200km

Basra

Tigris and Euphrates rivers flood between April and June, too late for winter crops and too early for those of summer. Gains in agriculture must therefore be achieved through irrigation, which has come under increasing control of the central government since the creation of the Iraqi state. Irrigation requires not only a large agricultural labor force— some 30 to 40 percent of the present population[4]—but also the cooperation of many demographic groups having particularistic associations of

4. Recent census figures have not been released by the Iraqi government, although Kadhim A. Al-Eyd, *Oil Revenues and Accelerated Growth: Absorptive Capacity in Iraq* (Praeger, 1979), p. 30, states that 55.7 percent of the population was engaged in the agricultural sector in 1973. During interviews in June 1981 I was given current estimates of 30 to 35 percent and 40 percent employed in agriculture by the Ministry of Irrigation and the Ministry of Planning, respectively.

region, tribe, ethnicity, and religion. Moreover, rainfall and temperature differences between southern and northern Iraq give rise to three distinct growing seasons, extending from December to April in the south, April to July in the middle of the country, and July to the end of November or the beginning of December in the north.[5] One measure of the success of a central government is its ability to coordinate efforts to collect, store, and redistribute water in and among these disparate zones.

Another problem for the government is that salinization of the soil, resulting from the transpiration of plants, a high evaporation rate,[6] inadequate drainage, and a high water table, has rendered many fields sterile. From Tikrit toward the north, the quality of water after absorption by the soil is good. South of Tikrit, higher concentrations of salt present in the soil are dissolved by water and carried in solution to the wells. This factor, coupled with proximity to the sea, has restricted use of the southern wells primarily to animal husbandry. Salinity has also been a major determinant of the types of crops cultivated and their quality and yield. Barley and dates, both exceedingly tolerant of salinity, are two of the most widely cultivated crops in Iraq. Exports of Iraqi dates in fact account for 80 percent of the world supply.[7] Without attention by the

5. Interview with Minister of Agriculture Amir Mehdi Salih, June 24, 1981. More detailed information about the geographic characteristics, resource utilization, and patterns of settlement in Iraq can be obtained from a number of sources, including the following texts and their bibliographies: Marion Clawson, Hans H. Landsberg, and Lyle T. Alexander, *The Agricultural Potential of the Middle East* (American Elsevier, 1971); Georges Roux, *Ancient Iraq* (Penguin, 1980); Fisher, *The Middle East;* Christian E. Gischler, *Water Resources in the Arab Middle East and North Africa* (Cambridge, England: Middle East and North African Studies Press, 1979); Robert A. Fernea, *Shaykh and Effendi: Changing Patterns of Authority among the El Shabana of Southern Iraq* (Harvard University Press, 1970); Central Intelligence Agency, *Atlas: Issues in the Middle East* (Government Printing Office, 1973); Fahim I. Qubain, *The Reconstruction of Iraq: 1950–1957* (London: Atlantic Books, 1958); and Wilfred Thesiger, *The Marsh Arabs* (Dutton, 1964).

6. Both the Tigris and the Euphrates rivers, particularly the latter as it flows across the western Iraqi plains, are subject to a high evaporation rate, almost two meters from a free water surface annually, which is approximately the same evaporation rate as that in Death Valley, California. U.S. Department of Commerce, *Weather Atlas of the United States* (Dept. of Commerce, 1968), p. 186.

7. That the date palm has adapted well to the Iraqi environment is evident in that there are an estimated 20 million date palms in Iraq, 60 percent of which are concentrated in Basra. Of the more than 300 varieties of date palm, however, reportedly only 10 are of economic value. In many areas, the palm is used primarily to protect citrus crops, including lemon, orange, sour orange, mandarin, and pumellos (sindi), from Iraq's harsh sun. Although many families in southern Iraq depend on date agriculture, the skill required to make it profitable has discouraged young Iraqis from engaging in this

central government and the allocation of significant financial resources, Iraqi agriculture can only deteriorate.

The International Bank for Reconstruction and Development reported in 1952 that some 20 to 30 percent of cultivated land in Iraq had been abandoned because of soil salinization and that the productivity of land remaining under cultivation had dropped 20 to 50 percent in the two decades prior to its report.[8] Although a number of agricultural and irrigation projects were begun in the 1950s, there has been a renewed emphasis since 1973 on increasing Iraq's agricultural productivity through land reclamation. The minister of irrigation, 'Abd al-Wahhab Mahmud, said in an interview on June 29, 1981, that under the present Ba'th government this work began in earnest after 1975. Since then, 600,000 donums (approximately 150,000 hectares) have been reclaimed, and it is hoped that by 1985 a total area of 2.5 million donums (600,000 hectares) will be completed. The amount of gypsum in the soil does not exceed 8 percent, which works to Iraq's advantage in developing its agricultural potential. By contrast, Egypt lacks gypsum in some areas, resulting in hardening of the soil after leaching, and Syria has concentrations of more than 20 percent, causing problems of water retention.

A third major obstacle to efficient use of water in Iraq is that the rivers are subject to large and rapid fluctuations. Surface runoff from the northern border area adjoining Iran can cause daily fluctuations in the water level of the Tigris of as much as 3.6 meters during spring. Iraqi authorities thus confront the ever-recurring problem of storing water during the maximum seasonal flow for use during periods of minimum flow. These fluctuations, coupled with the large volume and swift current of the Tigris, have led to devastating floods, particularly during the high water levels of spring, when the average flood peak discharge of 3,200 cubic meters a second (measured at Samarra) may increase fourfold. Until the completion of the first stage of the Wadi Tharthar project in 1956 and other flood control facilities during the next decade, some residents of Baghdad were annually forced to leave their homes to avoid inundation during the rainy season.

The terrain through which the Tigris and Euphrates waters flow also

---

livelihood, and the future of some groves remains in doubt. Even before the Iran-Iraq war, labor shortages discouraged the development of date plantations, most of which are privately owned.

8. International Bank for Reconstruction and Development, *The Economic Development of Iraq* (Johns Hopkins Press, 1952), p. 17.

Figure 1-2. *Southern Iraq and Its Geographic Commonalities
with Khuzistan (Arabistan), Iran*

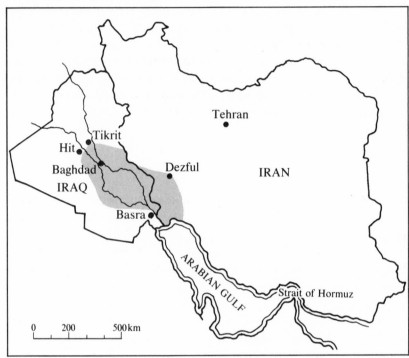

affects their use. Both rivers pass through two distinct regions—the
mountains of the north and the broad alluvial plains of the south—which
are separated by a zone of transition running roughly northeast from Hit
through Tikrit, north of Baghdad (figure 1-2).

In the region north of this transitional zone, the Tigris and Euphrates
meander in their own incised and distinct basins, separated by as much
as 300 kilometers at the widest point. The gradient of both rivers is
extremely steep. The Euphrates drops 240 meters between Jerablus (on
the Syrian-Turkish border) and Ramadi; the Tigris 300 meters from the
northern border of Iraq to Baghdad. This results in a swift current that
not only makes upstream navigation difficult,[9] but also has cut the

9. Several kinds of river craft have evolved in Iraq over the centuries—*mahaila,
ballam, danak, quffa, kalak, mashhuf*—each of which reflects in its design the adaptation
of man to the geographic complexities of the Iraqi environment. The *kalak*, for example,
was uniquely suited to the northern stretches of the Tigris. It was a buoyant raft
constructed from skins and timber, traveling the Tigris south from Mosul to Baghdad,

riverbeds so deep that in certain areas "hanging cliffs" as much as ninety meters high are a feature on their upper courses. The cliffs create obvious difficulties in that the water must be lifted in order to be used; but since the northern courses of these rivers have remained relatively unchanged, urban centers have not had to be relocated through time. Ancient cities such as Mari and Ninevah remain in the same proximity to the river, while other ancient sites have remained continually inhabited until now. Ancient Karkemish, for example, is the modern Jerablus (Syria), Haleb or Iamhad is Aleppo (Syria), and Ashur is Qal'at Shirqat (Iraq). Ninevah (Iraq) lies just across the river from Mosul, its modern counterpart.

Northern Iraq itself can be divided into two discernible regions. The first, lying north and east of the Tigris, can be further divided into an area known as Assyria, lying adjacent to the river, and in the extreme northeastern part of the country, an area sometimes referred to as Iraqi Kurdistan. Geologically, Assyria and Kurdistan are a series of parallel folds aligned southeast to northwest, which gradually change from rolling plains fronting the Tigris to increasingly steep ridges that culminate in the rugged Zagros mountain range (altitude 2,400 to 3,450 meters) on the Iraq-Iran frontier. Four large tributaries of the Tigris dissect these ridges. A favorable climate and annual rainfall ranging from 300mm to 1,000mm provide a variety of agricultural opportunities, from fruit and vegetable farming to the cultivation of grains. Nomadic pastoralism is practiced. Small oak and pine forests are also present, although many areas are denuded by overgrazing. This region has always been a highly contested frontier and one that the urban dwellers along the Tigris and Euphrates have viewed with suspicion. The rugged nature of the mountains makes them an almost impenetrable fortress, as was seen during the costly and bloody campaigns between the Iraqi government and Kurdish nationalists that officially ended in 1975. Between 40 and 50 percent of Iraq's oil production during the late 1970s, and perhaps more than 80 percent since the Iran-Iraq war began, was located in the more gently sloping terrain on the southwestern edge of Iraqi Kurdistan. The region therefore remains of vital concern to Baghdad, particularly because Kurdish nationalists have continued sporadic guerrilla activities and are in frequent contact with Iranian Kurds.

---

sometimes as far as al-'Amara. It carried from 4.5 to 28 metric tons of goods and upon reaching its destination was broken up, the wood being sold for fuel and the skins transported by land to Mosul for the creation of a new *kalak*. A complete discussion of these craft and their adaptation to specific geographic conditions in Iraq is found in Touvia Ashkenazi, "Native River Boats in 'Iraq," *Ethos,* nos. 1–2 (1957), pp. 50–56.

The second discernible region in the north is called Jazira, or "island," by the Arabs. It is a low plateau lying between the Tigris and the Euphrates where numerous small streams join to form the affluents of the Balikh and Khabur rivers. Much of this region is grazed by nomadic pastoralists, but in northwestern Iraq around Jabal Sinjar, at a slightly higher elevation of 900 meters, increased rainfall supports predominantly agricultural communities such as those of the Yazidis.[10]

South of the transitional zone is a region of vastly different character. The steep gradient of the Tigris and Euphrates north of Baghdad begins to level out, dropping only 4 centimeters per kilometer during the last 300 kilometers of the Euphrates and less than 8 centimeters per kilometer of the Tigris.[11] This southern region is primarily an extensive alluvial plain through which the two great rivers and their branches meander.[12] Spring floods regularly inundate the plain, depositing sediment and then retreating to leave extensive areas of marshland, isolated lakes, and braided channels. Archaeological sites such as Nippur and Ur, originally situated near the main river channels, are now stranded, illustrating the shifting nature of these rivers in their southern reaches. Baghdad exemplifies this phenomenon. Preceded by Babylon and Ctesiphon, it is the third major city that has dominated trade and exerted political control in that strategic position. Numerous other sites undoubtedly have been destroyed or submerged beneath silt deposits in the south. Even today, much community effort is required to prevent a buildup of silt in the irrigation channels and to protect against flooding. In contrast to northern Iraq, this region is accessible to central government control except when roads wash out during the wettest season.

The Shatt al-'Arab, formed by the confluence of the Tigris and Euphrates rivers, begins just below al-Qurna. During spring the region between Basra, al-'Amara, and al-Nasiriya frequently becomes an

10. The Yazidis are a tribe believed to be related to the Kurds. In the area around Jabal Sinjar they speak both Arabic and Kurdish, and some wear Arabic dress. They are distinguished by their devout adherence to their own religious beliefs, which over the centuries have synthesized elements of many other religions. They are socially exclusive and do not permit intermarriage with neighboring communities, even Kurdish tribes.

11. Fisher, *Middle East,* p. 369.

12. Although a number of meanings have been proposed for the word Iraq (*al-'Iraq* in Arabic), none is thoroughly convincing. Undoubtedly its origin is ancient. Some have said that it is borrowed from a lost language and means "a sunny land"; others that it means "coastland" or "the country of dark color," the latter perhaps referring to the fertility of Iraq's agricultural land. It also has been said to mean "a flat (or plains) area," an appropriate description of southern Iraq.

inhospitable salt marsh surrounded by date palms and, farther out, reeds. Rice is an important crop. Wilfred Thesiger, a British explorer, has described the life of the people who inhabit this area, al-Ahwar, in his book *The Marsh Arabs* (see note 5). Far removed from the political control of Baghdad and living in a very different environment, these people inhabit intricately structured homes built of reed bundles, eat rice and fish, and keep water buffalo, which provide milk and dung for use as fuel. Because most of their dwellings are surrounded by water, they travel by boat; in the wettest season the area is virtually untraveled except by its own inhabitants. Outsiders, even Iraqis, need a guide to navigate its complex waterways and to provide protection from its numerous hazards, such as wild boar and poisonous snakes. Even today the region's inaccessibility and unique geographic features have precluded the extension of electricity into its interior, though other remote areas of Iraq have benefited from government electrification programs.

The same features have made this marshy region an ideal place for smuggling between Iran and Iraq. It is believed that the predominantly Shi'i dissident movement in Iraq known as *al-Da'wa* has received arms and equipment from Iran at least since 1978 through the marshes of Misan Province, most of whose inhabitants are Shi'i. The Iraqi government has tentative plans to drain the marshes completely in conjunction with water projects elsewhere in the country. Realization of these plans would entail massive social adjustments that could saddle the government with new political problems, while diminishing other problems such as smuggling.

South and east of the marshy region is an area that Iran refers to as Khuzistan and Iraq as Arabistan. It is, in fact, a natural geographic and climatic extension of the southern Iraqi plain (see figure 1-2). An Iraqi schoolbook refers to the close links between Khuzistan and southern Iraq:

[Arabistan] is the region located in Iran to the southeast of our country—the region of al-Ahwaz. This is an Arab region which Iran has taken possession of. The land of al-Ahwaz stretches to our southern plains and its weather is the same as the weather of these plains. Its population is linked by language, religion, proximity and family ties to the population of our southern plains. Their customs and traditions are also similar. . . . The region is rich in oil and rice. Its most important cities are al-Ahwaz, Abadan, and al-Muhammara.[13]

Khuzistan was a highly contested area between Iran and Iraq in the

---

13. Iraqi Ministry of Education, *Jughrafiya al-'Iraq lil-Saff al-Khamis al-Ibtida'i (Geography of Iraq for the Primary Fifth Grade)* (IME, 1975), pp. 7–8.

war that began in September 1980, and it is precisely the geographic characteristics of Khuzistan that affected subsequent military planning. Iraqi tanks moved freely across this flat plain until the rains of winter and spring transformed it into mud unsuitable for further maneuvers. The Iranians flooded part of the plain by releasing water from behind a dam north of Dezful, compelling Iraqi troops to build raised roads and a network of dikes in order to maintain their advanced positions around 'Abadan. The Iraqi general in command of the southern front emphasized to the author that part of his wartime operations had included "returning the waters of the Karun to their banks."[14] President Saddam Husain praised the engineers whose efforts contained "threats posed by natural phenomena and the enemy's attempts to employ these phenomena." The government later announced that 37 million cubic meters of earth-works and 2,400 kilometers of roads were built between October 1980 and May 1981 to support military operations.[15]

Also included in this extensive southern region is the great Syro-Arabian desert. Because of the scarcity of water, it has been inhabited mainly by nomadic pastoralist tribes that move out into the desert during the wet winter season to find pasture and in summer move toward permanent wells and urban areas along the Tigris and Euphrates rivers and north into the Jazira. Until the mid-twentieth century, the central government in Baghdad found this southern and western desert difficult to control because of the size and military capability of the tribes and the extent of tribal authority, and because the tribal groups were dispersed throughout the desert during much of the year and hence not subject to central administrative control. Although the situation has been greatly ameliorated, it is nonetheless still difficult for the state to establish and maintain its sovereign legitimacy, collect taxes, and record accurate census data in this region.

The conditions characterizing the extensive and rugged mountains in northeastern Iraq and the vast expanse of the desert in the south and west have precluded intensive human settlement. Both regions are best suited for nomadic pastoralism. The intimate relationship between the nomadic pastoralists, or badu, of Iraq and land use had important

14. Interview with the commanding general in his military camp outside Khorram-shahr (al-Muhammara), June 14, 1981.
15. FBIS, *Daily Report: MEA*, November 12, 1980, p. E4, and January 7, 1981, p. E3; and Iraqi Press Office Press Release (Washington, D.C.), "Qaddasiyat Saddam," May 4, 1981.

consequences for the participation of various groups in the early political life of Iraq and on its policies of land reform. The badu were broadly divided into those who raised camels and those who raised sheep and goats. The camel breeders formed large, independent, and militant tribes. Because of the unique adaptation of the camel to its environment—specifically, its tolerance of salinity and its ability to browse a distance of twenty-five kilometers in a day—camel herders needed widespread access to water and grazing land. Cattle, sheep, and goats, being less adaptable, were kept closer to permanent water sources; their Iraqi owners usually lived near the rivers and sought protection from urban centers or larger camel-herding tribes. More than 9 million hectares are currently suitable for livestock raising in Iraq.

Outside the rainfed northeastern mountainous region, the Iraqi population is therefore relatively concentrated along the riverine systems (figure 1-3), where numerous cities have developed throughout Iraqi history.[16] Many of the larger urban centers attracted satellite settlements and associated tribes and became autonomous, self-contained political, economic, and social entities. In the twentieth century, economic and political authority became increasingly concentrated in only three urban centers—Baghdad, Mosul, and Basra—each of which occupies a strategic location, has a history dating back many centuries, and developed its own distinctive role in regional affairs. They are also the only cities in Iraq that currently have populations of more than half a million.

Baghdad lies in the transitional zone between north and south. Here the Tigris becomes navigable and irrigation on a large scale is possible. The city dominates an extensive surrounding region that traditionally was a center of trade and communication. Tribes in the deserts of the south and west were in frequent contact with Baghdad and the cities of al-Najaf and Karbala, as were the Persians to the east. Mosul, a northern focal point for trade between Assyria, Kurdistan, and Jazira, as well as to Aleppo and the Mediterranean, is a highly heterogeneous city. Before the delineation of the Iraqi nation-state, the inhabitants of Mosul were

16. Iraq's first deputy prime minister, Taha Yasin Ramadhan, emphasized this point during an interview on June 21, 1981, stating: "We are the home of ancient civilizations as is evident by Akkad, Nimrud, and Babylon. Iraq was a major center in Islam. In Egypt there are only the pyramids and in other countries there was only one civilization. In Iraq there were a series of civilizations. Kufa, Samarra, and Baghdad were all capitals."

Figure 1-3. *Limits of Settlement and Population Density in Iraq*

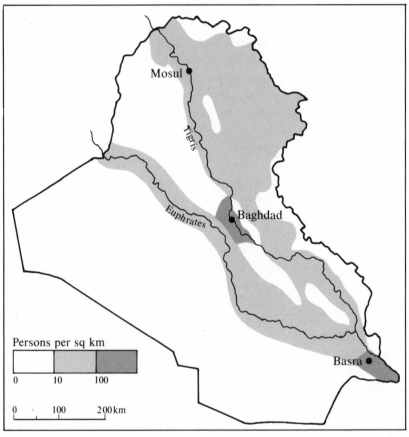

Source: Adapted from Central Intelligence Agency, *Atlas: Issues in the Middle East* (Government Printing Office, 1973), p. 11.

culturally and economically closer to the Arabs of Syria than to those of southern Iraq. When it chose, the Iraqi government could shift the direction of trade, but bonds of cultural affinity have a durability that remains. Basra, by contrast, has been oriented toward the Gulf region and India because of its role as a port city. During the latter half of the 1970s, the southern region around Basra has assumed greater importance in Iraq's economic life. The Rumaila oil field is located here, as is a pipeline linking Basra to Kirkuk that has a 900,000 barrels per day (bpd) capacity and is reversible. Approximately two-thirds of Iraq's total oil exports of 3.2 million bpd prior to the Iran-Iraq war moved from onshore facilities at and near al-Faw to two loading platforms in the Gulf, Mina al-Bakr and Khaur al-'Amaya.

While current population statistics for Iraq are not available, some general trends can be discerned. Between the first official census, held in 1947, and 1982, the population of Iraq grew from 4.8 million to an estimated 14 million, and the population of Baghdad from an estimated 500,000 to 3 million. In common with other urban areas in the third world, Baghdad's growth resulted both from natural increase, estimated in the early 1980s to be about 3.5 percent annually, and from migration from rural areas, where the population has shown no growth in recent decades. Stated differently, Iraq's urban population in 1947 was estimated to be 35 percent of the total population; in 1957 almost 40 percent; now it probably exceeds 60 percent. Baghdad and Basra have experienced the greatest percentage increases, with greater Baghdad containing 23 percent of Iraq's total population.[17] More than 40 percent of the population is under the age of twenty-five.

Pluralism: Sources and Trends

Centuries of linguistic, ethnic, tribal, regional, class, and religious identification in the Middle East now compete with newly defined nationalisms and party ideologies to provide linkages and divisions within individual states and in regional alliances. The nature of state formation, affected as it is by so many parochial interests, opens a Pandora's box in the question of Iraqi nationalism. Because of Iraq's pluralism, it has been said that there is no Iraqi nation.

Although 75 percent of Iraq's population speaks Arabic, the remaining quarter speaks Kurdish, Turkish, or Farsi. Farsi, the language of Iran, is spoken only in the privacy of homes even though the other so-called minority languages are spoken publicly. Moreover, while Islam is the religion of some 90 to 95 percent of the population, there are smaller

17. See Qubain, *The Reconstruction of Iraq: 1950–1957;* Hanna Batatu, *The Old Social Classes and the Revolutionary Movements of Iraq* (Princeton University Press, 1978), especially pp. 132–34, 1125; and Ihsan M. al-Hassan, "High Population Growth Rate in Iraq," *Iraq Today,* vol. 4 (June 1–5, 1979), pp. 20–21.

groups of Christians,[18] Jews,[19] Yazidis, Sabeans, and Shabaks. Of the Muslims, Shi'i Muslims comprise an estimated 50 to 55 percent of Iraq's total population and Sunnis about 40 percent.[20] While most of the population is Arab, some 18 to 20 percent are Kurds, who are predominantly Sunni albeit permeated with Sufi influences. There are smaller groups of Turkomans, Armenians, Assyrians, and Persians.

As is true elsewhere in the Middle East, the political implications of religious, ethnic, and regional identities in Iraq are complicated by trends that are either unique to or have accelerated in this century. These include fluctuations in the growth and distribution of populations, the changing roles of urban and rural institutions, intercommunal marriages, capital growth and development, the rise and competition of secular political ideologies and renewal of religion as an alternative political force, the exploitation of new resources and technologies, changing job markets, and improvements in communication and transportation. Economic development requires an educated, technically conversant population; transnational issues, such as the Palestine problem and Kurdish national aspirations, also intervene as major influences on Iraqi domestic

18. About 5 percent of Iraq's population is Christian. The Chaldean church, largest of the Christian churches in Iraq, has about 600,000 members. Smaller groups are Syrian Orthodox, Syrian Catholic, Armenian, Greek Orthodox, Nestorian (Assyrian), and Roman Catholic. During an interview with me on June 6, 1981, Fr. Avak Asadourian, head of the Armenian church in Iraq, stated that his membership is 20,000. He went on to say that "we are a minority in number, but not in status." My Muslim guide concurred, stating that Armenians had attained a comparatively high standard of education in Iraq and were known to be excellent physicians, lawyers, and craftsmen. In addition to contributions from their congregations, these Christian churches receive annual government subsidies. As is true of many sites in Iraq, the original Armenian church in Baghdad is so old that it has come to be regarded as sacred by Muslims, who can be found worshipping there alongside their Christian counterparts.

19. The Jewish community in Iraq is several thousand years old. A census in 1947 estimated that there were 118,000 Jews, concentrated mainly in Baghdad, Mosul, and Basra. During the 1940s, extreme Zionist groups in Iraq sought to assist the large-scale immigration of Jews to Palestine. Their assistance included propaganda and sabotage designed to create intercommunal strife. More than 120,000 Jews had emigrated by 1960, and it is roughly estimated that about 5,000 remain in Iraq today.

20. The distinction between Shi'is and Sunnis originated in the early days of Islam over the question of succession to the Khalifate. Because Shi'is believed that the person of the Khalifa should incorporate not only secular but also religious, indeed divine, ideals, they recognized 'Ali, the Prophet's cousin and son-in-law, and his descendants to be the legitimate successors after the Prophet's death. The proponents of this belief were known as 'Alids or Shi'is, an appellation derived from shi'at 'ali, that is, the adherents or party of 'Ali. While Muhammad is considered by Shi'is to be the Prophet of God, 'Ali shares divine proximity to God as his wali allah, the friend of God.

affairs. These factors have altered the form and degree of interaction among social groups, enhancing stability or intensifying internal divisions as social groups compete for access to and participation in economic and political life.

Britain's imposition in 1921 of the Hashimite monarchy in Iraq, which the British hoped would be accepted as a legitimate political authority because of the Islamic heritage of the Al-Hashim, who were descended from the Prophet Muhammad, was the first deliberate attempt to foster a nascent state patriotism in this century. Some Iraqis, however, questioned this "kingship" because of its association with the British and its non-Mesopotamian and Sunni origins. The hatred with which it came to be regarded was bloodily expressed in the revolution of 1958, which eliminated any possibility of a future Hashimite throne in Iraq. Perhaps the most poignant observation of the gap that had grown between Iraqis and the Hashimite monarchy is Majid Khadduri's statement that "it is an irony of history that the funeral prayers for the great grandsons of the Prophet Muhammad, killed by followers of the Prophet, should be given not in a mosque in Islamic lands but in a church in infidel lands."[21]

Subsequent governments, all secular and antimonarchic, have continued to confront the problems of internal political consolidation. This has meant that they have had to seek a broader base of political legitimacy, whether by force or by other more subtle political and economic means. Since the early 1920s authorities in Iraq have endeavored to eliminate divergent tendencies, and thereby centralize government control, through a variety of political maneuvers: settlement of powerful tribal shaikhs in urban areas, land reform, and moving or expelling from the country certain segments of the population.

As in all Middle Eastern countries, the interweaving of geography and history, temporal government and religion, regionalism and ethnicity colors political behavior, frequently providing a motive or a rationale for political action. Thus, for example, Ayatullah Khomeini of Iran refers to Saddam Husain, the Iraqi president, as an "infidel," to Iraq as a land of Satan, and to Iran's war as a *jihad*.[22] Husain in turn calls the Iran-Iraq war a second Qadisiya (an ancient conflict between Persians

21. Majid Khadduri, *Republican 'Iraq: A Study in 'Iraqi Politics since the Revolution of 1958* (Oxford University Press, 1969), p. 56.
22. *Jihad* used in this sense refers to a holy war or a war fought by Muslims in order to extend or to cleanse the Islamic community.

and Arabs) and asks that the swords of Imam 'Ali, Imam Husain, Khalid bin al-Walid, and Salah al-Din al-Ayyubi—the first three Arab Muslims and the last a famous Kurdish Muslim warrior—be unsheathed against tyrannical Iranian leaders. Thus by recalling Shi'i imams, Husain, whose family is Sunni Muslim, sends a message to Iraqi Shi'is that he reveres their heritage and their leaders who had a unique association with Iraq.

While governments use symbols of this kind as political tools to evoke emotional attachments and thus facilitate control, dissident groups have used and will continue to frame their opposition within the same lines of argument, whether through reinterpretation or the substitution of trigger symbols. Every Iraqi authority is acutely aware that pluralism has acted, at times violently, as a disruptive force in government affairs. The significance of this issue is illustrated by Saddam Husain's insistence that ethnic or religious associations should not displace one's first loyalty as an Iraqi national, as his following statements illustrate:

We in Iraq are one united people: Muslims and Christians, Shi'ites and Sunnis, Arabs and Kurds. The Muslims in the past came out with sects, a result of the interpretation of the Koran and history. Some said we are Sunnis and others said we are Shi'ites. So what? If the Iraqi people are made up of Sunnis and Shi'ites, does this make them two different peoples and not a united people, the people of the Ramadhan revolution [February 8, 1963] and the July revolution [1958]?[23]

Those who tell you that there is a contradiction between being a real Kurd and a real Iraqi do not seek your good.[24]

The present Iraqi government realizes that its ambitions for leadership in the Gulf and its capacity to achieve that goal will be affected by its ability to minimize internal conflict. The question remains, under what conditions may symbols of identification or association be brought into play and what might increase their effectiveness?

23. FBIS, *Daily Report: MEA*, February 11, 1980, speech by Saddam Husain to popular rally in Baghdad on February 8, 1980, pp. E1–E4. An Arab friend of mine was visiting Iraq when this speech or a variant on the same theme was broadcast. Husain paused midway through his exposition on Shi'is and Sunnis, Arabs and Kurds, and showed political acumen when he playfully added, "Soon some will say that Iraq is made up of women and men."

24. FBIS, *Daily Report: MEA*, August 28, 1979, excerpt from a meeting held by Saddam Husain with officers of al-Mansur forces in Sulaimaniya governorate on August 25, 1979, p. E1.

Causes of Concern

A major concern for government authorities is that a number of the potentially dissident groups are geographically separate from other parts of Iraqi society. The Kurds tend to be clustered in the north around Kirkuk, Mosul, and Sulaimaniya, though large numbers can be seen working in Baghdad, wearing the traditional Kurdish dress. Shi'is are concentrated in the southern regions; Sunnis comprise the majority of people in central and northern Iraq. Political unrest in the Kurdish-dominated regions, for example, could threaten economic activity in the rest of the country, since in normal times the northern oilfields produce as much as 50 percent of Iraq's petroleum. After the outbreak of war with Iran, the northern share of the diminished output rose to 70 or perhaps more than 80 percent.[25] More than half of Iraq's associated natural gas is also found in the Kurdish region, which in addition is crossed by pipelines carrying oil from Basra to the Mediterranean Sea through Turkey and Syria (figure 1-4).

A second concern is that in Iraq, as in most of the Arab countries where associations such as labor unions and professional clubs are forbidden or tightly controlled, the one form of public gathering to which the government cannot deny its people access is the mosque. Fridays and other Islamic holy days thus become potential occasions for agitation by opposition groups. This is particularly so in Iraq, within whose borders lie one of the holiest Shi'i mosques, al-Kazimain,[26] and two of the most revered Shi'i cities, al-Najaf and Karbala.[27] One such public

25. These percentages were obtained in an interview with the minister of oil, Qasim Ahmad al-Taqi, on August 10, 1982. See also John Rossant, "Iraq Sets BD-Goal, Confirms Massive Oil Reserves," *Petroleum Information International,* December 7, 1981, pp. 1–2.

26. The mosque of al-Kazimain is notable because it is the burial place of both the seventh and ninth imams in Shi'i Islam. The district in which it is situated, al-Kazimiya, is inhabited primarily by Shi'is of Persian origin.

27. The Imam 'Ali was assassinated in A.D. 661 at al-Kufa. Adjacent to al-Najaf, it is one of several cities established in Iraq during the early Islamic period. 'Ali's traditional resting place is al-Najaf, also called Meshhed 'Ali, literally "the place where the martyr 'Ali died (or is buried)." It is at the mosque in al-Najaf that Ayatullah Khomeini prayed every day for fourteen years after he was exiled from Iran and before he returned in the early fall of 1978. 'Ali's son, Husain, eventually succeeded to the Khalifate and was martyred in A.D. 680 at Karbala, also referred to as Meshhed Husain. The most important Shi'i holy day, 'Ashura, commemorates the martyrdom of Imam Husain.

Figure 1-4. *Kurdish-dominated Areas in the Middle East and Their Relation to Iraqi Oil Resources and Facilities*

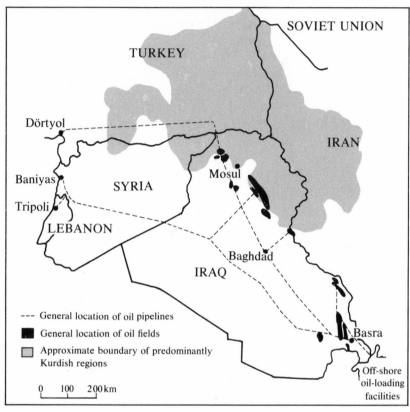

Sources: Adapted from CIA, *Atlas*, p. 7; and *International Petroleum Encyclopedia*, 1979, pp. 145, 152.

gathering held yearly in the Muslim month of Muharram is the *ta'ziya*, the procession and passion play in which Shi'is lament the death of the Imam Husain and other imams martyred centuries ago by Sunnis. In open outpourings of grief, spectators press *muhr*—cakes of soil from Karbala—against their foreheads and perform acts of self-flagellation. This tendentious history, which incorporates some forty to fifty individual stories, makes no distinction among Sunni groups, and during performances of the play the presence of non-Shi'is is not welcomed. Some governments in the Middle East, including those of Iraq and Iran, have attempted at various times to restrain or even abolish these rituals because of their potential to become politically disruptive.

Although disagreements over nationalism and the place of religion in society have discouraged the spread of Communist ideology in the Middle East, the Communist party itself has been well aware that institutionalized religion offers secular political movements opportunities to extend their operations. 'Aziz Muhammad, the exiled first secretary of the Iraqi Communist party, acknowledged in a 1979 interview that religious movements are indeed political and, moreover, that religious festivals are centers of opposition activity that can be organized.[28] The following excerpt from an article written and distributed clandestinely by a certain "Comrade Nasir" in prison advocates the use of such gatherings for revolutionary purposes:

Lenin said: "Act where the masses are"; and I doubt whether the masses can congregate in such numbers anywhere in Iraq other than in these places of pilgrimage. . . . In a country like Iraq where . . . laws prohibit gatherings and demonstrations except for religious purposes . . . it is incumbent upon us to think seriously of utilizing these legal possibilities in the interests of the democratic movement and for the cause of peace. . . . The government will long hesitate before meddling with the processions. . . .[29]

Yet another cause of concern to the Iraqi government is that, in addition to internal opposition groups like the Iraqi Communist party, other countries, notably Iran and Syria, seek to exploit and deepen Iraq's internal divisions for their own purposes, just as Iraq has done in other countries. By late November 1980 a number of Iraqi opposition groups had joined under Syrian auspices in Damascus to form the Democratic National and Patriotic Front. Its three main factions are the Kurdish Democratic party, the Iraqi Communist party, and the Unified Socialist party of Kurdistan. A former Iraqi general in opposition to the Iraqi government, Hasan al-Naqib, has had important contacts with the front; indeed, he has been alleged to be the leader of the opposition's military wing. At various times he reportedly has been in Lebanon, in northern Syria under cover of the Palestine Liberation Organization—his contacts with the PLO are said to date from 1969, when he commanded Iraqi troops in Jordan—and even in Iran. Al-Da'wa, the clandestine Shi'i opposition group, apparently refused to work with the front because of the inclusion of the Iraqi Communist party and what it termed nationalistic trends in the front.

28. 'Aziz Muhammad interview with Dave Lloyd, "Iraq's Communists Optimistic," *Morning Star* (London), December 28, 1979.

29. Quoted in Batatu, *The Old Social Classes and Revolutionary Movements,* pp. 695–97.

The Iranians themselves have put forward the name of Muhammad Baqir al-Hakim as a successor to Saddam Husain and the Ba'th party. As the son of Muhsin al-Hakim, the leading Shi'i spiritual leader or *mujtahid* in Iraq from 1960 to 1970, Muhammad had assumed great personal prestige and was therefore expected to rally all of Iraq's opposition parties. His father in fact had proposed in 1963 to Khomeini and other senior Shi'i religious leaders in Qum, Iran, that they come to al-Najaf and Karbala to escape further violent confrontations with the shah's forces.[30]

Although Muhammad Baqir al-Hakim traveled to Damascus once the Iran-Iraq war began, he was said to have been discouraged by disagreement among the front's leaders and returned to Tehran. He then became the spokesman in Iran for the Supreme Assembly of the Islamic Revolution of Iraq, set up in November 1982 to mount an Islamic revolution against the Iraqi Ba'th government. The Iranian news media accused Iraqi authorities of executing six and arresting ninety members of the al-Hakim family during May 1983. Iran also claimed that Iraq threatened to continue its crackdown if Islamic opposition groups did not stop their activities.[31] There can be no doubt about Muhammad's opposition to the Iraqi Ba'th, however, as the following statements make clear:

The Islamic leadership in Iraq has defined it [the attitude of the religious leadership to the Iraqi Ba'th party] on more than one occasion, and in more than one appropriate way. The earliest definition took the form of the well-known position of the late Imam al-Hakim. The latest was the position of the martyr Ayatullah al-Sadr.[32] This martyr has been able to lead the Iraqi masses several positive steps forward. The shedding of his pure blood was the latest event which really boosted the surge of the Moslem movement.

And now, we continue to support the position of the world religious leadership represented by the ever steadfast Imam Khomeyni. . . .

The position of al-Hakim was well known. My late father was determined in his reflection of and opposition to the regime. . . . I can say that he died, under circumstances similar to those of a martyr, in opposing this regime. He dedicated the entire latter part of his life to intensify this opposition. . . .

Anyone who believes in martyrdom as a principle and a philosophy of life will inevitably conclude that the blood of martyrs is a beacon which illuminates

30. Mohamed Heikal, *Iran: The Untold Story* (Pantheon, 1981).

31. British Broadcasting Corporation, *Summary of World Broadcasts*, "Middle East"/7364/i, June 20, 1983.

32. Muhammad Baqir al-Sadr was a leading Shi'i religious leader. Although his ancestors were Persian, he was born in the Shi'i section of Baghdad called al-Kazimiya and played an active role in the support, if not the actual foundation, of two Shi'i groups opposing the Iraqi government. He occasionally is referred to as a martyred imam because he was executed by the Iraqi Ba'th in April 1980.

the path of those who are on the move. Martyrdom strengthens the spirit of the opposition, and extends it to wider segments of the masses. . . .

God willing, the future in Iraq, the region and the world belongs to Islam. We are optimistic of victory, with God's will.[33]

Many clandestine opposition movements within Iraq are largely Shi'a in orientation. Of these, the Party of the Islamic Call (*Hizb al-Da'wa al-Islamiya*), or al-Da'wa, appears to be the best known in the West, primarily because its members were implicated in several attacks against leading members of the Ba'th party, including an assassination attempt against Revolutionary Command Council member Tariq 'Aziz in April 1980, during which innocent bystanders were killed. Believed to have been formed in the late 1950s, al-Da'wa allegedly had early financial links to the shah of Iran but seemed to take its ideological impetus from Muhammad Baqir al-Sadr in Iraq, who had close ties with the Iranian clergy. Before his death, he was referred to by Iranian radio as "the Khomeini of Iraq."[34] His execution by the Iraqi government in April 1980 is credited by some for the decline of al-Da'wa, though other important causes were a mass deportation of Persian Shi'is in May 1980, a simultaneous crackdown on al-Da'wa members, and the start of the Iran-Iraq war, which may have led many Shi'is to identify themselves more as Iraqi nationals than as Shi'i Muslims. According to one Iraqi official, 1,000 active al-Da'wa members remain as well as a considerable number of additional supporters, some 90 percent of whom are said to be Shi'is of Persian extraction.[35] Its present leader, at least nominally, is said to be Muhammad Baqir al-Hakim. Since the Iran-Iraq war began, Syria, which sided with Iran, has been accused by Iraqi officials of

33. Interview in *al-Shahid* (Tehran), December 24, 1980, reprinted in Joint Publications Research Service 77558, *Near East/North Africa Report*, no. 2284 (March 11, 1981), pp. 35–37. (Hereafter JPRS no., *NE/NA Report*.)

34. Hanna Batatu, "Iraq's Underground Shi'a Movements: Characteristics, Causes and Prospects," *Middle East Journal*, vol. 35 (Autumn 1981), p. 590. For further information see Eric Rouleau, "Khomeini Grooms Successor to Saddam Husain," *The Guardian*, November 2, 1980; *Islamic Echo* (London), vol. 15 (December 1980–February 1981); Abu Ali, "A Glimpse of the Life of the Martyred Imam: Mohammad Baqer al-Sadr and His Last Three Messages" (date and place of publication unknown); and Abu Ali, "An Iraqi Corrects *The New York Times*," *Islamic Revolution* (place of publication unknown), October 1981.

35. FBIS, *Daily Report: MEA*, May 16, 1980, interview by Huda al-Murr in *al-Majalla*, May 10–16, 1980, with Sa'dun Shakir Mahmud, Iraqi minister of the interior, pp. E1–E3. Activities attributed to al-Da'wa have continued throughout the Iran-Iraq war. These have included the cutting of telephone wires, blowing up of ammunition dumps, and other such acts, the most spectacular of which was a car bomb explosion at the Ministry of Planning that killed approximately 20 persons and injured more than 130 on August 1, 1982.

training persons such as these in terrorist tactics for use against the Iraqi government, while the Syrians have as often accused the Iraqis of intervening in their affairs.

Despite little reliable reporting, three other Shi'i underground movements are thought to exist: the Islamic Action Party of Iraq *(Munadhamat al-'Amal al-Islami fil-'Iraq)*, the Movement of the Iraqi Ulama *(Harakat Jama' al-'Ulama al-Din al-'Iraqiyin)*, and Islamic Warriors *(Mujahidun)*. It is not clear whether the last mentioned is an autonomous functioning group or simply refers collectively to participants in such movements as "Islamic warriors."

Chronic Dissidence, Sporadic Unity

Although the Kurds are the fourth-largest ethnic group in the Middle East, religious, national, tribal, and linguistic differences have all acted to thwart their nationalist or separatist movements. The long history of their agitation, dating to the 1800s, and the extent to which they have pursued their aims have ensured that the so-called Kurdish question has remained a persistent problem for governments in the region, including that of Iraq.

During the twentieth century Iraq has conducted at least seven major military campaigns against Kurdish guerrilla groups and witnessed almost continual trouble between the 1958 revolution and 1970, when the Ba'th government signed an agreement granting autonomy to Iraqi Kurds. The government made concessions more extensive than any made previously, allowing the Kurdish guerrillas to remain armed and to extend their influence territorially and through the news media. But relations with the government disintegrated as the Kurds demanded a greater percentage of Iraq's oil revenues and equal rights with Iraqi Arabs. Fighting broke out again in March 1974, when the autonomy plan was unilaterally resubmitted with minor revisions by the government. In reality it gave only limited self-rule in a region that excluded Kirkuk.

The rebellion did not end until Iran and Iraq concluded the Algiers Declaration of 1975 in which both governments agreed not to aid each other's minority groups. Security was increased in northern Iraq, some population groups were resettled, and the government resumed military operations as was necessary in 1978. The authorities tried to offset these unpleasant measures by expanding development projects in the Kurdish region, which accounted for 30 percent of the 1979 budget, and occasionally by granting amnesty to prisoners and exiles. While subsequent negotiations between the Kurds and the Iraqi government were unsuccessful, a combination of the government's policies and factional strife among the Kurds had reduced separatist activity to a relatively low intensity by the late 1970s. A number of active Kurdish dissident groups nevertheless remain. At least one of them, led by Jalal Talabani, advocated terrorism and allegedly had accepted Syrian and Soviet assistance until a political and security agreement was reached in December 1983 with Saddam Husain. Whether the agreement will prove to be of lasting significance remains to be seen.

Both Shi'is and Kurds have traditionally sought political influence through political organizations such as the Iraqi Communist party and even the Ba'th party, but their percentage of the total membership of these parties has varied substantially. Between 1949 and 1955, for example, Kurds and Shi'is accounted for 31.3 and 46.9 percent, respectively, of the central committee members of the Communist party in Iraq; Shi'is comprised only 5.7 percent of the top Ba'thist command from 1963 to 1970, but numbered 53.8 percent between 1952 and 1963.[36]

An irony of Iraqi life is that diverse interest groups have formed durable and mutually beneficial associations across social cleavages. Paradoxes abound: Christian Kurds, Shi'i and Sunni elements in a single tribal group, and both Muslims and Christians worshipping at the same place, such as the old Armenian church in Baghdad. Moreover, Shi'is, often portrayed as being passively manipulated by Sunnis, have actually dominated commercial sectors of the economy in certain periods.[37] It has been noted elsewhere that despite the dire straits of many Shi'is, some of the richest Iraqis have been Shi'is, including by 1958 six of the seven largest landowners in Iraq.[38] Their position has been attributed to the fact that they had less access to formal education than Sunnis and therefore developed commercial skills. The British in the

36. Batatu, *The Old Social Classes and Revolutionary Movements*, pp. 700, 1078–79.

37. During my first trip to Iraq, I asked Iraqis about the expulsion of approximately 30,000 Persian Shi'is from Iraq in mid-1979 before the outbreak of the Iran-Iraq war. Several Iraqis in Baghdad related that not as much resentment existed toward the government as might have been expected because this group had monopolized certain sectors of the economy, particularly in the south. Whether or not this is accurate, it is a perception held by at least some Iraqis.

38. See Batatu, *The Old Social Classes and Revolutionary Movements*, pp. 49 and 271.

twentieth century also attempted to assist less privileged groups such as Shi'is in order to balance internal political forces in Iraq. Moreover, when the Jewish population, which had held a dominant commercial position in Iraq, began to emigrate in large numbers by the late 1940s, Shi'is became the major merchant group in Baghdad, especially in the textile and wheat markets.

There are also numerous historical examples of economic and political cooperation between Shi'i and Sunni Muslims, various tribes, regional groups, Kurds and Arabs, and among Jews, Christians, and Muslims. The twentieth century has brought a number of occasions when communal schisms were submerged for the commonweal of modern Iraq—specifically *al-thawra* (the revolt) of 1920, the thirty-day war of 1941, the *wathba* (awakening) of 1948, the *intifada* (uprising) of 1952, the revolution of 1958, and the Iran-Iraq war that began in 1980. In the first five cases, diverse associations based on tribal, ethnic, regional, religious, class, military, and political groups in Iraq found themselves united at different times and to varying degrees in opposition to Britain and to the Western-oriented Hashimite monarchy. In the revolt of 1920, for example, joint religious celebrations were organized in Baghdad in which Sunni *mawlid*s, festivals on the occasion of the Prophet's birthday, were followed by *ta'ziya*s enacting the Shi'i theology of salvation. Although the causes and intensity of each event differed, all shared a common goal—the restoration of Iraqi control over internal Iraqi affairs. Each contributed to the gradual, albeit painful and at times halting, emergence of an increasingly cohesive national community within the Iraqi state. While it is too early to know the long-term domestic consequences of the Iran-Iraq war, the early phase of the conflict produced examples of intercommunal cooperation. The large-scale disturbances that might have been expected in the Shi'i or Kurdish areas had not occurred.

Encouraging Nationhood

One of the main objectives of the Iraqi Ba'th government of the 1970s was to systematize the development of national consciousness, both theoretically and practically. To this end the Ba'th articulated a policy on minorities in the Arab world in general, although it cannot be doubted that the party was concerned about the Iraqi case in particular. The report, produced by the eleventh national congress of the Arab Ba'th

Socialist party in 1977[39] and published in 1979, begins by asserting that the history of the Arab nation is several thousand years old and embraces numerous nationalities whose intermingling with the larger Arab nation has been extensive and profound. The party thus disavowed race in treating pan-Arab or national problems. An Arab, according to the broad definition in the Ba'th constitution, is "one whose language is Arabic, who lives on Arab land or seeks to live on it and believes in his membership in the Arab nation." The report states that conflicts with nationalities living within the Arab world whose population is significant and whose cultural characteristics are distinct must be resolved and a unity of goals pursued. It concludes by affirming that the Ba'th represents all the people, whatever their origins, and must be a party both of nationalities and of the Arab nation.

The lengthy discussion of the Kurds in the Ba'th national congress report on minorities indicates their importance to the Iraqi government. Clearly no Iraqi government, including the Ba'th since 1968, has been willing to accommodate full separatism in the northern Kurdish region of the country. During the early 1970s, Ba'th authorities concluded and have since reiterated that the Kurds must have autonomy—but as the central government in Baghdad defines it. Autonomy in no case is to undermine the unity of Iraq.

Iraqi Ba'th authorities in recent years have increased the flow of financial resources to the Shi'i and Kurdish areas of greatest potential concern. A $33 million government contract was devoted in part to urban reconstruction in the Shi'i areas surrounding the mosque of al-Kazimain in Baghdad, $60 million was allocated for the renovation of the two shrines of Husain and 'Abbas in Karbala, and $220 million for the renovation of the mosque of 'Ali in al-Najaf and for the construction there of a new city for pilgrims. An additional $52 million was donated for the construction of a hospital in al-Najaf.[40] Funds were provided in 1981 to complete a dairy, a poultry farm, and a housing project in Karbala, among a number of other projects.

In 1974 an autonomous administrative region was established in the

39. "Problem of Ethnic Minorities in Arab Homeland," *al-Thawra* (Baghdad), April 9, 1979, and "Theoretical Expression of Vital Fact," *al-Thawra* (Baghdad), April 10, 1979 (part 1), and April 11, 1979 (part 2), as translated and reprinted in JPRS 73694, *NE/NA Report*, no. 1983 (June 15, 1979), pp. 79–87.

40. *Middle East Economic Digest*, vol. 25 (December 11, 1981), p. 17, and interviews conducted in Iraq between May and July 1981. (Hereafter *MEED*.)

three Kurdish provinces of Irbil, Dahuk, and Sulaimaniya, and money began to be directed there for development. Projects costing almost $72 million were completed during 1980, additional projects worth $488 million were in progress in 1981, and almost $3 billion overall was allocated for development up to 1985.[41] It is important to note that these statistics are misleading in one sense. The central government in Iraq has often allocated larger sums to projects than could actually be absorbed, owing to inadequate infrastructure.

Numerous other actions have been taken by the government to emphasize the shared cultural unity of Iraq. Informal appearances by President Saddam Husain in various outlying regions of Iraq are one example. Stopping at random in badu areas, the marshes, Mosul, and the war zone, among other places, Husain has visited Christian shrines, prayed in mosques, and met with schoolchildren. His primary objective is to make personal contact with the people, to share their food or coffee, and to ask about their problems, such as salinization of their wells or their children's education. The first such visits by any Iraqi leader in memory, they are intended to increase not only Husain's prestige but also the legitimacy of the government itself. Another purpose of these trips is to demonstrate that cultural diversity is acceptable, that the central government is interested in the development of all of its peoples regardless of their differences, and that everyone is foremost an Iraqi belonging to a unified state.

Each of Husain's visits is videotaped and televised in the evenings throughout the country. Gifts of television sets by the government and the extension of electricity to rural areas ensure a wide audience. For a time, Husain also gave weekly interviews to the press and opened the presidential palace daily to visiting groups; Baghdadis said that at prearranged times he could be reached directly at his residence by dialing a published telephone number. By the summer of 1982 the frequency of Husain's appearances had been diminished by the demands of the Iran-Iraq war and by preoccupation with plans for the conference of non-aligned nations scheduled to be held in September 1982. Nevertheless, visits to the families of Iraqis killed in the war, trips to the battlefront,

---

41. "724 Million Dinars Allocated for the Autonomous Region," *al-Jumhuriya* (Baghdad), March 1, 1981, reprinted in JPRS 78363, *NE/NA Report*, no. 2352 (June 23, 1981), p. 4; and "Completion of 275 Projects and Continued Implementation of 734 Other Projects in Autonomous Rule Region," *al-'Iraq* (Baghdad), February 24, 1981, reprinted in JPRS 78121, *NE/NA Report*, no. 2334 (May 20, 1981), pp. 35–37.

and military ceremonies continued to give Husain much public exposure. In the Arab world such occasions—especially Husain's public appearances before the war—transcend the immediate event in that they symbolize both national unity and central authority.

Similarly the links in the Middle East between the past and the present—between archaeological discoveries, historical symbols, and their translation into a modern vernacular and context—have acquired relevance as social and political tools.[42] Because their findings may be of political and social value to the modern states of this region, archaeological excavations have been politicized to a degree unequaled in the West. As one example, excavation in Israel is given strong impetus by both the government and the military. Archaeology is also important to Iraq, one of the few Arab countries that is actively seeking to excavate and restore even its pre-Islamic past.[43]

The lion of Babylon, portrayed as the protector of Iraqi peoples, and Sargon, the first ruler to unite the northern and southern divisions of the Tigris-Euphrates basin under a single political authority, shortly after 2400 B.C., have become symbols intended to transcend more recent schisms in modern Iraqi society. As one Iraqi said, "Iraqi life is contradictory because Iraq is rich in its tradition and history." It is notable that more than 110 archaeological sites were either being excavated or restored in 1980, including two Jewish sites at Hezekiah near Babylon and al-Kifl near al-Kufa. Plans are also under way to help the Yazidis with the restoration of their historical sites. Great emphasis is placed on the training of additional Iraqi archaeologists, and there are now twelve holders of doctorates and thirty-six of master's degrees at the Baghdad Museum alone. Television, newspapers, and even the primary schools have undertaken programs to acquaint Iraqis with their cultural heritage. An estimated 12,000 to 28,000 people monthly visit the

42. Occasionally this can operate in reverse, as in the mid-1970s when Qaddafi, the Libyan leader, dynamited the Arch of Philaeni, known by British soldiers in World War II as the Marble Arch. It was originally erected by the Italian government to commemorate the ancient border between Tripolitania and Cyrenaica. Qaddafi's intention in destroying it was to demonstrate the symbolic end of divisions between the eastern and western portions of his country.

43. It is revealing that one of the few individuals who have commented on the role of archaeology in Iraqi political life is himself a Middle Easterner from Israel. See Amazia Baram, "Qawmiyya and Wataniyya in Ba'thi Iraq: The Search for a New Balance," *Middle Eastern Studies*, vol. 19 (April 1983), p. 196; and "Culture in the Service of *Wataniyya*: The Testament of Mesopotamian-Inspired Art in Ba'thi Iraq," *Asian and African Studies*, vol. 17 (November 1983), pp. 265–313.

site of Babylon during good weather, while the Iraqi Museum in Baghdad receives 12,000 visitors a month during summer and some 22,000 a month during winter.

Contemporary Iraqi artists frequently employ the ancient symbols of their past. As one artist said, "Our civilization is still in front of our eyes."[44] It is particularly noteworthy that the budget for Iraq's Ministry of Culture and Information was $2 million in 1975 and was believed in 1981 to be more than $30 million. Iraq's recent oil wealth cannot fully explain these large expenditures, nor can it be doubted that the government firmly believes that pride in the ancient past can function as a uniting force.

Although divergent tendencies may continue or even intensify if opposition groups exploit the appeal of symbols that are readily available to them, the process of nation-building is continuous and was fairly successful during the 1970s. Iraqi authorities undoubtedly will continue to confront the problem of pluralism despite the factors that operate as cohesive forces in Iraq. The present Ba'th government has instituted new measures to encourage those forces, as is discussed in part 2, yet it is clear that during the remainder of the twentieth century, one of the main goals of any Iraqi government must be to continue its efforts to convince Iraq's various interest groups that they have a common ancestry of shared geographic, economic, and political interests and that there is value in belonging to a central state as well as to their own particularistic groups.

44. Interview on June 1, 1981. Some 1,000 students are enrolled in the Institute of Fine Arts in Baghdad and 500 at the Academy of Fine Arts of Baghdad University. After graduation they tend to become schoolteachers or to be employed by the government on cultural projects. Iraq has a large museum of modern art in Baghdad that has encouraged exhibitions not only by Iraqi artists, but also by others in the Arab world. Some sensitive political themes are in evidence, although there may be unspoken limits beyond which artists do not generally venture. While the Museum of Modern Art does not attract Iraqis as much as do the archaeological sites, modern art galleries can be seen along the main streets in Baghdad. Syria has also been recognized for the quality of its artists, but the wing of modern art in the museum in Damascus is usually kept locked. Other countries such as Jordan have only recently begun to devote time and resources to encouraging an artistic community.

CHAPTER TWO

The Emergent State

THE fifty years that comprise the history of the modern Iraqi nation-state can be viewed as the most recent and as yet brief stage in a continuous history of civilized occupation that predates modern Iraq by some five thousand years. The basic issues discussed by the European powers in delineating the boundaries of Iraq after World War I were similar to earlier concerns of the Ottomans. These concerns have eventually confronted all "Iraqi" authorities, whether they were British mandatory, Hashimite, military, or current Ba'thist. This is so because many aspects of Iraqi political life—such as family, extended familial relationships, tribalism, religion, climatic and geographic constraints, and regionalism—have historical continuity and even now remain important elements in governmental decisionmaking.

Iraq's present boundaries, creations of the twentieth century mandate authorities, do not correspond to the entire geographic unit that is primarily defined by the Tigris-Euphrates river systems, one-quarter of which lies outside Iraq (figure 2-1). It is therefore essential to understand the basic relationship between the historical evolution of the Iraqi state as a single socio-political structure and its individual physical and cultural units. This relationship continues to be a fundamental factor motivating Iraqi political behavior.

Origins

The half millennium during which the present state of Iraq gradually evolved was a history of numerous negotiations, memoranda, mapmaking, lost records, procrastination, contradictory evidence, and little accord. Iraq inherited 1,472 kilometers of the old Ottoman-Persian

37

Figure 2-1. *River Basins of the Tigris and Euphrates*

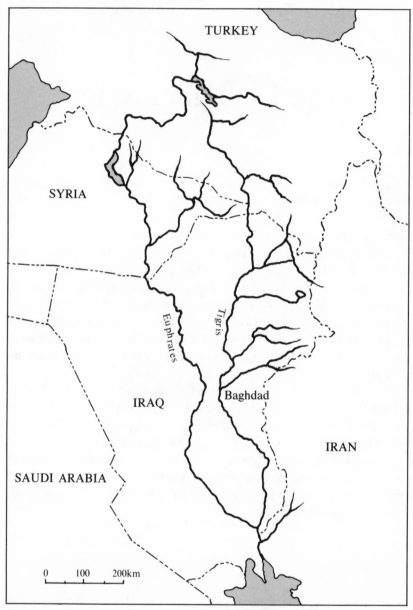

Source: Reprinted by permission of the publisher from Marion Clawson, Hans H. Landsberg, and Lyle T. Alexander,
The Agricultural Potential of the Middle East, p. 203. Copyright 1971 by Elsevier Science Publishing Co., Inc.
      Note: The map has been deliberately distorted to emphasize the Tigris and Euphrates river systems. It also illustrates
the relation between this riverine complex and the overlapping and artificial state boundaries.

frontier, which extended some 1,888 kilometers from the Gulf to Mount Ararat. Approximately 700 of the 1,472 kilometers pass through the region known as Kurdistan.[1] The complicated negotiations that defined this Ottoman-Persian frontier were clouded by intrigue, the extent of which may only be surmised. The earliest surviving document relative to the boundary settlement is dated at Zuhab in 1639, but was itself preceded by negotiations known to have occurred about one hundred years previously. The Zuhab treaty was followed by numerous attempts at further adjustments, most important in 1746 (Kurdan), 1823 and 1847 (Erzurum), 1911 (Tehran), and 1913 (Constantinople). All of these agreements were accompanied by the efforts of numerous commissions and cartographers, and interspersed with border strikes and general unrest. On one occasion there was a massacre of as many as 30,000 Persian Shi'is in Karbala when the Ottomans established their suzerainty over the city in 1843.[2]

After World War I, the fate of this territory was taken up in a new series of treaties and conferences: the Treaty of Sèvres in 1920, the Cairo Conference in 1921, the Anglo-Iraqi Treaty in 1922, the Treaty of Lausanne in 1923, and the Anglo-Turkish Treaty in 1926. Subsequent agreements—including, among others, the Algiers Declaration of 1975 and subsequent protocols with Iran—sought to define Iraq's frontiers with the neighboring states.

Iraq itself was assigned as a British mandate in 1920, despite widespread public resentment. The mandate encompassed roughly the three former Ottoman *wilayas*, or administrative districts, of Mosul, Baghdad, and Basra, which had been established during the mid- to late nineteenth century. (Kuwait, once part of the *wilaya* of Basra even though the Ottomans never established real control there, is now an independent state.) There was some doubt about the fate of the *wilaya* of Mosul, disputed by both France and Great Britain. It remained a "dark incubus of uncertainty"[3] until it was allocated to Iraq in 1925 after much

---

1. C. J. Edmonds, *Kurds, Turks and Arabs: Politics, Travel and Research in North-Eastern Iraq, 1919–1925* (Oxford University Press, 1957), p. 125.
2. Karbala was in effect an independent enclave whose social and political life was dominated by Persian Shi'is. See J. G. Lorimer, *Gazetteer of the Persian Gulf, 'Oman, and Central Arabia*, Historical Part 1B (Farnborough, England: Gregg International Publishers, 1970), pp. 1348–59.
3. Edmonds, *Kurds, Turks and Arabs*, p. 117.

international bartering. The territorial content of the mandate was not finally defined until 1926, and Iraq was not recognized as an independent state until 1932. The British simultaneously brought about the enthronement of Faisal bin Husain Al-Hashim as king, a position his successors inherited until the revolution of 1958 eliminated both the title, which many considered to be foreign to Iraqi political experience, and the man, who had become increasingly remote from popular sentiments.[4]

Iraq's borders have continued to be a source of constant tension within Iraq and with its neighbors. Not only did the new state include many diverse cultural groups, but some groups and even resources such as water were divided among the other new states delineated during the mandate period. For example, large areas predominantly inhabited by Kurds are found in Iraq, Turkey, Syria, and Iran, while scattered Kurdish enclaves are also found in the southern Soviet Union (see figure 1-4). Conflicts over resources such as oil and water at times have become intense.

It is useful to consider briefly the strategic and economic factors that influenced Britain's formulation of Iraq's borders and to view them within the context of Iraq's current interests. Britain's foremost concern in the post–World War I period in the Middle East was to secure economic and strategic interests that revolved primarily around India and Egypt. Whether or not it was accepted as a moral commitment, the founding of a Jewish home in Palestine under the terms of the Balfour Declaration constituted other political and strategic concerns. British officials felt that if they could control Iraq and Egypt, they could secure all these interests. A primary factor in the delineation of Iraq was to allow for potential railway, pipeline, and air routes between Palestine and Mesopotamia.[5] A glance at a map of the Middle East shows that Iraq

---

4. The Arabic word *malik,* or king, is derived from the triliteral verb root *malaka,* which means to exercise authority or to take possession of. The Arabic noun *mulk,* similarly derived, means not only supreme authority but also right of ownership or possession. There is an obvious relationship between the *malik,* king, who exercises *mulk,* power, over his subjects, although the term *malik* is used in the Quran only in reference to non-Muslim leaders; *mulk* belongs only to God and to whomever he wishes to grant it. Many Muslims therefore regard the assumption of the title king as antithetical to Muslim political theory. This is one reason for Ayatullah Khomeini's opposition to the self-proclaimed monarchy of the Sa'udi family after he returned to Iran in 1979. A further discussion of this title in the context of the Sa'udi and Hashimite families in central Arabia and al-Hijaz, respectively, is found in Christine Moss Helms, *The Cohesion of Saudi Arabia: Evolution of Political Identity* (Johns Hopkins University Press, 1981), pp. 109–10.

5. Ibid., pp. 186–89.

and Transjordan together formed a strategic corridor linking the Gulf to the British mandate of Palestine on the Mediterranean Sea. Britain also had secondary obligations to the Hashimite family, which had supported Britain's war effort and was considered a potentially useful political tool in the aftermath of the war. Members of this family were installed as leaders in the two adjoining states. Britain hoped that they would provide a chain of Hashimite control across northern Arabia that would remain under the protection and influence of the British.

Iraq's northern region, including Mosul, had originally included territory the French hoped to control. It became a major issue between the two mandatory powers. When the British realized that Russia would not have a common border with Iraq after the war, they sought to include Mosul within Iraqi territory, promising France 10 percent of any oil revenues derived from the region or part ownership in any oil concession. Although recent studies have stressed that the British government recognized the potential of Mosul's oil resources, London was at least as concerned about the economic and political viability of Iraq as a state.[6] British authorities worried in particular lest the waters of the Tigris be drawn off before reaching lower Iraq and lest the civil administration lose its revenues from tobacco, wood, and grain—commodities that were produced in the north but were scarce or lacking altogether in the south.

The justification for the delimitation of Iraq's southern border involved radically different concerns. A straight line through the desert was delineated by the British on the initial assumption that this region was largely uninhabited, but large and powerful tribes and tribal confederations moved throughout the territories now included within Syria, Iraq, Saudi Arabia, and Kuwait. These seminomadic and badu groups frequently returned to the cities along the Tigris and the Euphrates rivers for *musabala,* or trade. Now their freedom of movement was being constrained and traditional concepts of authority challenged. Tribes in territory controlled by the Sa'udi family of central Arabia were adopting the tenets of the Wahhabi, or *muwahhidun,* movement and gradually

---

6. For more information about this period, especially British interests in the Middle East, see Edmonds, *Kurds, Turks and Arabs,* p. 398; Ghassan R. Atiyyah, *Iraq, 1908–1921: A Political Study* (Beirut: Arab Institute for Research and Publishing, 1973); Edith and E. F. Penrose, *Iraq: International Relations and National Development* (Westview, 1978); Helms, *Cohesion of Saudi Arabia*; Christopher T. Rand, *Making Democracy Safe for Oil: Oilmen and the Islamic East* (Little, Brown, 1975); and Peter Sluglett, *Britain in Iraq, 1914–1932* (London: Ithaca Press, 1976).

moving north toward Iraqi tribes of the southern desert, proselytizing and collecting *zakat*, an Islamic tax. Within the ideological context of the Wahhabis, as they are frequently called, and of local tradition, the collection of *zakat* effectively signified political tribute. Military authorities in London and Baghdad foresaw that if the *muwahhidun* encroachments continued, they might threaten Iraq's sovereignty over the southern tribes and endanger urban areas along the Tigris and Euphrates rivers as well as the communication routes of the Transjordan-Iraqi corridor. Police and military posts were constructed along the southern border to provide a line of defense for the urbanized area toward the north.[7] Iraq's territorial integrity, and indeed its sovereign rights as a nation-state, were now to be strictly enforced.

These territorial disputes have not ended. Ever since the mid-twentieth century, negotiations have continued over the formal legal status of many of these boundaries. Iraq, for example, laid claim to all of Kuwait as recently as 1961[8] and to its islands of Warba and Bubiyan in 1973 on the historical grounds that they were all formerly part of the Basra *wilaya*; it settled the issue of the Neutral Zone with Saudi Arabia only in 1975, and signed an additional boundary agreement with Saudi Arabia in 1981 to which two protocols were appended in February 1982.[9] The celebrated Algiers Declaration of 1975 between Iraq and Iran was one of a long series of efforts to establish secure borders and to adapt to the ever-changing economic and political needs of the states concerned. Perhaps motivated by a desire to consolidate support from other Arab governments during the Iran-Iraq war, Iraq since 1980 has settled some of its outstanding boundary issues with, for example, Jordan, with which it had discussions in 1980–81 and signed an agreement over their international border in 1984.

Wellsprings of Foreign Policy

Three considerations involving authority, strategic vulnerability, and statehood help to determine the foreign relations of Iraq. The first arises

7. The Iraqi and Saudi perspectives on this dispute are presented, respectively, in Lieutenant-General Sir John Bagot Glubb, *War in the Desert: An R.A.F. Frontier Campaign* (London: Hodder and Stoughton, 1960); and Helms, *Cohesion of Saudi Arabia*, pp. 186–88, 202–06, 212–13, 227–35, and map on p. 229.

8. Embassy of the Republic of Iraq (Washington, D.C.), "'Kuwait as an Integral Part of Iraq," press releases, June–July 1961.

9. FBIS, *Daily Report: MEA*, February 25, 1982, pp. C7–C8.

from the nature of society and authority in the region known historically as Mesopotamia and now as Iraq. Economic and political links developed between nomadic pastoral tribes inhabiting the deserts and merchant agricultural groups bordering the rivers. These relations were institutionalized by either customary or Islamic law and endowed with inherent rights and obligations. Yet the political authority wielded by either urban leaders or tribal shaikhs was constantly in flux. Whole areas might lapse from the control of a central authority, whether urban or tribal; conversely, control could be extended and centralized so efficiently as to increase the productivity of irrigation-based agriculture through the cooperation of groups whose interests formerly diverged. More extensive interregional exchanges were primarily economic, except when a political power attempted to centralize authority over smaller autonomous units by threat of force. The creation of the Iraqi state formalized a central state apparatus, but the exercise of its authority was limited because tribal and urban structures remained intact, as did their traditional patterns of exchange across the new international boundaries.

Second, this region's inherent attractions as well as its strategic position on communication routes within the Middle East and between Europe and Asia made it the object of successive invasions and the home of several indigenous cultures, among them the Sumerian, Akkadian, Babylonian, Hittite and Hurrian, Kassite, Elamite, and Assyrian civilizations and the three Persian empires of Seleucia, Parthia, and Sasania. In A.D. 750 Baghdad became the capital of the Abbasid Khalifate, which lasted until the Mongol invasion in A.D. 1258. There has hardly been a time, in fact, in the recorded history of the territory now included within Iraq when it was not experiencing the pull of outside powers competing for their own strategic, economic, or political advantage. Ottomans and Persians vied for dominance until the Ottomans gained at least nominal control from 1638 until World War I; Britain, France, Germany, and Russia joined the competition in the nineteenth century; since World War II, the Soviet Union and the United States have been the two major powers seeking to control, or at least influence, the political behavior of the states in the oil-producing Gulf region.

This turbulent history sharpens Iraqis' awareness that their country bestrides a coveted and dangerous area of the world. They often refer to Iraq's vulnerable geographic position and its effect on their personality, as individuals and as a nation.[10] As if to strengthen what might be

10. 'Ali al-Wardi, an Iraqi sociologist, wrote a book *Dirasa fi Tabi'at al-Mujtama' al-'Iraqi*, or *A Study in the Nature of Iraqi Society* (Baghdad: Matba'at al-'Ani, 1965),

interpreted as subjective observations, Iraqis frequently refer to episodes in Iraqi history, naming, among other events, the Mongol invasions of 1258 and 1401 during which Baghdadis were massacred. The first invasion also delivered the coup de grâce to a declining irrigation system that had contributed to the region's former economic prosperity. Iraqis also relate that Karbala and the shrine of Imam Husain were sacked and reputedly 3,000 inhabitants slain in 1801 by Wahhabis under the authority of the Sa'udi Imamate of central Arabia, and that as recently as the 1920s the Wahhabis were again raiding southern areas of their country. That history can influence perceptions of current events is further illustrated by the Iraqi government's repeated references to the war with Iran as a second Qadisiya, the first having been a battle in which Arab Muslim forces in the seventh century overthrew the Persian Sasanid Empire, establishing Baghdad in a preeminent position during 500 years of the Abbasid Khalifate of Islam.

A final factor affecting Iraqi foreign policy is the relationship between Iraq's turbulent political past and Western attempts to impose boundaries as political solutions for Western problems. At least twelve states have appeared as newly created political entities in the Arabian Peninsula since World War I; almost without exception, subsequent acceptance of their borders by native inhabitants was accompanied by turmoil. Some areas were so contested that boundaries remained totally undefined, while neutral zones between Iraq and Saudi Arabia and Kuwait and Saudi Arabia evolved as the only workable solution to intractable political problems. One study has estimated that there have been at least twenty-two active boundary disputes in the region since 1900,[11] and no fewer than twenty-one instances in which redress was sought by military means. International boundaries have ostensibly been settled only to be brought once again to the negotiating table. Overlapping claims to grazing and water resources, interfamily rivalries, and assertions of historical rights by aggrieved groups have thwarted the efforts of seemingly impartial adjudicators. As anomalies became commonplace, justice was

in which he discusses what he has termed the dual personality of Iraqis and the historical and sociological factors that led to it. For those unfamiliar with the Middle East, it is worthwhile to note the inevitable response of non-Iraqi Arabs when they are asked to characterize Iraqis. They say that Iraqis are affectionate and generous with those they trust but can also be hard, pragmatic, and ruthless. The latter characteristics are not ascribed to other Arabs.

11. Lenore Greenschlag Martin, "A Systematic Study of Boundary Disputes in the Persian Gulf, 1900 to Present" (Ph.D. dissertation, University of Chicago, 1979).

increasingly replaced by an arbitrary political decision or imposed by the side most capable of enforcing a solution, however temporary.

Current Perceptions of Strategic Interests

Iraqi concerns about the vulnerability of the state have not varied substantially since the 1930s. Understandably, however, domestic and foreign policy priorities have shifted in response to ever-changing economic, social, and political forces. It is important to understand how the current Ba'th government perceives the vulnerabilities of the state in the context of geographic constraints, the party's political ideals, and the economy's dependence on water and oil.

Assuring Water Supplies

That the Tigris-Euphrates river system plays a vital part in the economic, social, and political life of Iraq is clear. The confluence of the two rivers in the Shatt al-'Arab is referred to by Saddam Husain as "the vital vein of Iraq's economy." Although nearly three-quarters of the entire system lies within Iraq, more than 80 percent of the country's measurable water supply comes from outside its borders. Both rivers arise in the mountains of eastern Turkey, the Euphrates passing south and east through Syria and the Tigris flowing along Syria's easternmost tip before entering Iraq. In Iraq they flow separately before merging as the politically contested Shatt al-'Arab waterway.

Since the 1960s the riparian states of Turkey, Syria, and Iraq have made multiple claims to the water of the Euphrates, whose annual flow is almost 29 billion cubic meters. About 90 percent of its catchment area is in Turkey; its two main tributaries, the Balikh and the Khabur, also arise in Turkey but enter the Euphrates in Syrian territory. Both Turkey and Syria have begun to develop this resource despite Iraq's wish to reach a prior agreement about equitable distribution of the water. Turkey has planned or undertaken five dams on the Euphrates since 1963. The Keban dam was completed in 1974 and the Karakiya and Ataturk dams are scheduled for completion by 1987 and 1990, respectively. It has been estimated that the Turkish dams will impound 13 billion cubic meters annually, or close to half the annual flow of the Euphrates. Syria undertook its Tabqa dam project on the Euphrates in 1965. While the reservoir was being filled from 1974 to 1976, the downstream flow was reduced by one-half to only 250 cubic meters per second, depriving, it was said, some 3 million Iraqi farmers of water for irrigation and livestock. The spread of the Shi'i underground movement al-Da'wa has been attributed to this water shortage, which ruined the rice fields and orchards of small agriculturalists in the south.[12] The Iraqi government also blamed the Tabqa dam project for delaying Iraqi development projects such as the Habbaniya dam. Turkey, Syria, and Iraq tentatively reached a tripartite agreement in 1974, but it was linked to other complicated matters such as the construction of oil pipelines from Iraq. The conflicting claims on the Euphrates consequently have not been resolved.

By contrast, the waters of the Tigris have aroused little controversy. Although approximately 40 percent of the Tigris water comes from Turkey, it originates in a mountainous and politically turbulent region where in any case there is sufficient rainfall to satisfy local needs. The rest of the aggregate water volume comes from the Zagros mountains in Iran and northeastern Iraq; all of the numerous and substantial tributaries are Iraqi and originate in the Zagros. Given its tendency to flooding, the greatest problem the Tigris presents to the government is to contain and make use of its waters. Numerous projects to provide hydroelectric power, to reclaim and extend cultivated areas, and to prevent flood damage have been undertaken on the Tigris and its tributaries. The Dokan dam, the Derbendi Khan dam, and the Hamrin dam were finished in 1958, 1962, and 1981, respectively. Another three dams are expected to be completed before 1990 at Mosul, Dahuk, and Bikhma. The importance of these projects to domestic development plans aroused concern for the safety of these sites after the outbreak of war with Iran in 1980.

Overcoming Landlock

Iraq's coastline on the Gulf is only about fifteen kilometers long. Noting Iraq's disadvantage in this regard, Saddam Husain has said that

---

12. Hanna Batatu, "Iraq's Underground Shi'a Movements: Characteristics, Causes and Prospects," *Middle East Journal*, vol. 35 (Autumn 1981), pp. 589–90. Some Iraqis, however, expressed the belief during interviews with me in August 1982 that the movement existed earlier, at least by the late 1950s, although it may have gained impetus during the mid-1970s.

Iraq "has only limited outlets" to the sea while Iran, in comparison, "has a coast 2,300 kilometers long."[13] Following the Algiers Declaration of 1975, Iraq accepted the thalweg—the midpoint of the main navigational channel—of the Shatt al-'Arab as the boundary between itself and Iran. Basra, which before the war handled many of Iraq's imports and exports other than oil, is accessible only through the narrow, vulnerable throat of the Shatt waterway (figure 2-2). In order to protect and facilitate its oil exports, the Iraqi government earlier had built two alternative ports, al-Faw and Umm Qasr, and extended two offshore loading terminals into the Gulf. It also continued to press Kuwait to lease, on a long-term basis, the islands of Warba and Bubiyan. The proximity of Iraqi and Kuwaiti interests here have created and probably will continue to create tension between the two states.

The narrowness of the Shatt and Iraq's constricted frontage on the Gulf are only two of the problems affecting the use of the rivers. The steep gradient of their northern reaches and the shallowness and silting of the channels in the south, for example, prohibit the movement of large watercraft far upstream except for those designed with shallow draft. It has been estimated that following the end of hostilities with Iran, a minimum of six months will be necessary to dredge the southern channels before the shipment of goods from or to Basra can be resumed. The longer the war continues, the more time will be required to remove the accumulated silt.

Economic constraints imposed by the war on the southern region and the increasing need for consumer goods and for equipment related to development have intensified governmental efforts to expand and diversify Iraq's overland transport capacity. This objective has obvious foreign policy ramifications for Iraq, a state almost totally landlocked by Iran, Turkey, Syria, Jordan, Saudi Arabia, and Kuwait. The Ba'th government sought gradually during the 1970s to improve its economic

13. FBIS, *Daily Report: MEA*, September 29, 1980, text of Saddam Husain's address to the nation on September 28, 1980, pp. E1–E8; and Klaus Reinhardt and Adel S. Elias, interview with Iraqi President Saddam Husain, *Der Spiegel*, June 1, 1981, as translated and reprinted in JPRS 78302, *NE/NA Report*, no. 2348 (June 16, 1982), pp. 33–42. See also information in FBIS, *Daily Report: MEA*, December 29, 1980, text of Saddam Husain's cabinet address on December 24, 1980, pp. E1–E7; FBIS, *Daily Report: MEA*, November 12, 1980, text of Saddam Husain's press conference on November 10, 1980, pp. E2–E19; the text of Nicola Firzli, ed., *The Iraq-Iran Conflict* (Paris: Editions du Monde Arabe, 1981), pp. 37–63; and British Broadcasting Corporation, *Summary of World Broadcasts*, ME/6653/A/6, February 19, 1981.

Figure 2-2. *Iraq's Access to the Arabian Gulf*

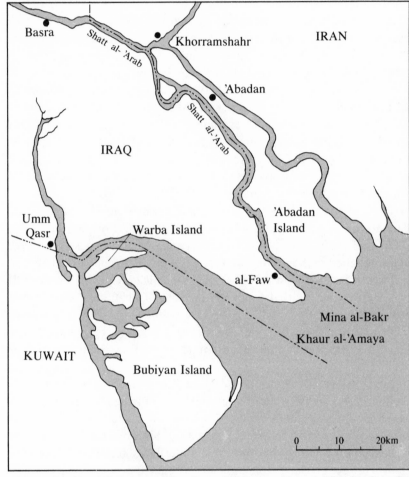

Source: Adapted from U.S. Department of State, Bureau of Intelligence and Research, Office of the Geographer, "International Boundary Study: Iran-Iraq," no. 164 (July 13, 1978), p. 3.

Note: There are several features unique to this area that are too detailed to include in the map but are worth noting. Many small islands can be found in the Shatt al-'Arab from the Gulf to Basra, which makes navigation hazardous. Much of the coastal land is so low that it is either inundated frequently or remains an area of marshes or mud flats.

relations with its immediate neighbors, sometimes unsuccessfully, while consolidating and extending political alliances throughout the Middle East and the third world in general. The outbreak of war in 1980 made diversification of Iraq's overland transport even more imperative.

Iraqi road traffic in 1981 increased 50 percent over that of the previous year, and feverish road-building was under way from Baghdad toward

Kuwait and Jordan. The latter country has received substantial Iraqi aid to develop its Red Sea port at 'Aqaba and to improve the highway from 'Aqaba to 'Amman. Stimulated by the war, imports at 'Aqaba rose from 3 million tons in 1980 to 6.2 million tons in 1981 and probably reached 8 million tons in 1982. One European transport company alone shipped to Iraq in 1980 more than 500 truckloads daily from 'Aqaba and 200 truckloads from Lataqiya and Tartus in Syria, where roll-on/roll-off ships speeded the unloading.[14] Although Saudi Arabia has its own transport problems, it cooperated with Iraq once the Iran-Iraq war began by accepting shipments for Iraq at several of its ports, including Qadima and Dammam. From the Turkish ports of Mersin and Iskandarun, 1,000 to 1,300 trucks a day left for Baghdad in 1981. Kuwait's ports of Shu'aiba and Shuwaikh were also busy in the first two years of the war, with 500 to 1,000 heavy trucks daily transporting goods to Baghdad. Cargo bound from Kuwait to Iraq increased nearly threefold between 1979 and 1982 to approximately 3.5 million tons, although the volume dropped in 1982 as a result of financial pressures caused by the war. During this period, the two governments began to consider plans to construct a railroad linking the two countries; additional plans contemplated railway lines extending from Baghdad to Hussaiba on the Syrian border and from Baghdad to the port of Umm Qasr.[15]

Protecting Oil Exports

Iraqis are acutely sensitive to the vulnerability of the oil resources upon which their economy primarily depends. Vulnerability reflects both the remote location of important oil fields and the need to transport oil over long distances either to the Gulf or to the Mediterranean Sea. Most of Iraq's proven oil reserves and refineries have been concentrated around Kirkuk in the Kurdish Autonomous Region and in Basra province, exposed to any internal political unrest that might arise in north-

---

14. *8 Days*, March 6, 1982, p. 41; *MEED*, vol. 26 (March 19, 1982), pp. 28, 30; "War Spurs Transport Development in Jordan and Iraq," *Wharton Middle East Economic Service*, vol. 1 (November 12, 1982), pp. 1–7; and personal interviews.

15. For further information see *MEED Special Report*, February 1982, p. 18; *MEED*, vol. 25 (July 31, 1981), p. 15; *MEED*, vol. 25 (May 22, 1981), p. 35; Iraqi Ministry of Culture, *Revolution and Development in Iraq* (Baghdad: Iraqi Ministry of Planning, 1980), pp. 90–93; *MEED*, vol. 25 (May 15, 1981), pp. 16, 19; *Financial Times*, July 23, 1981, p. 9; *8 Days*, March 6, 1982, pp. 42–43; and *MEED Special Report*, May 1982, pp. 81–82.

eastern Iraq and to external threat (see figure 1-4). Since the beginning of the Iran-Iraq war, both of these regions and their economic facilities have been primary military targets for Iranian warplanes. The oil terminals at Khaur al-'Amaya and Mina al-Bakr in the Gulf were put out of service during the early stages of the war.

Prior to the 1970s, Iraq's only means of shipping oil by land was a pipeline through Syria. Dependence on Syria led Iraq to construct two new pipelines, one through Turkey and the other from Haditha near the border with Syria to al-Faw on the Gulf. As part of the 1974 agreement on the Euphrates, Iraq agreed with Turkey to construct an oil pipeline 1,000 kilometers in length, 625 of which are in Turkey, ending at Yumurtalik on the bay of Iskandarun, about 10 kilometers from Dörtyol and about 20 kilometers from NATO's easternmost airbase at Incirlik. This pipeline opened in 1977. That Iraq's leaders considered these new pipelines to be part of a policy of independence from foreign interference had been made clear by Saddam Husain when the other project—a reversible line between al-Faw and Haditha capable of carrying 1 million bpd of Kirkuk oil to the Gulf or 900,000 bpd of Basra oil to the Mediterranean—was completed and inaugurated in 1975 as "the strategic pipeline." Referring to "this vital project and its role in protecting our national economy . . . and our political independence," Husain declared that it would "ensure the transport and marketing of crude oil with great flexibility according to the requirements of economic planning and the exigencies of political and military action."[16]

Since the mid-1970s Iraq's three main outlets for oil toward its west have been the pipelines to Turkey, with an export capacity of 650,000 to 700,000 bpd; to Syria's Mediterranean port of Baniyas, with a capacity of 700,000 to 800,000 bpd; and a 57-kilometer spur on the Syrian line diverging to Tripoli, Lebanon, with a capacity of some 400,000 bpd. The line terminating at Baniyas, more than half of which lies within Syria, has been a source of frequent disputes. Syria halted throughput from December 1966 to March 1967, nationalized the Syrian portion of the line in 1972, and imposed a doubling of transit fees on Iraq in 1973. The

16. *Middle East Economic Survey,* vol. 19 (January 2, 1976), p. 2. Syria's leaders had objected to construction of the Turkish pipeline for two reasons: they had hoped to earn increased pumping dues and gain political leverage over Iraq, and they bore a grudge against Turkey for its assumption of control over the province or region of Hatay in a rigged referendum held in 1939. Hatay, generally called Alexandretta by the Arabs (and currently known as Iskandarun), had been part of the French mandate in Syria.

whole Syrian-Lebanese pipeline was closed in April 1976 because of the Lebanese civil war and the failure of Iraq and Syria to agree on transit fees. In February 1979, with talk of an Iraqi-Syrian rapprochement, the pipeline again began to operate, but the Lebanese spur was not reopened until late December 1981. There are estimates that Syria then accepted 300,000 to 500,000 bpd, or 30 to 50 percent of Iraq's exports, of which it kept 80,000 to 100,000 bpd for its refineries at Homs.[17] On April 10, 1982, Syria again stopped oil shipments through the Kirkuk-Baniyas line and therefore the Kirkuk-Tripoli line after signing an agreement to purchase Iranian oil. Turkey then carried the bulk of Iraq's oil exports, or 600,000 to 650,000 bpd; by the fall of 1983, enlargement of the line and the addition of chemicals to increase throughput allowed Iraq to move well over 800,000 bpd through Turkey. Approximately 100,000 bpd were also carried by truck through Jordan and Turkey in 1983.

Both the Syrian and Turkish pipelines have been prime targets for saboteurs. Iraq's prewar oil exports of nearly 3.2 million bpd were reduced to slightly less than 1 million bpd by Iranian military action after the war began; following three acts of sabotage in early January 1982, they were temporarily reduced to just 300,000 bpd.[18] These acts included an explosion five kilometers south of the Syrian border in Lebanon and a second in Kurdish terrritory some seventy kilometers inside Turkey. The third incident was the shelling of a tanker loading Iraqi crude at Tripoli.

Throughout the war the Iraqi government has continued to seek means of reducing the vulnerability of its oil industry. Oil exploration continues in regions other than Kurdistan. Plans are being formulated to disperse facilities and storage depots, to install underground equipment, and to stockpile oil. Although a proposed pipeline through Kuwait has been postponed indefinitely, discussions with Turkey began in April 1982 to increase the capacity of the line from Kirkuk to Dörtyol to almost 1 million bpd. Work is proceeding to that end and is expected to be

17. Interview with Iraqi oil minister Qasim Ahmad al-Taqi, August 10, 1982; *MEED*, vol. 27 (February 25, 1983), p. 24; and Khadduri, *Republican Iraq*, pp. 287–88.

18. *Petroleum Intelligence Weekly*, January 4, 1982, p. 6, and January 11, 1982, pp. 2, 7; *Financial Times*, October 14, 1982, p. 6; "Hard-Pressed Iraq Sees Its Oil Exports Slashed by Attack on Pipeline to Turkey," *Wall Street Journal*, January 12, 1982; and *8 Days*, January 16, 1982, p. 3. It was also noted in *MEED*, vol. 26 (February 19, 1982), p. 12, that five Turks were accused by Turkish authorities of two separate sabotage incidents against the Kirkuk-Dörtyol pipeline. The men said they were commanded by Jalal Talabani, a Kurdish guerrilla leader.

completed no later than early 1985. Construction of a new pipeline through Saudi Arabia was proposed in July 1981; but as was the case in Kuwait, it met with resistance on the part of the host country. If it were built, the Iraqi-Saudi line would cost as much as $4 billion and transport perhaps 1.5 million bpd. Although continuance of the war with Iran raised doubts about the feasibility of constructing the line, Iraq announced unilaterally in 1982 that a consortium of companies would finance it against future oil revenues or debt borne by the Iraqi government. The line as proposed by the Iraqis would begin at Rumaila near Basra, turn south and west, then either join (as a first stage) or parallel (as a second stage) the Saudi pipeline from Ghawar oilfield to the Red Sea port of Yanbu', where it would diverge to a new terminal to be built by Iraq on the Red Sea coast. From there the oil would move both north through the Suez Canal and south through the Gulf of Aden. Completion was tentatively set for 1986.[19] Another project under discussion in 1984 was a pipeline tentatively planned to carry 1 million bpd of oil from Haditha in Iraq to the port of 'Aqaba, Jordan.

Approximately 55 percent of the world's recoverable oil reserves are located in the Gulf states, and some 65 percent of the world's non-Communist oil supplies are shipped through the Strait of Hormuz. Iraq shipped through the strait about 70 percent of its oil exports and other products such as dates before the 1980 war. The Gulf, which had gained prominence in Iraqi calculations after 1960, assumed an even greater priority when the shah of Iran in November 1971 militarily annexed three islands in the Strait of Hormuz—Greater Tunb, Lesser Tunb, and Abu Musa—that were also claimed by amirates in the southern Gulf.[20] In 1973 the shah exacerbated tensions by announcing his personal ambition to establish and maintain military superiority over this region. An Omani proposal in 1976 for the "protection of the waterways"—that is, Hor-

19. The Middle East Reporter, December 5, 1981, p. 23; Karen Elliott House, "Saudis Allow Iraq to Build Pipeline to the Red Sea," Wall Street Journal, February 22, 1983; and Petroleum Intelligence Weekly, February 28, 1983, p. 2.

20. For additional information see John Duke Anthony, Arab States of the Lower Gulf: People, Politics, Petroleum (Washington, D.C.: Middle East Institute, 1975); Enver M. Koury, Oil and Geopolitics in the Persian Gulf Area: A Center of Power (Chicago: Catholic Press for the Institute of Middle Eastern and North African Affairs, 1973); Jean J. A. Salmon, "The Conflict on Sovereignty Over Abu-Mussa and the Lesser and Greater Tunb Islands," Le Monde Diplomatique (Paris), November 1980, as translated and reprinted in JPRS 77099, NE/NA Report, no. 2241 (January 5, 1981), pp. 69–71; and Eric Rouleau, "A Policy of Power," Le Monde (Paris), December 2, 1971.

muz—was no comfort to Iraq when Oman was so closely associated with Great Britain, Iran, and later the United States—countries against which Iraq has held political grievances. After the fall of the Pahlavis in 1979, Iraq hoped for a change in Iranian foreign policy toward the Gulf. Instead, the new Islamic Republic called for extension of an Islamic revolution into other Gulf states and renewed its historical claims to Bahrain, which ironically were not dissimilar from those Iraq had made on Kuwait in 1961. Iraqi discomfort with Iran increased when it became known that Baghdad might be within the range of surface-to-surface missiles launched from Iran, or at least was more vulnerable to attack than Tehran.[21]

Iraq also has an interest in the Red Sea that was clearly stated in *al-Thawra*, an official newspaper of the Iraqi Ba'th party: "The Red Sea is of distinctive strategic importance politically, economically and militarily. This importance stems from the fact that it is the shortest sea route linking the West to the East, and is the link between the Mediterranean on the one hand and the Arabian Sea and Indian Ocean via Suez and the Bab el Mandeb Strait on the other."[22] Iraq and other Gulf countries have criticized Israel, the United States, and the Soviet Union for interfering in the internal affairs of African and Arab states that border the Red Sea.[23]

In the 1970s, Saudi Arabia began to express its own concerns. The Saudis held conferences in July 1972 and March 1973 (the latter attended by the two Yemens, Sudan, and Somalia) in which natural resources, sovereign rights, and security needs in the Red Sea were discussed. An Arab deterrent force was also proposed but did not materialize. After the Suez Canal was reopened in 1975, Saudi Arabia began to develop its Red Sea ports, as did North Yemen with its port at Hodeida. Saudi port development in part reflects the diminished importance of the trans-Arabian pipeline (Tapline), which has been little used since it became more economical in the mid-1970s to ship Saudi oil through the Gulf than through the pipeline to the Mediterranean. Taking its place is Petroline,

21. FBIS, *Daily Report: MEA*, November 12, 1980, text of Saddam Husain's press conference on November 10, 1980, p. E9.

22. FBIS, *Daily Report: MEA*, September 5, 1979, article entitled "The Red Sea: A Vital Extension for Arab Territories," by Barzan Ibrahim al-Takriti in *al-Thawra*, August 20, 1979, pp. E1–E3.

23. L. Thomas Walsh, "Bab-el-Mandeb: The Gateway of Tears for the U.S.?" *Armed Forces Journal International*, vol. 118 (September 1980), pp. 74, 76.

opened in June 1981 to link the oilfields of Ghawar and Abqaiq to the new port at Yanbu'.

Supporting Arab Consensus

Iraq's sphere of political interest includes the larger Arab nation, in which the present Ba'th government sees Iraq as providing strategic depth and serving as the eastern flank. There is a feeling among some Middle Easterners that their common heritage as Arabs is the basis for a politically stronger and more cohesive region. Those who hold this view are in contrast to those who believe that Islam is a more binding and widely shared foundation for unity. The Ayatullah Khomeini, who is one of the latter group, distrusts Arab nationalism because he considers it an essentially antiprogressive and obstructionist philosophy. Arab nationalists, on the other hand, perceive the division of the Arab world into twenty-two states as the outcome of deliberate efforts by the West to undermine an Arab consensus. According to Saddam Husain, this policy continues, for "powers are still trying in every possible way to divide these 22 parts into at least another 22 parts."[24]

The concept of an Arab consensus—that is, Arab unity or Arab nationalism—is central to Ba'thist ideology, and there have been numerous unsuccessful attempts by Arab nationalists to make it a reality. The rationale for such attempts includes not only common political ideologies but also common strategic and economic interests. Various formulas for unity between Iraq and Syria, for example, were proposed in the mid-1940s and the early 1960s. They failed. Unity between the Iraqi and Syrian governments again was put forward after Egypt and Israel signed a peace agreement in 1978, but met with failure in the summer of 1979. The benefits to Iraq from such a union were stated by Saddam Husain:

24. FBIS, *Daily Report: MEA*, November 12, 1980, text of Saddam Husain's press conference on November 10, 1980, pp. E2–E19. Precisely this policy of stimulating further divisions in the Arab Middle East has been proposed by an Israeli, Oded Yinon. Among the countries Yinon singles out for attention are Egypt, Syria, Iraq, Saudi Arabia, and the smaller Gulf states. See his original article, "A Strategy for Israel in the 1980s," in *Kivunim* (Orientations), no. 14 (February 1982). Moreover, an Israeli official was quoted as saying in 1982 that "ideally we'd like to see Iraq disintegrate into a Shiite, Kurdish and Sunni community, each making war on the other." See *Newsweek*, July 26, 1982, p. 32.

As in the past, geographical, political, and strategic requisites continue to push Iraq toward unity with Syria. Indeed, the neighboring territories and close relations established as a result; the common river; the complementary economies; the internal strength in the face of foreign threats; and the need for sea outlets, particularly in this age of oil—Iraq being one of the most important oil-exporting states—all these requisites make Iraq feel the need to establish a binding relationship with Syria. Naturally, the best, most useful, and guaranteed relationship would be that of unity. Indeed, Iraq would benefit from unity at a time when it is offering sacrifices for it. Therefore, the sacrifices which Iraq might have to offer for such a unity would not diminish the importance of the benefits which such unity would bring.[25]

Ba'thists are pan-Arabists, theoretically believing that the artificial and Western boundaries imposed on the Middle East must someday be dissolved in order to reunite the Arab nation. There is, however, a difference between the theoretical formulation and the practical implementation of this philosophy that is evident to many persons, including Arabs. Unequal geographic distribution of resources, competition among leading Arab politicians and their political ideologies, and the presence of diverse cultural groups ensure disagreement, however desirable the ultimate goal of unity appears as an alternative to superpower domination. Perhaps because of Iraq's reliance on many Arab states during the war with Iran, the idea has undergone reformulation in Iraq, as will be seen in chapter 4. High-ranking Iraqis said in 1981, after the war began, that unity remained an ideal and a useful political tool, though it would not necessarily be implemented through the deliberate elimination of borders in the near future and perhaps not implemented at all.

Iraq's perceptions of its immediate strategic interests and those of concern to the broader Arab world are the framework in which the Ba'th party sets priorities in foreign affairs. Geography and politics are related not only in Iraqi politics but also in relations between the Arab world and international powers. Husain warned before the war that if the Arab countries ignored the realities of present political trends, there would be a "shift from the outer perimeter to the inside perimeter," a reference both to the strategic concerns of individual Arab countries and to the collective political responsibility of the Arab nation.[26]

25. FBIS, *Daily Report: MEA*, September 17, 1980, text of message by Saddam Husain to the Kuwaiti newspaper *al-Watan*, pp. E2–E4.

26. FBIS, *Daily Report: MEA*, September 5, 1979, quoted in "The Red Sea: A Vital Extension for Arab Territories," article by Barzan Ibrahim al-Takriti in *al-Thawra*, August 20, 1979, pp. E1–E3.

Conclusion

Geography and history produce similar and recurring challenges that confront all Iraqi governments, regardless of their political coloration or the foundations of their support. In domestic affairs, governing authorities have had to deal with serious problems of resource utilization, transportation, and communication in the context of the difficult climate and topography of Iraq and the patterns of human settlement there. Iraqi pluralism, a consequence of Iraq's geographic location and human adaptation to its diverse environmental conditions, not only affects patterns of human interchange but also requires that all Iraqi governments unrelentingly seek political legitimacy. They have done so either by force or by the use of shared or invented symbols of sociopolitical identification across the spectrum of Iraq's pluralistic associations. Because Iraq is virtually landlocked and is bordered on two sides by strong non-Arab powers, Iraqi governments also have had to seek ways to minimize the vulnerability of the state.

While Iraqi modernization involves revolutionary methods, it too is shaped by the environment, as we shall see in part 2. Even Iraq's oil wealth has not diminished the impact of the recurring themes in Iraqi history on the formulation of domestic and foreign policy, though it has increased economic flexibility. Unfortunately for Iraq, the resulting political competition has often been an impediment to progress.

PART TWO

The Iraqi Ba'th Party

CHAPTER THREE

Years of Growth and Conflict

THOUGH all Iraqi governments have had to grapple with the problems presented by Iraq's physical environment, its historical variables, and its ever-changing political, economic, and social currents, the domestic and foreign affairs of Iraq are strongly influenced today by one factor unique to the twentieth century: control of the government since 1968 by a single dominant political organization, the Arab Ba'th Socialist party. The ideology, objectives, and even the structure of the party influence virtually all governmental decisions. It is therefore essential to examine the Ba'th political elite in order to understand how the government functions.

Such a discussion is limited by a scarcity of information about the party and by the difficulty of access to it. The reasons for this are straightforward. Before 1960 the Ba'thists in many Arab countries were struggling to attain recognition and expand their following; members were frequently jailed and their organizations occasionally forced underground. In Iraq the prevailing political environment even as late as the 1960s compelled the party to operate clandestinely as it struggled against the central government and competed for adherents against other political movements, particularly the Communist party. Moreover, the Ba'th party itself has not been free of intraparty disputes, as all its members are well aware. As recently as 1980, Tariq 'Aziz, a prominent Iraqi Ba'thist and writer, remarked on the party's clandestine and revolutionary heritage: "The ABSP [the Arab Ba'th Socialist party] is not a conventional political organization, but is composed of cells of valiant revolutionaries. . . . They are experts in secret organization. They are organizers of demonstrations, strikes, and armed revolutions. . . . They were the knights of struggle."[1]

1. Tariq 'Aziz, *On Arab-Iranian Relations* (Baghdad: Ministry of Culture and Information, Summer 1980), p. 51.

59

The historical legacy and complex problems of maintaining Ba'thist control of the government during the 1980s amid numerous competing political forces have led to a natural reluctance on the part of Iraqi Ba'th members to discuss publicly the internal affairs of the party. Communication is restricted by the hierarchical structure of the party and even among the Ba'th's governing elite. In addition to affecting the quality of research on contemporary Iraq, clandestinity has profound consequences for the functioning of the party and the state. Despite this constraint, five aspects of the Ba'th's position in Iraqi life are readily discerned:

—The party is ubiquitous. Its organs function alongside or in place of the government bureaucracy, thereby imparting to government a dualistic nature.

—Although the Iraqi Ba'thists may deviate from a strict interpretation of Ba'thist ideology, their doctrine nevertheless sets the guidelines for policy formulation by Iraqi leaders. Some of the party's concepts, such as nonalignment, pan-Arabism, and accommodation with diverse religious and ethnic groups, have become hallmarks of Ba'thist thought to greater or lesser degrees throughout the party's history. These concepts have been formally translated into standard Ba'th positions on the superpowers, revolutionary movements, royalist and conservative regimes, and the issues of Palestine and Israel, though they have not necessarily been practiced with unswerving devotion.

—The Ba'th regime is further distinguished from those of the other Arab Gulf states in that it is not hereditary.

—Iraqi Ba'th policies, as distinct from Ba'thism in the Arab world generally, are of necessity directed to specific Iraqi problems and therefore diverge from an extreme pan-Arab stance when deemed necessary by the Ba'th leadership in Iraq.

—Since Ba'thists took control of Iraq in 1968, their leaders increasingly have had to deal with practical problems of governance rather than concentrate primarily on party ideology or organization. Because Iraq is a less-developed country, Iraqi leaders devote considerable resources to internal development, such as improvement of irrigation and the agricultural sector and construction of the industrial sector. Because Iraq is an oil-producing state, they must also cope with complex problems in the sectors of oil and finance that have consequences far beyond the state's borders. These needs have resulted in a series of related party decisions regarding Iraq's labor force, infrastructure, and educational system.

This chapter and the following one examine so far as is possible those aspects of the Ba'th party that are relevant to understanding Iraq's current domestic and foreign policies, including the history of the party, its relation to other political parties, the evolution of its doctrine, and the means by which it now influences the determination of priorities. How the party functions and the means by which it seeks to reach the broader public are also considered, as are the social and educational background of the ruling elite, the extent of party membership, and its hierarchy. Within this framework, indeed throughout this study, special attention is devoted to Saddam Husain; however long his tenure as president of Iraq, he has been a primary formulator of Iraq's domestic and foreign policies since 1968 and as such provides the most visible evidence of "mainstream" Ba'thist thought in Iraq.

Both in the present discussion and in that of the Iran-Iraq war that follows, which is essentially a case study of Iraqi policy formulation, conjecture is required to understand sensitive and less-accessible areas of Ba'th politics. Speculative topics include the relationship between Ba'thists and non-Ba'thists, between the central decisionmakers and those to whom they delegate authority, and finally among Ba'th party members in the government bureaucracy, in the military, and among the technocrats. The discussion does not resolve whatever contradictions already exist in the literature. Its purpose is rather to explain wherever possible the general structure, processes, and membership of the Ba'th in relation to other institutions and individuals within Iraq as the party guides decisionmaking and garners public support for its domestic and foreign policies.

Origins and Development of the Party to 1968

Before the Iraqi Ba'thists took control of the government in 1968, party members were exposed to a variety of formative influences. One was the gradual but determined systematization of Ba'th doctrine and organization that had begun in the 1940s. Another was the clandestine mode the Iraqi Ba'thists adopted in the early 1950s and retained, with only a brief respite in the early 1960s, until they seized power in 1968. A third was their observation of the Ba'th party's struggles in other Arab countries, particularly Syria, which had assumed public dimension by the late 1950s. Yet another was rivalry, manifest as early as 1959 and acute throughout the 1960s, between the Iraqi Ba'th and other political movements, particularly the Communist party. The present domestic and foreign policies of the Iraqi Ba'th and Iraq's relations with other states, such as Syria, thus can be better understood by viewing the party's development within a historical framework.

Responses to Foreign Influence

Various kinds of foreign intervention in the Middle East during the past century created the alembic in which Ba'thists, and indeed modern political thinkers in this region generally, developed much of their ideology. The power vacuum created after World War I by the dismemberment of the Ottoman Empire, which had exercised control in the Arabian peninsula and North Africa for half a millennium, was filled by Great Britain, France, and Italy following intense competition for political dominance in the region. The subsequent delineation of fixed boundaries and nation-states led to further competition not only between the European governments and indigenous political forces within the new states, but among the indigenous people themselves.

Political conflict was sharpened by additional factors: competition among and diminution in the strength of traditional rulers, the discovery and exploitation of oil, fluctuations in the rates of population growth and migration, the search for new communication routes, diverse forms of social identification, disparities and shifts in the distribution of wealth, the development of state nationalism as a unifying political force, and the establishment of a Jewish national home in the mandate of Palestine. Significantly, Arabs perceived all of these factors in varying degrees either as tools useful for achieving the political and economic goals of the European mandate authorities or as by-products of their policies.

Resistance by Middle Easterners to foreign influence has taken two general forms that resemble each other in their diagnosis of the problem but are diametrically opposed in their solutions. The first is that in which Islam provides the raison d'être for unity. Within this broad category are subsumed a variety of belief systems, such as Islamic modernism, reformism, conservatism, and fundamentalism. The extent and diversity of these movements are such that an accepted scheme that conveniently categorizes them has not yet emerged. In the so-called post-modernist period, when foreign interference in the Muslim world was increasing and profound in its consequences, many Islamic movements that may simply have sought the purification of their Islamic society began to adopt political goals. Broadly speaking, those subscribing to these movements think that the humiliating events of this period were possible and persist because their own society has undergone a moral crisis so enfeebling as to preclude effective resistance to foreign domination.

The solution of Islamic conservatives in particular, although formulated in numerous ways, is to return to the perceived purity of Islamic values, especially those of early Islam. Islam thus becomes a common rationale for unity transcending all other associations, including nationalism. Membership in the Islamic community, *umma*, effectively makes all Muslims equal before God and subject to the same rights and responsibilities. All daily acts, whether religious or secular, are then guided by the exclusive precepts of Islam. This concept of Islamic unity or an Islamic nation has become a major political force in the Middle East today. The *muwahhidun,* or so-called Wahhabis, of Saudi Arabia and the Islamic revolution in Iran represent two well-known examples. The most visible opposition groups that engage in terrorist activities against the Iraqi government have chosen this path.

Believers in the principle of Arab unity or Arab nationalism—the second Middle Eastern response to foreign interference, which assumed its momentum only after World War II—have proposed a "revolutionary" or "visionary" solution directly at variance with that of the Islamic movements. While recognizing the importance of Islam, Arab nationalists think that as an ideology it does not fully encompass the needs of the Middle East, for three reasons. First, although the vast majority of Arabs are Muslims, some countries include concentrated populations of other religious groups, however small. Second, there are differences in the interpretation and practical application of Islam within the Islamic world as a whole. Third, it is felt that those who subscribe to Islamic fundamentalism cannot effectively adapt themselves to the ever-changing phenomena of the twentieth century because their interpretation of Islam tends to be immutable, being theoretically based on the "pure" early Islamic nation.

Arab nationalists believe that if Arabs are to compete in the modern world, they must acquire the knowledge and skills used by more advanced nations and be prepared to contend in the international marketplace with technologically advanced non-Muslim countries, within the framework of secular international legal systems. Advocates of the nationalist ideology believe that it circumvents the potential problems the Islamic movements confront, particularly those affecting economic development, and they theoretically would diminish sectarian affiliations for the sake of concerted action.

Nasirism, established in Egypt by President Jamal 'Abd al-Nasir, is considered by many to be the best-known representation of Arab nationalism. Ba'thism, however, represents an even more consequential evolution of Arab nationalism and political thought in the Middle East. In sharp contrast to Nasirites, whose activities were mobilized around the cult of a single personality, Ba'thists attained a high level of organization, systematizing the party's structure and functions, its determination of policy priorities, its standards of membership, and its rules of conduct and election. Although an individual might acquire considerable prestige or even absolute power within the Ba'th, the party was designed to function in the event of his ousting or death. Party ideologues were responsible for the formulation of doctrine and for commentary on current events. Newspapers officially designated as organs of the party were published even during periods when the party was illegal in the states in which it operated.

Since its inception, Ba'thism has spread from Syria to Jordan, Iraq, and Lebanon, and to a lesser extent to Sudan, Morocco, Saudi Arabia, Yemen, and Libya. The spread of Ba'thist ideology in Egypt was hampered by Nasir's overwhelming charisma during the 1950s and by the fact that Cairo was Egypt's educational center rather than Beirut or Damascus, which were the formative arenas of Ba'thist thought.[2]

Compared with the broad-based Islamic movements, Arab nationalism and its extreme expression in pan-Arabism have seemed to the spectrum of Middle Eastern populations to be remote and abstract, hence less appealing. Evidence of this is found in the originally narrow membership and slow growth of Arab nationalist movements such as the Ba'th, whose first adherents were mainly students and intellectuals. It is instructive in this regard to consider the backgrounds of three Arabs—Zaki al-Arsuzi, Salah al-Din al-Bitar, and Michel Aflaq—who were major contributors to the early development of Ba'thist ideology.

2. Numerous articles and books have been written about or relating to the Ba'th. Five useful studies in English are Hanna Batatu, *The Old Social Classes and the Revolutionary Movements of Iraq* (Princeton University Press, 1978); John F. Devlin, *The Ba'th Party: A History from Its Origins to 1966* (Hoover Institution, 1976); Kamel S. Abu Jaber, *The Arab Ba'th Socialist Party: History, Ideology, and Organization* (Syracuse University Press, 1966); Majid Khadduri, *Republican 'Iraq: A Study in 'Iraqi Politics since the Revolution of 1958* (Oxford University Press, 1969); and Khadduri, *Socialist Iraq: A Study in Iraqi Politics since 1968* (Washington, D.C.: Middle East Institute, 1978).

Neither in their shared attributes nor in their dissimilarities could any of these men be considered typical of their communities. They were linked by three unusual characteristics: all had middle-class origins, all received part of their education at the Sorbonne in Paris, and all returned to the Middle East, where they became educators. They were distinguished by the diversity of their early religious affiliations: Arsuzi was a Nusairi, Bitar a Sunni Muslim, and Aflaq a Greek Orthodox Christian.

These associations at times were as controversial as they were diverse. The term Nusairi, for example, is generally used to refer to an extreme Shi'i sect, but it also has been employed diversely to describe an administrative area around Lataqiya in Syria where there are concentrations of Nusairis and to identify various social groups, scattered from northern Lebanon through western Iraq, who adhere to Nusairi beliefs. Nusairis are more commonly known today as 'Alawites. Although persecuted since the twelfth century, the 'Alawites, among them President Hafiz al-Asad, have come to dominate the political and military life of Syria.

The story surrounding Aflaq is revealing not only of the relationship between politics and social affiliations in the Middle East but also of the propaganda value of symbols. During the tensions between Nasir and the Ba'thists in the late 1950s and early 1960s, Nasirites claimed that Aflaq was a Greek from Cyprus because he belonged to the Eastern or Greek Orthodox Church. Ba'thists retaliated by claiming that Nasir was really an Iranian because his wife's family was of distant Iranian origin. After Ayatullah Khomeini's return to Tehran in 1979, Iranian propagandists sought to discredit the Iraqi Ba'th by claiming that Aflaq had a Jewish mother. At other times rumors were spread that Aflaq was a secret convert to Islam.

Each of the three men eventually acquired a reputation as an intellectual and an Arab nationalist, concerned above all with the possibility of a moral and intellectual revolution among Arabs. For an Arab, this was to entail self-recognition of his Arabness and striving on the part of all Arabs to join in a united and independent Arab state against foreign opposition. Arsuzi, on the one hand, and Aflaq and Bitar, on the other, expounded these views during the 1930s at political meetings that attracted small groups of high-school students. At first each group numbered only a few dozen; but as the young men pursued higher education, they shared their thoughts with other students and frequently became educators themselves, thus widening their circles of influence.

Four events, either prompted by or in reaction to foreign influences, have been identified by writers on the Middle East as the primary catalysts in extending and solidifying Arab nationalist opinion, particularly in Iraq and Syria during the later 1930s and the 1940s. The first was the Arab revolt that occurred in Palestine between 1936 and 1939 in response to the increasing number of Jewish immigrants, to the fact that Jewish groups were smuggling in weapons, and to the announcement in 1937 of a partition of the Arab and Jewish communities. The second was France's transfer of Alexandretta, a former *sanjaq,* or administrative district, of the Ottoman Empire, to Turkish suzerainty in 1939 despite strong protests by Armenian and Arab residents, among whom was Arsuzi. The episode culminated in the emigration to Syria of thousands of refugees, many of whom were later to become Ba'thists. The first Ba'thists influential in Iraq reputedly were from Alexandretta. Third, after the fall of France in World War II, Free French and British forces invaded Lebanon and Syria in June 1941, promising that those areas henceforth would be independent. The immediate outcome differed greatly from Arab expectations. Not until 1946 was an agreement reached, under the auspices of the United Nations, which stipulated that British and French troops withdraw by the end of that year. Finally, during the spring of 1941, the government of Rashid 'Ali al-Gailani in Iraq protested Britain's increased military presence in that country, and fighting broke out as Iraqis tried to capture Britain's military base at Habbaniya, about seventy-five kilometers west of Baghdad. Following the failure of this attempt, Gailani was exiled from Iraq until after the revolution of 1958.

The four years following the events of 1941 brought many changes, particularly for Aflaq's and Bitar's followers. During the early 1940s, as Arsuzi was withdrawing from public life, Aflaq and Bitar began to concentrate on politics rather than teaching.[3] They published bulletins and organized demonstrations in Damascus in support of Gailani's government in Iraq. They advocated pan-Arabism, the elimination of artificial boundaries imposed by the mandates, and the union of all Arabs

---

3. The lives of these men were not easy. Not long after a term of imprisonment, Arsuzi retired from active political life and died a natural death in Damascus in 1968. Bitar was assassinated in his office in Paris on July 21, 1980, reputedly by Syrian Ba'thists. Aflaq is currently the secretary-general of the Iraqi Ba'th party, although he is rarely seen and is often referred to in Baghdad as a man who is well respected but past his prime. There have been rumors that he opposed the way in which the Iran-Iraq war had been conducted and thus deliberately kept a low profile.

in a single state under a single leadership. Strength was to be derived from *ihya*, literally revitalization or reflection on the heritage of Arab culture, in order to infuse the continuing struggle with common goals and vigor. By 1943, *ihya* had been replaced by the term *ba'th*, literally resurrection or renaissance; the name of their movement, *Harakat al-Ba'th al-Arabi*, the Arab Renaissance Movement, was first mentioned in that year. The membership was estimated then to be fewer than ten.[4] By 1945, they replaced the term for movement *(haraka)* with that for party *(hizb)*. On July 10, 1945, Aflaq, Bitar, and Midhat al-Bitar sought from the Syrian government formal recognition of their *Hizb al-Ba'th al-Arabi*, the Arab Ba'th party. Although denied licensure, the party continued to expand laterally and to develop a hierarchy of leaders. Its estimated membership was then in the hundreds, with affiliated groups in Aleppo, Homs, Lataqiya, and Jabal Druze. The first party newspaper, *al-Ba'th*, appeared in mid-1946 bearing the party's slogan: "One Arab nation, (with) one immortal message." This was the beginning of a large and ever-evolving body of Ba'thist thought to appear in speeches, articles, books, magazines, newsletters, and journals.

The Path to Power

The increasing geographic diversity of the party's membership and its numerical expansion did not abate. In 1947, Aflaq and Bitar sought to include Arsuzi's followers within their party. Arsuzi agreed. The first Ba'th party congress was convened in Damascus on April 4, 1947, which came to be recognized as the party's date of founding. Attended by about 250 persons, including students from neighboring Arab countries, the congress approved a constitution as well as a statute defining the rights and obligations of members. Michel Aflaq was elected secretary-general with a three-man executive committee. An additional union took place in 1952 between the Ba'th and Akram al-Hurani's Arab Socialist party. Although socialism had entered into some earlier Ba'th writings, it was after this union that greater lip-service was paid to it and the term socialism first was included in the party's name.[5] This union extended the party's influence into the middle ranks of the Syrian military and the region around Hama.

4. Batatu, *Old Social Classes*, p. 727.
5. Hurani and the Ba'thists dissolved their union in 1962. Since 1976 he has been living in Baghdad; by some accounts he engages in business, by others, in politics.

Between the founding congress of 1947 and 1953, when it became known as the *Hizb al-Ba'th al-Arabi al-Ishtiraki*—the Arab Ba'th (Renaissance) Socialist party—the organization achieved considerable expansion in the larger cities and towns of Syria. The debacle in Palestine in 1948 further increased the party's appeal and extended it for the first time beyond the borders of Syria, as many Arabs identified with the humiliation and loss of rights of the Palestinian Arabs. Collateral branches were established in that year in Transjordan and the following year in Lebanon. During the first half of the 1950s, Ba'th activity also expanded into Iraq, Saudi Arabia, Yemen, Libya, and Jordan. It is estimated that Syrian party membership grew from approximately 200 in April 1947 to 500 at the beginning of 1953, with an additional few hundred Ba'thists in other countries.[6]

Despite its potential influence, the appeal of the Ba'th remained restricted until the mid-1960s. A partial explanation is that party members sought to recruit those closest to them in their professional and personal lives. This practice led to a concentration of Ba'thists in Iraqi towns such as Tikrit, 'Ana, Samarra, and Haditha, and in areas populated by the Druze and the 'Alawites in Syria. Since the late 1930s the Communists also had discouraged lateral expansion of the Ba'th in that they had developed well-organized clandestine cells that were already entrenched in so-called people's organizations—a tactic not yet systematized by the Ba'th. Finally, the appeal of pan-Arabism was less attractive than religious, geographic, or ethnic associations. Many groups, especially the military, generally perceived the Ba'thists as a young educated civilian elite.

Although Iraq later became a major center of Ba'thist thought, its evolution in that country was particularly slow because the party's activities, beginning as early as 1949 and 1950,[7] had to be clandestine. The first official branch was established in 1952 or 1953, but its first notable activity did not occur until January 1955, when students went on strike against the recently announced Turkish-Iraqi defense treaty, more commonly known as the Baghdad Pact. The strike was followed some five months later by government raids against Ba'thist centers in which more than a hundred persons were arrested, twenty-two of whom were brought to trial.

6. See Devlin, *The Ba'th Party*, pp. 60–61 and other relevant sections of his book, for detailed accounts of this period.

7. Interview on August 10, 1982, with Naim Haddad, a member of the Ba'th's Revolutionary Command Council and president of the National Assembly.

By the time of the revolution of 1958, the Hashimite government of Iraq had so alienated the general public that opposition existed in virtually all quarters. There were many sources of criticism, but at their core lay the concentration and perpetuation of political power within a small ruling elite whose influence originated in and continued to be supported by the West. The 1950s were already a volatile political period in the Middle East. Among the events of that decade were the signing of the Western-supported Baghdad Pact in 1955; the British, French, and Israeli attack on the Suez Canal in 1956; and the Lebanese civil war, which erupted in part over the question of Lebanon's neutrality in foreign relations and in which the West intervened. Meanwhile, Nasir's prestige was high, and his emphasis on Arab rights and freedom from foreign interference struck a responsive chord in many people. The predictable stand of the Iraqi government in support of Western security needs eroded popular support for the government to such an extent that the government's overthrow took only hours and the demise of the Hashimite monarchy went virtually unmourned, at least publicly.

At no time before 1958 does it appear that the Iraqi Ba'th organization made a substantial contribution to political change within the country, though it had achieved the status of a regional command with branches in Kirkuk, Mosul, and Basra by the end of 1957. Its ideas remained essentially restricted to students who had returned from Damascus, Beirut, London, and the United States and then had congregated in the urban centers, particularly Baghdad.

Only after the government tried to reform certain students by sending them to military-supervised camps in 1955 did some army officers allegedly become favorably disposed to Ba'thist doctrine.[8] Only a few Ba'thists, however, were among the military officers associated with the planning of the July 14, 1958, revolution. Among them was Colonel Ahmad Hasan al-Bakr, who was appointed by the Free Officers as one of a three-member court of martial law on the day of the revolution and became the first Ba'thist president of Iraq when his party took control in 1968. Various estimates place the number of Free Officers at 150 to 300, the latter figure probably including sympathizers in addition to active participants.

The Free Officers were directed by a clandestine entity known as the Central Organization, composed of fourteen men aided individually by groups of trusted supporters. The fourteen held a variety of political

8. Devlin, *The Ba'th Party*, pp. 108–09.

views but all were to some degree Arab nationalists. Within several months after the revolution the leader of the Central Organization, 'Abd al-Karim Qasim, had emerged as the sole leader of the government at the expense of many of the Free Officers. It is nevertheless notable that in addition to Qasim, two other members of the Central Organization later became presidents of Iraq: 'Abd al-Salam 'Arif took control in 1963 and was succeeded by his brother, 'Abd al-Rahman 'Arif, in 1966. Another member, 'Abd al-Wahhab al-Shawwaf, might also have become president if a revolt he led against Qasim in 1959 had been successful. Of the fourteen, all but three were born or reared in Baghdad; except for two Shi'is and Qasim, who had a Shi'i mother, all were Sunnis. There were no Kurds in the Central Organization nor any Ba'thists, although there were other pan-Arabists.[9]

That the Ba'th had only limited influence at this time is also evident in that only one Ba'thist, Fuad al-Rikabi,[10] the first Ba'th regional secretary in Iraq, was appointed to the new cabinet after the revolution of 1958. Yet the revolution, which had eliminated the Hashimites, and Communist-sponsored riots in Mosul in 1959, which alienated Iraqis generally, presented the first opportunity for Ba'thists to extend their appeal to more diverse segments of the Iraqi population. The party deliberately reduced its standards of admission, increased its efforts to infiltrate workers' organizations and the military, and agreed in principle that participation in popular front activities was advantageous. Significantly, these were all directions in which the Ba'th party of the 1970s also moved.

These tactical innovations in recruitment, however, were short-lived. The 1960s became a decade of drastic change for the Arab Ba'th Socialist party in its organization, its membership, and its doctrine. Three events were largely responsible. Two flowed from the policies of Arab leaders—

9. See Khadduri's *Republican 'Iraq*, pp. 15–85, for an informative account of the planning and execution of this revolution.

10. Fuad al-Rikabi was a Shi'i from al-Nasiriya in southern Iraq. He appears to have gained control of the Iraqi Ba'thists by 1951 or 1952, after which time the party began to increase in size, including a number of Shi'is from Rikabi's home province. When the attempt was made to kill Qasim in 1959, Rikabi escaped to Syria and was ousted as secretary of the party. In 1961 he was expelled from the party because of activities the party had engaged in while he was its regional secretary. After that he became a Nasirite but returned in 1964 to Iraq, where he served in various government posts until he was arrested by the Ba'th in 1968. Sentenced to three years in jail, he was stabbed to death by an unknown assailant in 1971 shortly before he was due to be released.

Qasim and Nasir—while the third was the failure of Iraqi Ba'thists to maintain control of the Iraqi government after they seized it in 1963.

First, within three months after the 1958 revolution, 'Abd al-Karim Qasim had asserted himself as the predominant political force in Iraq, stressing Iraqi and Arabian Gulf concerns rather than pan-Arab, pro-Nasir goals. In October 1959 the Ba'thists made an unsuccessful attempt to assassinate Qasim, who had supported both the Communists and the Ba'thists against each other in hope of weakening his political opponents. Saddam Husain, who became the president of Iraq in 1979, was a member of the assassination squad. (After being shot in the attempt, Husain fled to Syria and then to Egypt, where he studied at the Cairo University Law College before returning to Baghdad in 1963.) The attempted assassination was a departure from previous Ba'thist policy and had important consequences. Qasim's security police made a broad sweep for party members. Many in the Iraqi Regional Command, the highest office of the Ba'th party in Iraq at the time, either dispersed or were brought to trial. These men, including Fuad al-Rikabi and many Shi'is, were ousted from the party's top leadership and never reentered it. Moreover, there were splits, defections, and resignations in the party as a whole following public condemnation by Syrian and Lebanese Ba'thists of violent action as a means to attain political power and of inadequate long-term planning by the Iraqi Ba'thists. The rules for recruitment consequently were made more restrictive as early as 1960.

The second event arose from Egypt's union with Syria in 1958 as the United Arab Republic, which was initially welcomed by Ba'thists as an achievement in Arab unity. But Jamal 'Abd al-Nasir's increasingly personalized control came to be viewed as autocratic, deliberately excluding independent political parties and well-known Arab nationalist leaders. The Ba'th party was forced to dissolve in Syria in 1958, and some leading Ba'thists resigned government posts in the United Arab Republic in December 1959, a move that did not trouble Nasir. In September 1961 a group of independent Syrian army officers unilaterally announced the secession of their country from its union with Egypt. A period of internal power struggles followed in Syria during which the Ba'th, one of the few well-organized political parties, seized the government in 1963.

Lastly, the Iraqi Ba'th, joined by non-Ba'thist sympathizers, succeeded in overthrowing Qasim's government on February 8, 1963. The Ba'thists were ill prepared to manage a government bureaucracy, however, and their energies were expended chiefly in eliminating Communists, their principal political opponents. In the ensuing intraparty feuding, Ba'th moderates had to request assistance from nonmembers to end the violence. The first Ba'th government fell in November, only nine months after it had taken charge. It was succeeded by a government composed of other Arab nationalist military officers and civilians with technical expertise. Plans for another Ba'thist attempt to unseat the government were discovered in September 1964, after which the party again adopted a clandestine mode.

The long-term impact of these events of the early 1960s was profound and led to a searching reappraisal of Ba'th "failures," as members themselves expressed it. Saddam Husain remembered it as "a difficult learning period." Two of its lessons for the Ba'th were insistence on party loyalty and distrust of non-Ba'thists, especially those in the military.

In addition, events of the 1960s brought about two basic shifts in Ba'th party policies. The first was to establish stronger regional—that is, state—autonomy within the party as a whole; and the second, to concentrate on practical questions of governmental policies, such as agrarian reform, rather than on theoretical formulations of doctrine. During this period the old Ba'thists, those who initially favored Nasir's leadership and unity with Egypt, were ousted by a new wave of members seeking a broader-based party organization among the populace and revolutionary means of change if they were the only way to attain participation in government. Many of the older members therefore were expelled or left voluntarily, and the military, particularly in Syria, began to see the usefulness of the Ba'th organization as a political tool. By contrast, Iraqi civilian Ba'thists who witnessed the Syrian events became warier of military control of party organs.

Throughout the 1960s the conflict between so-called regionalists in Syria and the National Command of the Ba'th continued and intensified, ultimately resulting in a split within the party. In Syria, military officers who had maneuvered themselves into positions of political dominance within the Ba'th organization took complete control of the government and the party apparatus on February 23, 1966. A new Regional Command of the Ba'th was elected, effectively eliminating the old guard. The subsequent election of a new National Command in that year spelled the end of a major period in the party's history, for it resulted in the formation of two Ba'th parties, each claiming to have a command called national, respectively headquartered in Syria and in Iraq.

On July 17, 1968, the Iraqi Ba'th party regained control of the Iraqi government with the help of non-Ba'thist army officers. Learning from its defeat in 1963, the party endeavored to expand its appeal among diverse elements of the population, reinforcing among them its oft-stated goals, and to consolidate its control by eliminating non-Ba'thists who initially supported the revolution. Because the elimination of non-Ba'thists from the government this time was bloodless, it was called the white revolution. Saddam Husain played a major part in the arrest and exile of these officials to ambassadorial posts abroad. Some of the civilians who participated in these events acquired considerable prestige in Iraqi Ba'th politics of the 1970s and early 1980s even as the party continued to experience internal upheavals.

Ba'thists and Communists: An Uneasy Relationship

Modern political parties in Iraq have confronted major obstacles in their development that are not confined to overcoming the opposition of a central government. In a country as heterogeneous as Iraq, with its long history of competing interest groups, the first task of any political movement is to appeal across particularistic associations, a task compounded by the historical and geographic factors discussed earlier. Ironically, the two most successful parties in Iraq—the Iraqi Communist party and the Iraqi Ba'th—have been major competitors, even though—or perhaps because—they originally had a number of characteristics in common.

It is important to consider the depth and scope of this rivalry, which continues unabated, not only because it has contributed to the development of the Ba'th but also because the Iraqi Communist party is supported by a foreign non-Arab power, the Soviet Union. Soviet support is clearly intended to aid the Iraqi Communists wherever possible without seriously endangering state-to-state relations. At times, therefore, good relations between Moscow and Baghdad have resulted in a betterment of the Iraqi Communist party's position within Iraq while, conversely, antigovernment activities by Iraqi Communists have brought a cooling of Iraqi-Soviet relations.

Michel Aflaq and Salah al-Din al-Bitar allegedly had made their first contacts with the Communists by the early 1930s while both were students at the Sorbonne. Such contacts were not uncommon at the time, for early Arab nationalists tended to shun the West because of their experience of colonialism and because their traditional rulers, whom they perceived as corrupt, were associated with Western powers. As two of the few opposition parties in the Middle East that were well organized, the Ba'th and the Communist party at first had much in common in their calls for popular support, for basic changes in the economic system, and for the eradication of foreign influence and overthrow of traditional ruling elites. But periods of actual cooperation between the two parties were brief and fragile. Ultimately they were not destined to succeed. Their basic disagreement hinged on two factors: competition for adherents and ideological differences that could not be reconciled.

Although Aflaq had turned on the Communists by the early 1950s, the disagreement was not yet apparent in Iraq, where the Ba'th was still a young party struggling to organize itself. The Ba'th did not receive much attention even from the Hashimite government, given its small membership and perceived lack of support from foreign non-Arab powers, unlike the Communists. This period, which marked the party's first venture into the public arena, helped to shape Ba'thist attitudes toward participation in politics and government in the coming decades.

This benign interlude was interrupted by demonstrations against the Baghdad Pact in 1955, then dramatically transformed by the revolution of 1958 and the policies of the new regime. The Ba'th party's membership had expanded rapidly from several hundred persons in mid-1958 to perhaps twice or thrice that number in the subsequent year. The growing ranks of Ba'thists were angered by Communist criticism of Nasir, which reflected communism's fundamentally "internationalist" bent and evinced little sympathy for the struggles of Arab nationalists or for an ideology that stressed above all the principles of Arab unity and the potential of the Arab nation. Ba'thists also were frustrated by the Communists' ability to organize and gain the support of workers' organizations to the detriment of the Ba'th.

Tension rose in Iraq when 'Abd Al-Karim Qasim, the army general who had taken control after the revolution of 1958, sought to weaken his political opponents by giving them all a degree of freedom. The result, as Qasim had anticipated, was that the opposition groups began to direct their activities against each other instead of the central government. Events reached a climax in early March 1959 when Colonel 'Abd al-Wahhab al-Shawwaf led from Mosul an unsuccessful countercoup against Qasim, apparently timed to coincide with a Communist rally to be held in Mosul. In the ensuing pandemonium the Communists, whose demonstrators came from throughout Iraq, seized the opportunity to mass in the streets, identifying and eliminating political opponents. Victims were frequently tortured, some dragged behind cars until dead. Government troops eventually took control, but bloody skirmishes led primarily by the Communists and consequent reprisals by other groups continued throughout the following months. Casualties from this period are estimated to have numbered as many as 5,000.

Taha Yasin Ramadhan, the first deputy prime minister of Iraq, was a young lieutenant in Mosul in 1959. In an interview on August 14, 1982, Ramadhan related the events of March 1959, stating that hundreds of people, including women, had been killed and that thousands more had been injured. Ramadhan ironically noted: "This was a time when it was better to be arrested and put in jail than to be free on the streets and killed." Exactly one year after the July 14, 1958, revolution, the Communists instigated further strife, this time rekindling old antipathies between the Turkomans and Kurds in Kirkuk and Irbil. The outcome was perhaps even bloodier; according to one report, forty persons were buried alive by the Communists.[11] Minor street skirmishes between the two parties continued from 1959 until Qasim's overthrow on February 8, 1963. Some of Qasim's troops and the Communists, who recognized the consequences of a Ba'thist victory, fought with desperation, killing at least eighty civilian and military sympathizers of the Ba'th.

The series of events that began in mid-1959 had profound consequences. The memory became indelibly etched on the minds of Iraqi Ba'thists, many of whose colleagues had been ruthlessly killed by the Communists, and it helped to form their judgment of all future relations with the Communist party in Iraq and, at times, with the Soviet Union. When referring to this period, a Ba'thist told the author that at the time of the February 1963 revolution, Ba'thists were acutely aware that they had only 700 members while the Communists had a membership of between 5,000 and 10,000.

When the Ba'th eventually did take control, it was able to maintain power for only nine months. One reason frequently advanced to explain its short tenure is that the Ba'th disregarded government affairs as it unswervingly sought revenge against the Communists. Although the Ba'thists then were singularly unprepared to take the reins of govern-

11. See Khadduri, *Republican 'Iraq*, p. 124.

ment, this argument has merit. It has been estimated that in the two weeks following the downfall of Qasim's government, between 500 and 3,000 persons were killed, the majority of whom were Communists or their allies.[12] Six influential members of the Communist party, including the first secretary, were executed by the Ba'th in succeeding months. Others who were executed included 149 Communists charged with the Mosul and Kirkuk incidents in mid-1959 and with activities against the February 1963 revolution, both before and after its success.[13] The Communist party in Iraq was ruthlessly uprooted, just as the Arab Ba'th Socialist party publicly had said it would be.

When 'Abd al-Salam 'Arif, who was an army colonel at the time of the revolution of 1958 and a major political rival of Qasim, consolidated his control in late 1963, he excluded Ba'thists from the government, and both the Ba'thists and the Communists began regrouping their forces. The former tried to increase their support in the military and in popular organizations, while the latter adopted a more cautious position under the new leadership of 'Aziz Muhammad. Eager to further their influence against that of the Ba'th, the Communists indicated a desire to ally themselves with 'Arif or groups that supported him. Fearing that the Ba'thists would create an environment conducive to overthrowing the government, the Communists, the Muslim Brotherhood,[14] and the Kurdish Democratic party made an alliance against them. During an interview, one Ba'thist described this period with bitterness, saying that the Communists had helped the government to identify and follow Ba'thist students.

12. Devlin, *The Ba'th Party*, pp. 235, 255–56; and John K. Cooley, "The Shifting Sands of Arab Communism," *Problems of Communism*, vol. 24 (March–April 1975), pp. 22–42.

13. This is an official number. Hanna Batatu has stated in correspondence that the actual figure is 162.

14. As early as the 1930s the Iraqi government had sought to outlaw public performances during the Shi'i celebrations during Muharram because of their potential to become politically explosive. The festivals nevertheless became difficult to control in the rural areas during the 1940s, and during the 1950s and 1960s they spread even to Mosul. But religious movements never seemed to profit from the Ba'thist-Communist rivalry; in fact the Communists began to make use of them and apparently attempted to organize among the clergy. One Ba'thist said in an interview that Ba'th members sometimes went to the mosques offering security to imams who wished to speak about the evils of communism. He went on to say that some of the religious movements disintegrated in the early to mid-1970s and that one group, the Muslim Brotherhood, never gained a foothold in Iraq as it had in Syria. Later, however, the perceived failures of pan-Arabism gave fresh stimulus to these groups and opened them in particular to the new influence of Khomeini's Iran.

In 1967 the Iraqi Communist party split. Although the newer group led by 'Aziz al-Hajj is generally reported to have been oriented toward Maoist China, it pursued an independent line. Its leadership became known as the Central Command of the Iraqi Communist party, as distinguished from the Moscow-supported Central Committee of the Iraqi Communist party. The offshoot continued sporadic acts of violence and in the late 1960s was severely repressed, whereupon many of its members returned to the pro-Moscow faction. When Ba'thists returned to power in 1968 they did not repeat the 1963 purges of the Iraqi Communist party, although they made clear through occasional intimidations and executions that Ba'thists, and only Ba'thists, were in command.

During the late 1960s and the first half of the 1970s, the Iraqi Ba'thists and Communists achieved the highest level of cooperation they had ever experienced, though their relationship could not be characterized as one of trust. Their rapprochement was not a consequence of greater interparty cooperation but rather a direct result of the Iraqi government's reliance on Moscow in the face of domestic and foreign pressures. Among those pressures were the shah of Iran's claims to the Shatt al-'Arab in 1969 and his seizure of three strategic islands in the Arabian Gulf in 1971, an increase in the early 1970s of Kurdish guerrilla activities in northern Iraq sponsored by the United States and Iran, Iraq's nationalization of the Iraq Petroleum Company and its affiliates in 1972, and the October 1973 war with Israel.

Iraqi dependence on the Soviet Union had become manifest as early as April 1972 in a treaty of friendship between Baghdad and Moscow. The treaty, coupled with a Soviet arms shipment to Iraq during the early part of the Kurdish dispute, brought a predictable improvement in the position of the Iraqi Communist party, which was legalized in July 1973 with the formation of the Progressive National and Patriotic Front. Two Communists, one of whom was a woman, were subsequently appointed to the Iraqi cabinet, but the period of cooperation was brief. Relations between the Iraqi Ba'th and Communist parties became gradually more contentious after mid-1975, and by the late 1970s most Communists who had been appointed to government positions had resigned or fled the country.

Several factors contributed to the renewal of tension. One was that after the revolution of 1958, Iraqi governments sought domestic popularity and greater flexibility in foreign affairs through policies of neutralism, or positive neutralism. The Ba'th party's conception of nonalignment was a particularly forceful and refined version of neutralism, a natural evolution of what many Iraqis perceived to be a remedy for the country's strategic weaknesses. Another was that most of the conditions responsible for Iraq's initial dependence on the Soviet Union had been ameliorated by 1975, particularly after the Algiers Declaration between Iraq and Iran ended overt border hostilities between the two states and concurrently stopped those of the Kurdish guerrillas. Yet another was that the position held by the Iraqi Communist party in the National Front had allowed it to expand its membership as against that of the Ba'th. Even elements of the army who were dissatisfied with the 1975 settlement with Iran were said to be attracted to the Communist party. Civilian Iraqi Ba'thists were wary of a recurrence of the military's persistent interference in politics, particularly in light of the cooperation of Afghan military units with Soviet forces in Afghanistan.

Moreover, the intervention of the Soviet Union in regional affairs generally—whether overt, as in Ethiopia in 1977[15] and in Afghanistan and the People's Democratic Republic of Yemen in 1979, or covert, through the manipulation of local Communist parties—precipitated Ba'thist alarm about Soviet intentions toward Iraq. It was alleged that either Iraqi Communists or Syrian Ba'thists were responsible for disturbances in the Shi'i-dominated southern areas of Iraq during 1977. Whatever doubt remained in the minds of Ba'thist leaders was eliminated by 1978, when the Iraqi Communist party began publicly to criticize Ba'thist policies. It is significant that Iraq's announcement of an Arab charter calling upon the Arab states to reject foreign bases or access to military facilities was made in February 1980, shortly after the Soviet invasion of Afghanistan.

The intensity and duration of the Ba'th's response to the Communists since 1975 has demonstrated yet again the pervasive distrust and rivalry that separate the groups. The first new sign of impending trouble was Iraq's repetition in 1978 of an earlier request that the Soviets move their embassy, situated close to the presidential palace in a favorable position for electronic monitoring. When the Soviets refused, the Iraqi govern-

---

15. Iraq was strongly opposed to Soviet policies in the Horn of Africa, particularly Moscow's support of Ethiopia against both Somalia and the Eritrean Liberation Front. In consequence the Iraqi government tried to halt Soviet overflights to South Yemen in 1977, which Iraq believed were carrying cargo destined for Ethiopia. Iraq also offered aid to the Eritreans and to Somalia. See Arnold Hottinger, "Arab Communism at Low Ebb," *Problems of Communism,* vol. 30 (July–August 1981), pp. 22–24.

ment shut off their electricity and water, thus ending the stalemate. In May of that year the government reiterated an earlier announcement that no political activity would be allowed in the Iraqi armed forces other than that of the Arab Ba'th Socialist party. The Ba'th subsequently reported that twenty-one Communists were executed and many others purged from the military. A member of the Central Committee of the Iraqi Communist party claimed that those executed numbered thirty-six,[16] a discrepancy that may reflect the execution of a second group or a distinction between active and retired officers. An Iraqi law promulgated in July 1978 retroactively extended the death penalty to all military personnel who engaged in prohibited political activities after 1968 even if they had retired since that year.

The leaders of the Iraqi Communist party fled the country in April 1979, dispersing to Tehran, Aden, Beirut, Damascus, Moscow, and Eastern European countries, where the dispute, continuing unabated, assumed different forms. On the one hand, Iraqi security agents reportedly were assassinating exiled Communists in pro-Soviet countries such as the People's Democratic Republic of Yemen. On the other hand, Iraqi Communists either directly or through Soviet-supported states sought to discredit the Iraqi Ba'th government by a number of incidents. Iraqi students in Bulgaria, for example, were forced to return to Baghdad in December 1979 after being intimidated by Bulgarian government authorities. Some seventy students from the People's Democratic Republic of Yemen were caught publicly distributing anti-Ba'thist literature in April 1980 and expelled from Baghdad.

A report released in mid-1979 by exiled Iraqi Communists heaped virulent abuse on the Ba'thist government, even criticizing it for not supporting the Steadfastness and Confrontation Front against Israel.[17] During 1980 the Iraqi Communist party stated its desire to build a front, including the army, that would be loyal to the country and end Ba'thist rule. A number of Communists joined Kurdish resistance groups, particularly that led by Jalal Talabani, who between 1978 and December

16. John K. Cooley, "Conflict within the Iraqi Left," *Problems of Communism*, vol. 29 (January–February 1980), p. 89; and David Hirst, "After the Shah: How Do Iraq's Ba'thists Survive?" *The Guardian*, February 27, 1979, reprinted in JPRS 73065, *NE/NA Report*, no. 1927 (March 23, 1979), pp. 154–56.

17. "Report of the Iraqi Communist Party's Central Committee: The Situation in Iraq and the Arab Region," as translated and reprinted in JPRS 74485, *NE/NA Report*, no. 2038 (October 31, 1979), pp. 78–81.

1983, when a temporary alliance was made with the Iraqi government, had increased his anti-Iraqi government activities and was believed to be supported by Syria and the Soviet Union. The Iraqi Communist party's first secretary, 'Aziz Muhammad, personally addressed the Twenty-sixth Congress of the Communist party of the Soviet Union in Moscow in 1981. During the congress he continued his tirade against the Iraqi government, which abstained from sending a delegation although it had done so at the previous congress in 1976.[18] In February 1982 'Aziz Muhammad met in Damascus with Syrian President Hafiz al-Asad, who dislikes Saddam Husain's ruling faction of the Ba'th and hence is a primary supporter of dissident Iraqi groups. During the discussions, 'Aziz Muhammad continued his verbal attack against both Iraq and Jordan, Iraq's staunch ally since the start of the war with Iran.[19] Asad and the Iraqi Communist leader met at least two other times in 1983, once in January and again in June.

Although the Ba'thists made no ideological distinction between Communist parties in the Arab world and the Communist system as promulgated by Moscow, Iraqi frustration with the Soviet Union arising from its support of Communist activities against the Iraqi government and the Middle East generally was clearly demonstrated when Saddam Husain declared in 1978 that "they [the Soviet Union] won't be satisfied until the whole world becomes Communist."[20]

Between 1979 and the second year of the Iran-Iraq war, developments within the Iraqi Communist party are rumored to have weakened it further. Some Communist party members still residing underground in Iraq after 1978 reportedly have criticized their party on a number of important points.[21] First, they note that the exiled Iraqi Communist leaders appear disunited because they remain physically dispersed. Second, those leaders are inconsistent in labeling the Ba'th government

18. *Washington Post*, March 3, 1981. See also *Yearbook on International Communist Affairs* for 1981, 1982, and 1983 (Hoover Institution Press).

19. British Broadcasting Corporation, *Summary of World Broadcasts*, ME/6955/A/ 12, February 16, 1982, and ME/6957/A/4, February 18, 1982.

20. Interview with Arnaud de Borchgrave, *Newsweek*, July 17, 1978, p. 50.

21. Sulaiman al-Farzali, "Peaceful Observations in Time of War; Split between Iraqi Communists and Their Leadership Abroad," *al-Hawadith* (London), May 1, 1981, as translated and reprinted in JPRS 78345, *NE/NA Report*, no. 2351 (June 22, 1981), pp. 26–28. It should be cautioned that Farzali is supposed to be a member of the Lebanese Ba'th party. There have been no reports of major Communist activity in Iraq since 1978 except in the northern Kurdish areas.

a dictatorship after having consistently praised it as "revolutionary" in the years between the formation of the Progressive National and Patriotic Front in 1973 and their exile in 1979. Communist publications in Iraq had even lauded the achievements of the Ba'th party on both the economic and the Kurdish issues. Third, the critics condemn the Soviets for their involvement in Afghanistan and Poland and note the voluntary emigration of thousands of Cubans to the United States. Fourth, the war with Iran has divided the party's members into those who support the leadership abroad and those who contend that Iraqi nationalism should take precedence over the internationalism of Communist ideology. The latter group was especially critical of 'Aziz Muhammad's speech at the Twenty-sixth Congress of the Soviet Communist party in which he criticized Iraq in the war with Iran, even though the leaders of the Iraqi Communist party had openly discussed the danger of the aggressive Iranian stance toward Iraq before their exile.

An assessment of the Iraqi Communist party's position made in 1982 states that after the Iran-Iraq war began, the party's only substantial activity took place in Iraqi Kurdistan.[22] This has had two serious consequences for the party. One is that the Communists have become involved to their own detriment in intra-Kurdish quarrels; the other is that the party is becoming predominately Kurdish.

The release of some 60 to 200 Communists from Iraqi prisons in mid-1982 kindled speculation that the action was linked to an agreement by Moscow to resume arms shipments to Iraq and to send the arms directly rather than through third countries. During interviews in August 1982 the upper echelon of the Iraqi regime, including Saddam Husain and Taha Yasin Ramadhan, expressed satisfaction with Soviet actions in such remarks as "they [the Soviets] are quicker at realizing where their interests lie than the United States." They nevertheless qualified their statements by adding "at the present time" or "we have no reason at present to be dissatisfied [with the Soviets]." They were also quick to accompany these observations with expressions of hope that Iraqi relations with Europe would continue to improve and that France not only would continue to have good relations with the Arab world, but also would have a role to play in the future of the Middle East. The general tenor of these remarks on Iraqi-Soviet relations contrasts with

---

22. For more detailed information see John F. Devlin's article on Iraq in the *Yearbook on International Communist Affairs, 1982* (Hoover Institution Press, 1982), pp. 24–25.

the tone of interviews conducted in Baghdad between May and July 1981, when Iraqi leaders expressed their continued disappointment with Soviet actions. Whether temporary or not, the latest improvement in Iraqi-Soviet relations coincided in 1983 with a period of increasing anti-Communist activity in Tehran, including the arrest of the leader and many other members of the Iranian Communist (Tudeh) party, and the execution of a number of them in early 1984.

Although the Iraqi Communist party can be expected to continue its opposition to the Ba'th, it appears to have been weakened by internal disagreements. One disagreement is over the Iran-Iraq war: the criticism of the Iraqi leadership by the exiled Communists has made them, in contrast to those remaining in Iraq, seem sympathetic to Iran. Moreover, these same Communist leaders, who before the exile had openly praised the Ba'th for its economic achievements, were now blatantly taking an opposite line. This served to belie their credibility, especially when economic achievements in Iraq have been substantive enough to extend the appeal of the Ba'th. In any case, the Ba'thists have made it abundantly clear that they will not rule through a coalition of parties or tolerate parties that subordinate Iraqi interests to those of foreign powers. The occasional release of Iraqi Communists from prison may be a harbinger of improved Iraqi-Soviet relations, but so long as the Ba'thists are in power it is highly unlikely that they will stop their surveillance of Communist sympathizers or allow organized Communist activity unless it is carefully monitored.

CHAPTER FOUR

Party Organization
and Ideology

DECISIONMAKING in the Iraqi government is dependent on the Ba'th party, whose organization pervades the political system and whose vigorous recruitment policy strives to attract a wide following. Political parties other than the Ba'th may publicly participate in a controlled coalition of parties, the National Front, but only under the Ba'th's direction. Although membership in the party is not a prerequisite for government employment or even for advancement, a number of Ba'th and non-Ba'th Iraqis agree that "an incompetent Ba'thi is unlikely to be promoted, but all factors being equal a Ba'thi has a greater advantage than a non-Ba'thi."

The outstanding characteristics of the party are its discipline and secrecy. Cellular in structure, the Ba'th is designed to resist official suppression and violent attack by rival groups. As was mentioned earlier, the party in Iraq had to struggle throughout the 1950s and 1960s to attain recognition and to expand its following. It did so not only as a political party opposed to the established authority but often as an underground organization. Where the Ba'th has won political power, as it did in Syria and Iraq, the same structure provides an efficient means to extend and organize party activity. In the Middle East, where political activity frequently must be underground, two clandestine parties currently operating—the Communist party and the Muslim Brotherhood—employ the same organizational structure. It is said that because of their knowledge of clandestine operations, Ba'thists were frequently used in 1963 to interrogate arrested Communists.

A cellular organization such as the Ba'th allows no free transfer of information. Communication within the system occurs vertically, never

Figure 4-1. *Organization of the Iraqi Ba'th Party, 1984*

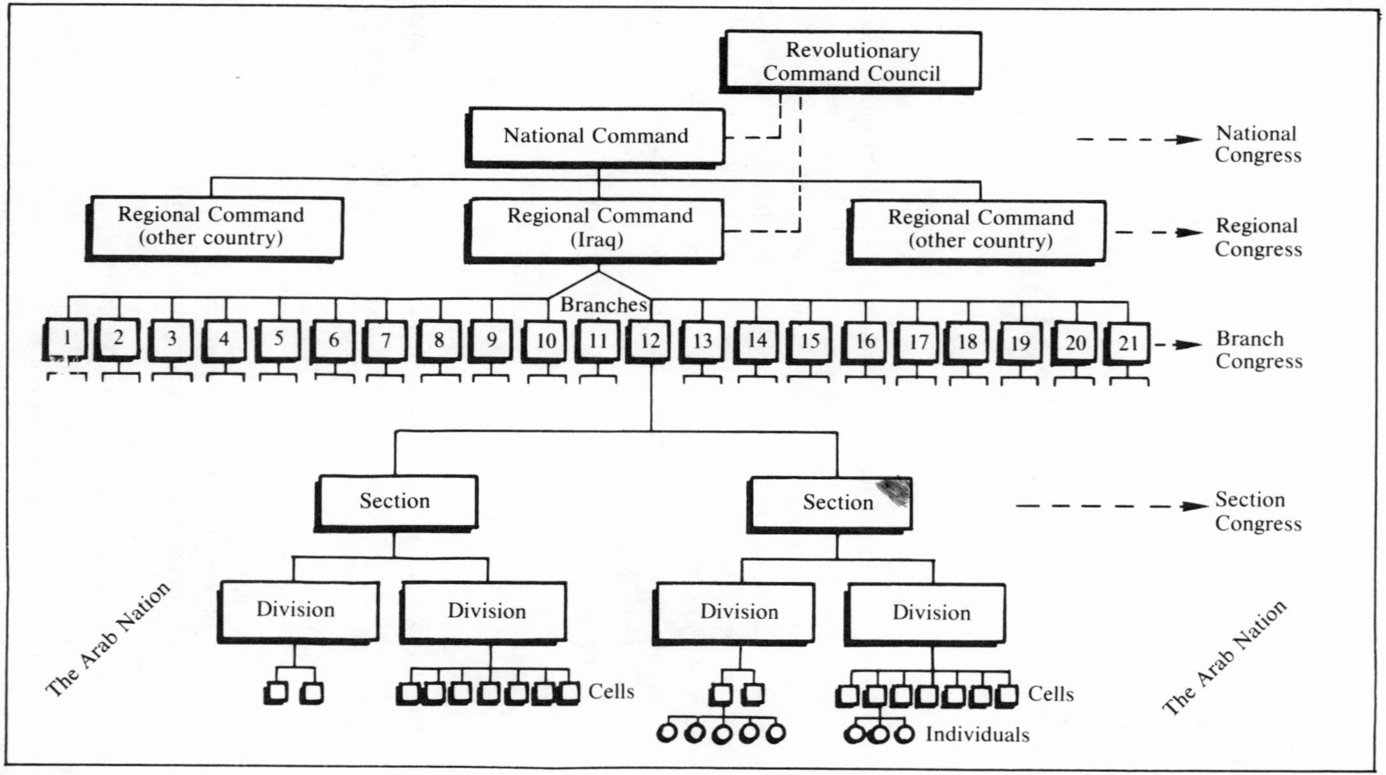

Source: Author's interviews with Iraqi Ba'th officials.

horizontally, so that recruitment can be carefully controlled, information effectively restricted, and individual cells isolated so that discovery of one cell does not endanger the entire network. Low- and middle-ranking Ba'thists therefore may be not only reluctant but unable to discuss the party machinery; and even though members of the upper echelon are exceedingly articulate about Ba'thist policies, they remain reticent in discussing decisionmaking and internal party debates. Many members hesitate even to discuss their personal histories, although this characteristic has been less pronounced since the party was legalized.

The Ba'th adopted formal statutes at its second national congress in June 1954, but frequent revision and reinterpretation by the Regional Commands have obscured their meaning in practice. Uncertainty increased after 1966 with the formation of separate National Commands in Syria and Iraq, accompanied in the mid-1960s by disputes among the Iraqi Ba'thists themselves. The party statutes thus contribute little to understanding the dissolution or reconstitution of Regional Commands, or the establishment of a command's credibility at a time of internal competition among cliques or individuals.

Structure and Decisionmaking

Despite these obstacles, several known features of the Ba'th allow general deductions to be made about how the party perceives its role, extends its influence, and determines policy. The most readily observable pertain to the party's structure. At its broadest organizational level is *al-watan* or *al-umma*, literally the nation or the entire Arab world, for whose unity it theoretically strives. Within the nation is a pyramidal structure of cells, each composed of several individuals and fixed within a hierarchical chain of command (see figure 4-1). The cell or circle (*khaliya*, plural *khalaya* or, as it is also known, *halqa*, plural *halaqat*) is the smallest organizational unit, composed of a minimum of three persons. A minimum of two and a maximum of seven cells form a division (*firqa*, plural *firaq*); at least two divisions form a section (*shu'ba*, plural *shu'ab*); and at least two sections form a branch (*far'*, plural *furu'*). There are twenty-one branches in Iraq, one in each of the eighteen provinces and three in Baghdad.[1] The union of all the branches forms a

1. Interview with Naim Haddad on August 10, 1982. He also stated that it was possible for only two branches to form a Regional Command.

Figure 4-2. *Options for String, or Bead, Organizations,*
Iraqi Ba'th Party

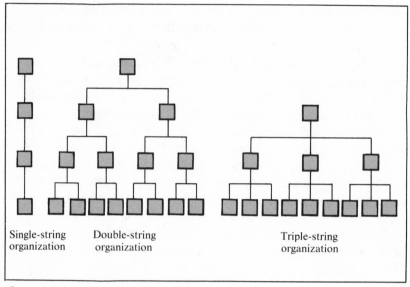

Single-string   Double-string   Triple-string
organization   organization   organization

Source: Author's interviews with Iraqi Ba'th officials.

region (*qutr*). At each level of the hierarchy are an elected command and
congresses that meet regularly. Four countries—Syria, Iraq, Lebanon,
and Jordan—are believed to have attained regional status in the history
of the Ba'th party, although the exact level of the party's current
organization in some countries, such as Libya, Saudi Arabia, Yemen,
and Sudan, remains guarded information.

According to one Ba'thist, during times of extreme pressure some
members of the party have broken away from the traditional structure
for their own safety. One alternative structure was called the "bead" or
"string" organization (*tanzim* or *jahaz al-khaiti*, see figure 4-2). In the
single-string organization a member knew only one Ba'thist above him
in the hierarchy and one below him. This kind of organization was used
in Iraq in 1964, in Syria after 1976, and in some other Arab countries. In
late 1962 in Iraq there were also alert committees (*lijan al-indhar*)
composed of Ba'thists carefully chosen from different ranks of the party
to warn of impending crackdowns by the government. Between late 1963
and a new government crackdown in September 1964, a situation also
arose in Iraq in which a select group of Ba'thists, including Saddam

Husain, functioned as an autonomous organization parallel to the Ba'th, its existence unknown to the rank and file of party members.

An estimated 1.5 million Iraqis, or 10.7 percent of the total population of 14 million, are supporters or sympathizers of the Ba'th; full party members number 25,000, or less than 0.2 percent.[2] By contrast, membership in the Communist party of the Soviet Union in 1976 numbered 6.1 percent of the total Soviet population; but because the Soviet Communist party accepts direct entrants and does not have conditional categories equivalent to sympathizers and supporters, the figures are not fully comparable.

Membership in or support of the Ba'th is closely identified with support of the government and the state. The Ba'th's recruiting efforts hence are directed primarily toward the young, both to tap this large population group—at least 40 percent of Iraqis are below the age of twenty-five[3]—and to build a sense of nationhood. Theoretically anyone can join the party, but the Ba'th's recruitment procedures resemble a system of apprenticeship in the sense that the recruit must pass successfully through several stages before becoming a full party member. At the earliest stage, that of sympathizer (*mu'ayyid*), a person at least seventeen years old may join and spend an average of two years before becoming a supporter (*nasir*) of the party for another period, usually a minimum of two to three years. Next he becomes a candidate (*murashshah*) for another year and a half and then a trainee member (*mutadarrib*). He remains at that level for one year, when he becomes a full party (or working) member (*'udw*).[4] Persons who have made outstanding contributions to the state of Iraq or to its people are the only exceptions. 'Abd al-Wahhab Mahmud is an example. As an engineer he was instrumental in completing the Hamrin dam and in planning the Tharthar canal project, and was rewarded with party membership and later with the position of

2. This information was obtained during interviews with high-ranking officials of the Iraqi Ba'th party.

3. Some 2 million members of this age group are in primary school, 2 million in secondary school, 1 million in universities, and 1 million in training schools of various kinds, and an unspecified number are infants or not in school. These figures were obtained in an interview with an Iraqi official concerned with education; however, the *Baghdad Observer* of October 17, 1981, reported that children in primary school numbered 2.5 million, and the figure for university students is probably too high.

4. This information came from a number of interviews and is correct to the best of my knowledge. Most people are reluctant to discuss the subject at all; the most frequent contradictions concern the time spent at each level of the party hierarchy rather than the categories. Never has a person told me the actual level that he or she has attained.

minister of irrigation. With such exceptions, advancement within the party hierarchy is competitive, bestowed not only on those who follow the party line and participate in party activities, including weekly meetings and a monthly symposium, but also on those who contribute in substantive ways to the productivity of their workplace or participate in the Popular Army, discussed later in this chapter.

Strict guidelines govern personal conduct. Gambling, heavy drinking, or adultery can result in expulsion from the party—perhaps reflecting lessons learned by the Ba'thists from their failures of 1963, when at least one Ba'thist was publicly associated with personal excesses. Even Iraqis critical of the Ba'th have admitted that members of its upper echelon are perceived to lead relatively pristine lives as family men or women with little time for social life. A few Iraqis go so far as to say that the leaders are not hypocrites like others in the Gulf who drink and do other things they deny their people. When asked about this during an interview, a high Iraqi official responded that "we [presumably the Ba'th or the government] cannot refuse to the people what we do in our own homes," adding that "everything should be done in moderation." In their dress and manners, the Ba'thists are unostentatious. Saddam Husain is an exception in that he is a dapper dresser; in his other personal habits, however, he appears to remain quite modest. He has frequently appeared in public with his youngest child, a daughter, and has occasionally been photographed as a family man in the company of his wife and children. His wife avoids publicity but nevertheless has continued working as a schoolmistress.

At the apex of the Iraqi Ba'th is the National Command, whose membership includes representatives of the Ba'th from other Middle Eastern countries as well as from Iraq.[5] Theoretically the National Command is the party's highest executive body, responsible for formulating doctrine, directing policy, coordinating the Regional Commands, participating in international organizations or conferences, and maintaining research bureaus concerned with finance and foreign affairs, among other things. In reality the National Command has been less

5. The National Command of the Iraqi Ba'th is as follows: Michel Aflaq (Syrian), founder and secretary-general; Saddam Husain (Iraqi), deputy secretary-general; Shibli al-'Aysami (Syrian), assistant secretary-general; 'Abd al-Majid al-Rifa'i (Lebanese); 'Ali Ghannam (Saudi Arabian); Qasim Sallam (Yemeni); Badr al-Din Muddathar (Sudanese); 'Izzat Ibrahim (Iraqi); Taha Yasin Ramadhan (Iraqi); Naim Haddad (Iraqi); Tariq 'Aziz (Iraqi).

significant since the party split in 1966, although the presence of Michel Aflaq as secretary-general of the National Command in Iraq is meant to increase its credibility because of his role as one of the founders and best-known ideologues of the Ba'th. Iraqis now emphasize the uniqueness of their party just as do the Syrians. The first deputy prime minister of Iraq, Taha Yasin Ramadhan, went out of his way to dispute the fact that Alexandrettans from Syria had played a major part in the formation of the Iraqi Ba'th in an interview in August 1982, saying that this assertion resulted from earlier Syrian propaganda. Ramadhan's reaction is easily explained. Since the split in the Ba'th party, Syrian Ba'thists have considered Zaki al-Arsuzi to be the founder of their party and have erected a statue in his honor in Damascus; Iraqis have attributed the founding of their party to Aflaq. The dispute thus represents only another manifestation of the rivalry between Syrian and Iraqi Ba'thists.

Regional Commands, technically under the direction of the National Command, may appoint and dismiss their own members, dissolve themselves or lesser Ba'th organizations within their regions, and monitor the affairs of government departments through Ba'th units emplaced in each. They also have general responsibility for party activities within each state and between states. In reality, however, all five Iraqis in the National Command—Saddam Husain, 'Izzat Ibrahim, Taha Yasin Ramadhan, Naim Haddad, and Tariq 'Aziz—are also members of the Regional Command and, more important, of the Revolutionary Command Council.[6] A ruling in 1977 provided that appointment to the Regional Command would be for five years, but internal party conflicts and the Iran-Iraq war have obscured the significance of this rule in practice. In any event, internal party maneuvering has reduced the membership of the Regional Command from a high of twenty-one in 1977 to only fifteen at present.

Both the National and Regional Commands are overshadowed by the Revolutionary Command Council (RCC), the most powerful decision-making body in Iraq. It meets as circumstances require, but usually once a week. Established in July 1968, the RCC fulfills both the executive and

6. The ninth regional congress of the Iraqi Ba'th party concluded its work on June 27, 1982. The following people were elected to the Regional Command: Saddam Husain (chairman), 'Izzat Ibrahim (deputy chairman), Taha Yasin Ramadhan, Naim Haddad, Tariq 'Aziz, 'Adnan Khairallah, Hasan 'Ali, Sa'dun Shakir, Muhammad Hamza al-Zubaidi, 'Abd al-Ghani 'Abd al-Ghafur, Samir Muhammad 'Abd al-Wahhab, 'Abd al-Hasan Rahi Faroun, Sa'di Mehdi Salih, Mizban Khider, and Sa'dun Hammadi.

legislative functions normally associated with the constitutional powers of Western governments.[7] In form, function, and name, it is a variant of the supreme command councils established in other Middle Eastern countries after a revolution. Parallels can be found in Egypt under Nasir as well as in Libya and Syria. After the revolution of 1968 in Iraq, the first Ba'th RCC was predominantly military, but its military members were rather rapidly replaced by civilians. The council theoretically may restrain actions of the president, who is chosen from and elected by its members. Because its internal business is never discussed publicly, the council's ability to restrain the president must remain conjectural. Most interviews with high-ranking Ba'thists indicated, however, that it is a consultative body whose meetings elicit discussion and even disagreement despite Husain's personal authority. Husain himself said in an interview with me that he relies on the knowledge of others when a subject is technical or of less personal interest to him than to others on the council.

Theoretically all members of the Regional Command also serve on the Revolutionary Command Council. Following elections to the regional congress in June 1982, however, those who were not reelected immediately lost their positions on the RCC, whose size therefore dropped from fifteen to nine, with an additional man, Khalid 'Abd al-Munim Rashid, appointed as its acting secretary-general. The remaining members of the council decided not to admit the newly elected Regional Command members until a later date. This was done on the pretext that there was no immediate procedural necessity, but both Saddam Husain and Taha Yasin Ramadhan indicated during interviews that the council's previously large membership had delayed decisionmaking on crucial issues and that some members who were cabinet ministers were neglecting their governmental positions. Thus, when Tayih 'Abd al-Karim lost his membership in the Regional Command and his post as oil minister, he was replaced by Qasim Ahmad al-Taqi, a skilled technocrat highly respected by persons in the ministry and the Iraqi National Oil Company. Others apparently lost their positions because they were praying in party locations and seeking to introduce religion as a measurement of being a good party member, a practice President Husain criticized at the regional

7. The Revolutionary Command Council in Iraq as of June 1982 was as follows: Saddam Husain (chairman), 'Izzat Ibrahim (deputy chairman), Taha Yasin Ramadhan, Naim Haddad, Tariq 'Aziz, 'Adnan Khairallah, Hasan 'Ali, Sa'dun Shakir, Taha Muhyi al-Din Ma'ruf, and Khalid 'Abd al-Munim Rashid (acting secretary-general of the RCC and head of the Presidential Office).

congress. One had even built a mosque in his own name. If, it was said, the public saw the Ba'th advocating Islam, particularly Sunni Islam, then the party would open itself to criticism from Shi'is and those who were pro-Iranian, thus creating the potential for greater divisiveness in Iraq. In any event, shrinkage of the Revolutionary Command Council did not constitute a "palace coup," as some foreign reports initially suggested, though its reduced membership does mean that Saddam Husain has less trouble guiding the council during the critical period of the Iran-Iraq war.

The Iraqi government has a dualistic nature in the sense that, although the bureaucracy is an autonomous entity, the Ba'th party can influence or directly control government policies by two distinct means. The first and most obvious is that a number of government employees are also members of the Ba'th. For military personnel, it is not only illegal but a crime punishable by execution to have political affiliations other than with the Ba'th. Less obvious but more important is the party's ability to influence governmental decisions at lower levels. Party units independently monitor activities in all government departments, and the party itself has bureaus that are functionally parallel to those of the government.

An example of duality is found in Iraq's Ministry of Foreign Affairs. Before the party elections of June 1982, Foreign Minister Sa'dun Hammadi—a Ba'thist of long standing—was not a member of the Regional Command. The director of the Foreign Affairs Bureau of the Ba'th was Tariq 'Aziz, who was also the deputy prime minister and a member of the Regional Command, the National Command, and the Revolutionary Command Council. In these circumstances, it is certain that the formulation of foreign policy was deliberately made subject to influences external to the Foreign Ministry—even though the exact means by which the Ba'th and the bureaucracy intermeshed are not clear, and though Hammadi's views may have received full consideration. The situation changed with Hammadi's election to the Regional Command in June 1982, and changed again when Hammadi because of ill health was replaced as foreign minister by Tariq 'Aziz in January 1983.[8]

8. Although rumors in the West suggested that Hammadi had fallen out of favor, it seems unlikely. Hammadi is known for his thoughtful and scholarly demeanor and did not seem to enjoy the constant attention he received as the Iran-Iraq war was prolonged. He traveled freely inside and outside Iraq after he was replaced, and party members continued to speak well of him.

The pervasiveness of the party is further illustrated by the fact that Iraqi embassies have their own Ba'th cell structures, and the highest diplomatic position—that of ambassador or chargé d'affaires—is not necessarily occupied by the highest-ranking Ba'thi in the embassy. Indeed, the ranking Ba'thist might not even be a member of the embassy staff or even an Iraqi. This is consonant with the pan-Arab philosophy of the party and perhaps is an additional safeguard in the party's system of monitoring the bureaucracy. The same concept at least partially explains why Iraq has offered welfare benefits and waived the requirements for entry visas for non-Iraqi Arabs.

Duality also prevails at the top levels of government. Of the four main branches—the presidency, Revolutionary Command Council, National Assembly, and judiciary—the first two are entirely Ba'thist, the third is interwoven with party mechanisms, and the fourth is subject to party influence. The president wields extensive powers in the party as well as in government. In addition to serving as chief executive, in which capacity he appoints cabinet ministers and senior members of the judiciary, and as commander-in-chief of the armed forces, Saddam Husain is deputy secretary-general of the Ba'th's National Command, chairman of the Regional Command, and chairman of the Revolutionary Command Council.

Under Saddam Husain's predecessor, Ahmad Hasan al-Bakr, the vice-president's functions were merged with the president's and the vice-presidency was made largely honorific. The present incumbent is a Kurd, Taha Muhyi al-Din Ma'ruf, who is believed not to be a Ba'thist. The president's temporary successor in case of his death or absence is not the vice-president but the deputy chairman of the Revolutionary Command Council, who is to serve until a new president is elected. Currently the deputy chairman is 'Izzat Ibrahim, a popular but unassuming Ba'thist whose role in the governmental hierarchy is distinctly overshadowed by the president.

Internal Party Dynamics

Three aspects of the Ba'th's leadership deserve special attention: trends within the leadership elite, collective leadership versus the cult of a single personality, and decisionmaking within the party. All are interrelated.

Factions within the Ba'th party sooner or later become evident as competition between those in dissent increases. Because policy decisions are announced only after internal party debate has produced a consensus, it is more difficult to observe within the party what may be termed trends. When Iraqis are asked about trends within the Ba'th, party members and nonmembers give different responses. Nonmembers do not portray the party as a dynamic and variegated institution. They rephrase the question by commenting instead on individuals they perceive as powerful or who command a power base. By contrast, party members attempt to obscure the question and its implications by conveying an impression of unanimity even if, as is evident in other conversations, they consider some party elites to be more influential than others. The leaders themselves try to deemphasize differences within the party. Taha Yasin Ramadhan said bluntly, "We try to discourage trends in the party." Dr. Sa'dun Hammadi explained that "we encourge an open, active debate over an issue, but once a vote has been taken it is expected that all members will accept the majority opinion as if it had been unanimous. No further public debate is allowed."

In the history of the Ba'th party, however, there have been internal differences, some with serious repercussions for the party. The first Ba'th president after 1968, Bakr, and his successor, Husain, can be said to have represented the prevailing political current during the 1970s. A salient aspect of their leadership was the consolidation of the civilian wing of the Ba'th party over that of the military, presumably in order to reduce debilitating internal conflicts, to establish continuity in the Ba'th's leadership, and to extend the legitimacy of the Ba'th and of the Iraqi government among the general population. Continuity was manifested in the public display of the leaders' photographs in government offices, in shops, and even in homes. This in itself was not unusual, as it is a custom in many countries of the Middle East. What was unusual was that when Bakr resigned and Saddam Husain replaced him, both of their photographs were displayed side by side until the summer of 1982, when Bakr's photographs were removed. Their removal caused some not unfounded speculation that Bakr was no longer a political alternative to Husain if the Iran-Iraq war continued and Husain's replacement was made necessary.

Throughout the 1970s, Bakr and Husain continued to consolidate their authority in what came to represent the moderate element of the party in both domestic and foreign policy. Broadly speaking, moderation included limited accommodation with the Kurds, greater moves toward political and economic nonalignment, attempts to curb the involvement of the military in government, efforts to increase public support for the central government, a gradual improvement in relations with Turkey and Iran, and a greater practical emphasis on domestic rather than foreign policy.

It is difficult to discern even now where dissent exists within the party in the absence of deliberate leaks to the press, such as those of American government officials who wish to dissociate themselves from or take credit for particular decisions. Occasionally the elimination of an individual by demotion, assassination, or execution may provide a clue, but it is not always clear whether the penalty was for an illegal or treasonous act or merely for challenging the established leadership of the party. Husain executed more than twenty persons for treasonous activities in mid-1979 when he assumed the presidency.[9] Demotions and transfers to overseas ambassadorial posts are also common methods of punishing extreme or challenging behavior within the party. Some have been dismissed suddenly from government or party positions, only to be as abruptly reinstated after their reform.

Such is presumably the case with Salah 'Umar al-'Ali, Iraq's permanent representative to the United Nations, who has been in and out of favor several times in his career and again "resigned" or was "dismissed" from his post in August 1982. Similarly, those who lost their positions in the elections of June 1982—for example, Minister of Transportation and Communication Sa'dun Ghaidan, who later visited the United States—were not arrested and were free to travel.[10] Riyad al-Ibrahim, the minister of health, was the exception in 1982. The government announced his execution on the grounds that imported medicines were contaminated and had caused several deaths. It is noteworthy, however, that the minister's demise was accompanied by rumors that

9. Details of this episode have not been fully disclosed or confirmed by outside sources. Ba'th members have long contended that it would be difficult to strike at the party except from the inside; this appears to have happened in 1979 when several Ba'thists, including associates of Saddam Husain, were linked to a plot to overthrow the government. The conspirators were accused of having a military wing and of maintaining ties with the Syrian government. A former Ba'thist related to me that the events of 1979 gave Husain an opportunity to remove persons who had long-standing party credentials and replace them with Ba'thists from the second rank in the hierarchy, thus giving him and the party a more broadly based legitimacy.

10. Even the Communist party leader, 'Aziz al-Hajj, who was arrested in 1969, was eventually pardoned and sent as an Iraqi representative to UNESCO in Paris.

he had links to Shi'i leaders in southern Iraq, was excessively anti-American at a critical point in Iraqi-American relations, and perhaps most important, had suggested that Husain resign his office in favor of Bakr. In any event, it is highly probable that there are powerful men or factions both in and outside the Ba'th party who are not well known outside Iraq because they prefer to operate in the background, their power base is developing, or their base is so strong that others will not speak openly against them.

One man in the Ba'th party usually occupies a dominant position. His authority resides, at least theoretically, in the fact that he has demonstrated his abilities through a skillful and perhaps ruthless consolidation of power. Nevertheless each leader, if only to a small extent, is constrained by the party and its practices: decisionmaking by consensus at several levels of the hierarchy, elections even if they are highly controlled, collective leadership or a concern simply to appear as a collective leadership, and the existence of competing interest groups within the party. Although many people have perceived the leadership of this individual as dictatorial, it is unrealistic to assume that within the party that person is not subject to the pressures of its various constituents. Someone like Husain can become extraordinarily popular and act as a symbol of unity, but the party elite accepts his popularity only so long as it is seen to advance the legitimacy of the party itself. Ramadhan explained the role of the party leader and President Husain's consolidation of power during the 1970s as follows:

Our purpose of education is to show the people that the party provides and is continuing. Any association [of the party] with a person means the beginning of the end, as happened with Nasir. Therefore we concentrate on the party. The first man acts as a symbol. When people support the first man, they are also supporting the party. The alternative will always be the party. In our organization the president is always secretary-general of the party and is respected as much as he expresses the ideology of the party and the will of the people.

We do not need a strong person, but one who can convince the people. Bakr [who was a military officer] led a certain stage of the party and at his side was Saddam Husain. This person came to an end because of his age and health. Leaders do not follow a certain program, but work hard. When Saddam Husain became president, he had enough power. Saddam Husain is almost like a son to Bakr.[11]

President Husain himself emphasized the importance of collective

11. Interviews with Ramadhan on June 21 and 22, 1981.

leadership in an interview on August 22, 1982, in which he also shed light on decisionmaking by the upper echelon of the Ba'th:

The Revolutionary Command Council is a constitutional body with vested authority. It has an agenda which is distributed a sufficient time before meetings convene. Decisions are taken by the majority. Usually a consensus develops through discussion so that it is rare an actual vote must be called. In fact, I can count these occasions [less than] the fingers of my hands. We are mostly interested in unanimous decisions, but not necessarily identical mentalities. I have no veto power, but my opinion as a question of courtesy is viewed in a different way. Sometimes outsiders, such as Sa'dun Hammadi, are called to present special issues. If there is a tie vote, the president's opinion carries. In very sensitive issues, we desire even more a consensus and consultation among the National Command, Revolutionary Command Council, and Regional Command.

Innovative Structures: The Party and the People

While the Ba'th has many ways to command the loyalty of its members, it is difficult to assess the attitude of Iraqis generally toward their government or toward the complex and sometimes turbulent political life of Iraq. It would be erroneous to assume that all non-Ba'thists oppose the central government, despite the radical and ruthless image in which the Ba'thist regime has been portrayed in the West or by opposition groups. Many Iraqis benefited from the Ba'th's economic and social policies during the 1970s and value the continuity of a single governmental authority since 1968, though they may not agree with the philosophy or tactics of the Ba'th or simply are not interested in politics. Moreover, the party attracts different segments of the population. During interviews in the summer of 1981, for example, many Iraqis who were aged forty and over said that they were not Ba'thists, but readily and with some pride added that their sons and daughters were members or sympathizers of the party. It would appear that success in a job as a taxi driver or shopkeeper was not enhanced by membership in the party, or that age itself made membership less relevant or useful. Such persons preferred to be independent, and "anyway the meetings take too much time."

Yet one of the Ba'th's most important goals is to broaden its base of support in Iraq's heterogeneous society. The task has not been easy: advancement in the Ba'th party depends upon one's education, but the illiteracy rate for persons more than ten years old was estimated in 1977 to be 44.5 percent in the cities and 77 percent in rural areas.[12] The party therefore embarked on the Campaign for Literacy, whose purpose was not only to improve the quality of manpower but also to provide another means by which the party could appeal to the people. Party spokesmen emphasized through the mass media the value of the ability to read and write, directing the message at some 2.2 million Iraqis between the ages of fifteen and forty-five. Each person was to spend fourteen months in the program, which was funded for three years. Registration was compulsory, and those who refused to register were subject to penalties. The response rate of 60 to 70 percent in rural areas exceeded that in the cities, apparently because the rural population welcomed the opportunity to socialize. Where teachers were lacking, soldiers or civil servants were trained for two to three weeks and assigned temporarily to rural classrooms.

The Ba'th has also extended its influence through the use of what may be called innovative structures. Among them are grassroots organizations such as the Federation of Iraqi Youths, the General Federation of Iraqi Women, and the Popular Army, as well as governmental or quasi-governmental entities such as the National Assembly, the Legislative Council for the Kurdish Autonomous Region, and the National Front. A review of them will aid in understanding some of the Ba'th's objectives.

The party has repeatedly emphasized that "the wealth of the country is in its children." The Vanguard Organization, founded in September 1973, is only one program within the Federation of Iraqi Youths, but it demonstrates the means by which the Ba'th seeks to extend its support even to this young group. The Vanguard includes both boys and girls of ten to fifteen years of age who participate in supervised sports, cultural and scientific activities, and training camps. They seek to acquire skills through "discipline and work" that will be used "in the service of their nation." In many ways, including the wearing of uniforms and taking of oaths of allegiance to their country, they are not dissimilar to international scouting groups elsewhere. The motto of the Vanguard, however, specifically recognizes that their efforts are also for the Ba'th party and its revolution. As is true of the Ba'th generally, there is an emphasis on competitive achievement. The Vanguard has an elaborate hierarchical

12. J. S. Birks and C. A. Sinclair, *Arab Manpower* (London: Croom Helm, 1980), p. 146.

chain of command that incorporates urban and rural areas and resembles the Ba'th party's structure even in having elected rather than appointed representatives. National, regional, and local congresses elect a central office, which in turn elects a core committee. Other childrens' age groups within the Federation of Iraqi Youths are accommodated in like fashion: the Pioneers organize primary school children, and the Youth organizes young people from fifteen to twenty years of age.

Iraq has a long history of advanced education for women relative to many other Middle Eastern states, the first Iraqi woman lawyer, for example, having been graduated in the 1930s. Since its founding in 1947 the Ba'th has maintained that women are equal to men, a position that demographic factors have reinforced. The Iraqi labor force has been depleted by the war, yet it must meet the need for large security and military forces as well as the demand for skilled labor in a developing country. Women therefore are important both for childbearing, which is now encouraged by monetary subsidies, and for their contribution to the labor force. They comprise 47 percent of agricultural workers—that is, approximately 60 percent of all active women—and 25 percent of the total labor force.[13] The Agrarian Reform Law of 1970, which decreed that women could own land on the same basis as men, was followed by a law granting women who work on agricultural cooperatives the same wages as their male counterparts. Subsequent laws have given married women the same tax exemptions as married men and provided for subsidized maternity leaves from work. Other laws enacted since 1970 have sought to provide women certain guarantees, protecting their rights before marriage and abolishing coercive divorce by men, prolonging their rights to child custody in case of divorce, and amending the inheritance laws in their favor. Women have the right to vote and after

13. Amal Sharqi, in *The Progress of Women in Iraq* (London: The Iraqi Cultural Center, 1978), p. 16, also noted that by 1977 women accounted for "38.5% of teachers, 31% of doctors, 30% of chemists, 25% of physicists, 15% of accountants, 11% of factory workers and 15% of civil servants . . . even a proportion of 3% . . . in senior management . . . two women ministers . . . a number of prominent women lawyers, including a Deputy Attorney-General, and head of the Juvenile Court." Women in high positions also include the dean of a school of dentistry in Baghdad, the chief veterinarian in charge of a major slaughterhouse, engineering supervisors at the Hamrin dam, the Tharthar canal project, and the Rumaila oil fields, and urban planners and architects. Of the 250 persons elected to the National Assembly in 1980, 16 are women. Before the Iran-Iraq war 40,000 women were volunteers in the Popular Army. In my own travels in Iraq I met many multilingual, politically aware, and achievement-oriented women.

1977 were admitted to the military, where the highest ranking woman holds a rank equivalent to major.

The General Federation of Iraqi Women is organized in a manner similar to that of the youth organizations and the Ba'th. There are 18 branches, one in each province of Iraq, 265 subsections based in major towns, 755 centers that incorporate villages with more than 200 families or quarters of cities with more than 6,000 people, and an additional 1,612 liaison committees that extend to all remaining villages and quarters.[14] Conferences are held regularly at the centers, where elections determine the membership of a general council from which a 38-member central council is elected. An executive bureau is chosen from among those members.

Relying on the desire of many women to meet socially, particularly in rural areas, the federation has been instrumental in the development of basic skills in child care, family health, nutrition, and hygiene, as well as in facilitating the progress of women in education. It was, for example, the basic tool by which women and children in the rural areas were incorporated into the Campaign for Literacy. The federation thus has enabled the Ba'th party to pursue some of its policies of social and economic development while inculcating Ba'thist ideas and a sense of Iraqi nationalism. Whether the federation has established a degree of loyalty to the Ba'th among women is difficult to know, but certainly it has helped to maintain consistent links between central government authorities and women throughout the country, exposing them in the process to larger governmental concerns.

The Popular Army, a national militia formally established in 1970, provides yet another means by which the Ba'th may extend its influence. The original concept can be traced to February 1963, when a force of some 2,000 Ba'th sympathizers rose from the Ba'th-dominated 'Azamiya quarter of Baghdad to fend off possible army intervention against the Ba'th's attempted takeover of the government. That force was later legitimized as the National Guard.[15] Its successor organization partici-

14. Information gathered from interviews with Manal Unis, president of the General Federation of Iraqi Women, and Shirmin Jawdat, formerly president of the Kurdish Women's Federation and now the secretary-general of the General Federation of Iraqi Women, on June 23, 1981. Manal Unis has been a Ba'thist since 1958, Shirmin Jawdat since 1973.

15. John F. Devlin, *The Ba'th Party: A History from Its Origins to 1966* (Hoover Institution, 1976), p. 233; Barraq H. 'Ali, *Baghdad Observer Weekly Supplement*

pated in the successful revolution of 1968 and evolved into the Popular Army. Since 1974 its commander-in-chief has been Taha Yasin Ramadhan, the first deputy prime minister and a member of the Revolutionary Command Council and of the Regional and National Commands of the Ba'th party. Some Ba'thists in Baghdad say that Ramadhan initiated the use of this militia in the 1968 revolution and employed it to watch the regular military for signs of intervention until the Ba'thists were firmly in control.

In addition to protecting strategic installations, guarding the frontier, and acting as a security force in rural areas, the Popular Army serves as a military reserve force and an instrument of political consolidation. During a two-month annual training period, members receive lectures on political vigilance as well as training in weaponry, mobilization, and military tactics from graduates of the Popular Army's own school, established in 1972. Several factors have contributed to rapid growth. At first the Popular Army, like its predecessor, confined its membership to supporters of the Ba'th over eighteen years of age, but in 1975 it began to accept non-Ba'thists and in 1976 admitted women. By the end of the decade it had evolved from a clandestine militia into a broadly based organization whose members came from throughout Iraq and had diverse backgrounds in the civil service, factory work, and teaching, and whose employers were reimbursed by the government during their absence. Its numbers grew from about 3,000 in the early 1970s to some 250,000 in 1980–81, when the war with Iran provided an additional spur to recruitment. In 1982 the Popular Army had some 450,000 participants, including approximately 40,000 women and 25,000 Kurds from the Autonomous Region.[16]

The institutionalization of the National Assembly and of the Legislative Council for the Kurdish Autonomous Region can also be seen as an attempt by the Ba'th to widen its base of support during the late 1970s, when the government was feeling the influence of Khomeini's return to Iran and pressure from the Iraqi Communist party. An additional factor was the proposed union of Iraq and Syria that began to be discussed in 1978. Bakr's resignation as president and the alleged coup attempt of

---

(Baghdad), as translated and reprinted in JPRS 72917, *NE/NA Report*, no. 1917 (March 5, 1979), pp. 29–31; and *Iraq Today* (Baghdad), vol. 5 (February 1–15, 1980), pp. 8–9.

16. Interview with Taha Yasin Ramadhan, August 12, 1982; interview at the General Federation of Iraqi Women, June 23, 1981; and British Broadcasting Corporation, *Summary of World Broadcasts*, ME/6642/A/7, February 6, 1981.

1979, when Bakr's successor Husain executed many prominent Ba'thists, may in part have reflected a split in the Iraqi Ba'th over this issue.
Although Husain initially was said to have supported union, he later
came to oppose union or any other power-sharing arrangement with
Syrian President Hafiz al-Asad. Those whom he executed allegedly had
favored union or conspired with Syrian officials.

Against that background, nationwide elections were held on June 20,
1980, in which 250 of 840 candidates were elected to the National
Assembly for a term of four years. The country was divided into electoral
districts with one representative for every 50,000 people; all Iraqis, male
and female, over the age of eighteen years were eligible to vote. The
candidates themselves did not have to be Ba'thists but were required to
be Ba'thist in spirit, signifying that they did not belong to an opposition
group not recognized by the Ba'th and were not among the so-called
former feudalists. In addition, candidates were to be over twenty-five
years old, be the offspring of an Iraqi father and an Arab mother (thus
eliminating many Persians), be married to an Iraqi, and be of sound
moral character.

The rights and duties of the National Assembly officially are said to
include ratification of the budget and international treaties, the right to
question and relieve any cabinet minister of his post, the debate of
domestic and foreign policies, the proposal and enactment of laws, and
the supervision of state institutions. In reality it is not known whether
this body will exercise real power, in part because the onset of war with
Iran a few months after the election required the continued centralization
of power in the Revolutionary Command Council.

An analysis of the social composition of the assembly prepared by
Amazia Baram[17] shows that 75 percent of those elected are Ba'thists,[18]
7 percent are women, some 50 percent have had higher education, about
40 percent are Shi'i and 12 percent Kurdish, 73.6 percent are between
thirty and forty-five years of age, and only about 3 percent come from
the military. Baram also notes that the majority of the elected Ba'thists
joined the party between 1958 and 1963, worked hard for their education
relatively late in their lives, gave their early party service in the provinces,
where they rose in the ranks and acquired administrative skills before

---

17. Amazia Baram, "The June 1980 Elections to the National Assembly in Iraq: An
Experiment in Controlled Democracy," in *Orient* (September 1981), pp. 391–412.

18. In an interview with Naim Haddad, president of the National Assembly, on June
28, 1981, he stated that 80 percent were Ba'thists.

moving to Baghdad, and generally came from modest socioeconomic backgrounds. In sum, there is reason to believe that in peacetime they would provide a stable and predictable support group for the civilian Ba'thists.

The Legislative Council for the Kurdish Autonomous Region consists of fifty elected members. The council is theoretically empowered to make decisions regarding development of the Autonomous Region, to propose its budget, and to exchange views with the region's ten-member Executive Council. The Legislative Council was an outgrowth of attempts by the Iraqi government to find a peaceful outlet for Kurdish nationalist aspirations. The Autonomy Law of March 11, 1974, recognized the Kurdish people as a distinct national group living within their own region and granted them specific rights, while safeguarding the territorial integrity of the Iraqi state. As was mentioned earlier, Kurdish nationalism has remained a persistent problem for Iraqi governments throughout the twentieth century, one that became acute in the 1960s. Because detailed accounts of the Kurdish issue exist elsewhere,[19] suffice it to say here that the government's "carrot and stick" approach to the problem has often been applied and has usually emphasized the latter. How legitimate or effective the Kurds perceive the Legislative Council to be is not known.

A National Action Charter made public in 1971 and operative in 1973 led to the formation of the so-called National Front, the last of the means mentioned here by which the Ba'th has sought to extend its appeal. The party invited opposing political groups to discuss national issues such as a constitution, Kurdish autonomy, development plans, and foreign policy, among others. A High Committee was created in hope of reaching a consensus. It was composed initially of eight Ba'thists, three Communists, three Kurdish Democratic party members, one Progressive Nationalist, and one independent. After divisions among the Kurds, its membership was increased from sixteen to eighteen, with five seats offered to the Kurds. Its composition changed again in the late 1970s with the exile of the Communist leaders.[20] It remains, as does the

19. See different accounts of the Kurdish issue in Edmund Ghareeb, *The Kurdish Question in Iraq* (Syracuse University Press, 1981); Gerard Chaliand, ed., *People without a Country: The Kurds and Kurdistan* (London: Zed Press, 1980); and Sa'ad Jawad, *Iraq and the Kurdish Question, 1958–1970* (London: Ithaca Press, 1981).

20. The contents of this charter and an analysis of its implementation are found in Majid Khadduri, *Socialist Iraq: A Study in Iraqi Politics since 1968* (Washington, D.C.: Middle East Institute, 1978), pp. 97–101, 199–229.

National Assembly, an innovative but highly controlled experiment in democracy by the Ba'th party.

"Unity, Freedom, Socialism": Goals in Theory and Practice

Although the Ba'th party still confronts difficult obstacles in its quest for a stable government with popular support, it must be asked what enabled the party in the 1970s to achieve its successes against other political groups, even Arab nationalist movements. Part of the answer is contained in the saying that "the man [or party] who controls the agenda carries the meeting." The party's turbulent history convinced a number of Ba'thists at least as early as the 1960s that only through reducing internal party conflicts could they gain the necessary advantage over rivals. Internal pacification was and is achieved through institutionalization of the party and its procedures, adherence to defined party policies, strict disciplinary action against deviant members, and periodic, occasionally public reappraisals of failures, although the last occurs within guidelines set by the party.

There is quite literally a stockpile of formalized Ba'thist thought or ideology that has been commissioned, sanctioned, and published by the party. Dating to at least the 1940s, this body of literature is remarkable among Middle Eastern political parties not only because it is so large but also because it provides guidelines for almost every aspect of domestic and foreign affairs. Problematic topics that have not yet been studied are referred to the party's research bureaus for evaluation and policy suggestions. Although some of these writings may be spontaneous short-term responses by the leadership elite to crisis situations, they should be viewed as Ba'thists view them—as a doctrinal foundation that may require further elucidation or modification.

The core of Ba'thist literature consists, at one extreme, of officially sanctioned ideological expositions intended for dedicated members and, at the other extreme, of magazines and newspapers directed to a broader readership. Designed to be palatable even to non-Ba'thists, the latter nevertheless reinforce the same Ba'th objectives.

Information disseminated to the public in Iraq by radio, television, and the press is censored by a government that itself is controlled by organs of the Ba'th party. Supervision of the media has the clear purpose of consolidating support for the government and the party, which has an obvious interest in presenting its own analysis of the news and in extolling its own achievements. The party also seeks to eliminate propaganda by political groups that oppose it. The authorities can do little to prevent anti-Ba'th broadcasts by foreign states such as Syria, or by Communist and Kurdish groups operating clandestinely, but it can and does expend considerable effort to eliminate the distribution of opposition literature and to identify those responsible for it. One aspect of government control is that the purchase of a typewriter requires a license and telex machines may be operated only by Iraqis or those officially approved by the government.[21] Another is that Western publications such as *Newsweek* and *Le Monde* disappeared from Baghdad bookstores after the war began, though copies inexplicably appeared on the desks of middle-level bureaucrats. Despite such restrictions, the party allows the broadcast media to provide a range of entertainment and education. Arabic music and readings from the Quran are intermingled with English, German, and French radio programs on, for example, marine biology, archaeology, and self-improvement topics such as water safety, hygiene, or the proper use of carpentry tools. American serials such as "Big Valley" and "Dallas" appear on Iraqi television as do children's cartoons, the last without Arabic subtitles.

Literature in Politics

Serious Ba'th party literature offers valuable insights into Iraq's domestic and foreign policy decisions. Consisting mainly of tracts, speeches, editorials, opening addresses, and even interviews, this body of writing prompts a number of general observations. First, its rhetorical and deliberately repetitious nature not only makes its study cumbrous but also obscures the underlying logic, contributing to a radical image. Second, it reflects the relative priority of concrete problems that confront the party. Careful reading may even disclose divergent opinions among the party's leaders. Third, although many observers perceive the party solely as a calculating tool of political power, as indeed it is, the Ba'th's leaders have consistently conveyed an intense, almost messianic sincer-

---

21. Off-the-record interview. During the Iran-Iraq war it was also rumored that frequent "breakdowns" in the long-distance telephone system were a frustrated reaction by the government to its failure to prevent direct-dial calls to Iran from families or friends in Iraq.

ity in expressing the main goals of the party.[22] Fourth, those leaders display a remarkable unanimity once a policy decision has been made. While this tends to mask internal party divisions, it does lend a degree of predictability to their actions. Fifth, Ba'thist ideology is used to inculcate Ba'thist goals, to unify members within a party organization, and to legitimize political decisions. Sixth, because there has not been a unified repository of Ba'thist thought since the party split into two National Commands in 1966, before which time Michel Aflaq held an unchallengeable position as chief ideologue, its current publications are distinctly representative of so-called regional concerns—that is, mainly Iraqi. Seventh, those to whom the authorship of Ba'thist ideology is credited can be seen to have acquired a modicum of prestige within the party hierarchy if for no other reason than that they are in its approved mainstream at the time of writing, or perhaps because their names have become readily identifiable.

Even though all high-ranking Iraqi Ba'thists are steeped in party ideology, very few are actually credited as writers and almost none as ideologues. For those few who are, the ability to write or to articulate ideas publicly is undoubtedly an important attribute in their repertory of political skills, though it is neither a prerequisite of success nor a requirement for advancement in the party. Aflaq, for example, the best-known of all Ba'thist writers and an influential force in the political life of several countries, never attained sole political authority in any state and in fact held only a cabinet post for one brief period.

When Iraqi Ba'thists are asked whom they consider to be Aflaq's successor as ideologue, the almost universal response is Saddam Husain,

22. When young Iraqis were asked how one became a high-ranking Ba'thist, the consistent response was "hard work and long hours." One manifestation of this is seen in the daily habits of the Ba'th command. My interviews took place at the appointed times; if cancellations had to occur, they were rescheduled in advance. One Ba'thist attributed this concern for punctuality to a trait inherited from the time party members were operating clandestinely; if a member was more than two minutes late, it was assumed that something had gone wrong. Interviews occasionally were held late at night or early in the morning to avoid interfering with the work of the ministries. There has also been an attempt to provide greater contact between the people and government officials and to increase the efficiency of the latter. In some cases this involved giving personal access to a minister each week or maintaining a daily staff for registering complaints. Before the Iran-Iraq war began, high-ranking party members made informal and sometimes incognito visits to health facilities to assess the helpfulness of the staff to the general public. It is difficult to imagine the equivalent of these activities in any Western political system.

under whose name have appeared more than 200 books, articles, and essays.[23] Although the choice of Husain may not seem surprising, it should be recalled that in Ba'th history the positions of head of government and ideologue have not been synonymous. Tariq 'Aziz, a member of the Revolutionary Command Council and deputy prime minister, is sometimes named in addition to Husain as a man of prolific writing ability and erudition. 'Aziz in fact was once an editor of the Ba'th party newspaper *al-Thawra*.[24] Dr. Sa'dun Hammadi, best known in the West as a foreign minister of Iraq, also has written a number of articles on political philosophy and current Arab affairs.[25] It is noteworthy that the party credentials of all three men—Husain, 'Aziz, and Hammadi—date from the 1950s.

During an interview on August 22, 1982, President Husain explained how he used writing as a means of furthering his own political goals, and also discussed the more encompassing social role of ideology within the party. The following quotation introduces a more detailed discussion of Ba'thist literature and its relationship to policy decisions, in addition to suggesting why Ba'thist discipline and organization have helped the party to endure where others holding similar ideas have failed.

23. Interview with Latif Nusayif Jasim, Iraqi minister of information, August 14, 1982. A number of pamphlets averaging at least fifty pages each have been published under Saddam Husain's name even since the start of the Iran-Iraq war, although there is almost certainly a bureau of the party that is responsible for the composition and dissemination of these publications. A cross section of those published in 1980 alone includes *al-Turath al-'Arabi wa al-Mu'asira* ("The Arab Inheritance and Modernity"); *al-Dimuqratiya: Masdar Quwa li al-Fard wa al-Mujtama'* ("Democracy: A Source of Strength for the Individual and Society"); *Li al-Sha'b Kull: al-Dimuqratiya wa al-Hurriya wa al-Huquq* ("To All the People: Democracy, Freedom, and Rights"); *Mubadi'una al-Qaumiya Tuhaddid 'Alaqatina bi al-'Alam* ("Our National Principles Define Our Relations with the World"); and *Iradat al-Insan al-'Arabi Ba'athat fi al-'Iraq* ("Aspirations of the Arab Man Are Awakened in Iraq"). All of these were published in Baghdad by Dar al-Hurriya.

24. When I visited Tariq 'Aziz at one of his offices in the summer of 1981, one bookcase was filled solely with English publications on economics, history, political theory, and current political affairs and personalities, and he indicated a desire to discuss several of his most recent acquisitions. His knowledge undoubtedly has been instrumental in propelling him to a position of public prominence. He is a frequent overseas representative of his government, and when Western correspondents visit Baghdad, Tariq 'Aziz is more often than not the single member of the Revolutionary Command Council they are allowed to interview.

25. Two of Dr. Hammadi's recent publications are *Mulahazat hawla Qadiyat al-Harb ma'a al-Iran* ("Observations on the Matter of the War with Iran") (Dar al-Hurriya, 1982); and *Muhawala fi Tafsir 'Amaliyat al-Taqaddum* ("An Attempt at an Explanation of the Process of Advancement") (Matba'at al-Majma' al-'Ilmi al-'Iraqi, 1982).

The truth is that I did not begin deep responsible thinking until after the revolution in 1963. That was the beginning. [Then] I was not a senior [party] member. I was in charge of a bureau of farmers.

I did not begin political writing, except small internal manifestos, until the beginning of 1964 when I was in hiding. Then I made a declaration to the provisional leadership after the setback of the revolution in 1963 . . . and [I decided to] face the dissent, which was posing Marxist ideas. Within the framework of the party I decided to declare that a regional leadership existed where it did not exist. . . . On my own responsibility I fired a number of leaders . . . and I defined the road for the party as the basic road upon which it had already started. . . . I [also] felt that they [presumably the party in its entirety] should be more concerned with development.

This was the end of 1963 and the beginning of 1964. [Our] problems were of an intellectual nature. They had to be dealt with. I decided that intellectual treatment and feelings . . . that ideology should be all encompassing in solving problems or finding solutions to problems of the future.

Suffering [however] has become more than reading itself. He [an Iraqi] rises, washes, meditates, and pinpoints all phenomena [around him]. We [as a party] began submitting all problems of an intellectual nature [to critical thought and to writing]. The judge will be [a better standard of] life itself.

The social role of Ba'thism alluded to in these last comments of Husain should not be dismissed as mere window-dressing. It is a common theme in all writings of the party regardless of their authorship. Every prospective Ba'thi from the first day he indicates a desire for party membership is urged to view himself as the vanguard of a social transformation (*inqilab*) and to evaluate his daily performance in both a professional and a personal sense. The importance of sacrifice for the betterment of one's moral character as well as for one's society therefore became a key aspect of Ba'thist doctrine. Saddam Husain in particular stressed the importance of self-criticism during the 1970s, contending that there was a difference between a "Ba'thist"—that is, someone who strives to achieve goals of self-improvement even if he is not a party member—and a "Hizbi," who is a Ba'thist but is more aptly described as simply a party-liner or yes-man.

Transformation is as vital a component of Ba'thist political thought as the Islamic concept of *jihad* is to Islamic movements. *Jihad*, contrary to its more generally recognized stereotype as a "holy war," signifies continued striving for a pure Islamic society even in routine activities that are usually considered secular by other religious groups. Therefore, *inqilab* and *jihad* can very loosely but with some usefulness be compared as political tools of reunification. Both concepts connote a reawakening of certain aspects of the past, a striving for the internal reformation of individuals and of the community (*umma*) in all aspects of life from mundane thoughts and daily rituals to the initiation and conduct of war, even to the overthrow of illicit governments. They both place the individual firmly within a framework of social responsibilities and, conversely, define the responsibilities of society to the individual.

Nevertheless, the Ba'thists are secular; theoretically they respect ethnic and religious differences while recognizing Islam as the religion of the state. Social transformation as they define it seeks to attain social and economic development within the framework of three goals: unity (*wahda*), freedom (*hurriya*), and socialism (*ishtirakiya*). The emphasis on development, a desire intensely expressed by the upper echelon of the Ba'th, is one of the things that has distinguished the party from other Arab nationalist groups, which are often unable to develop a comprehensive social and political platform, and from Islamic movements, which exist primarily for the furtherance of a pure Islam.

Because the three goals have had such a pervasive influence on policy, they are dealt with separately below to illustrate the framework within which Iraqi Ba'thists have perceived the socioeconomic and political needs of their country. These goals played a primary role during the 1970s in aiding the Ba'th to consolidate and extend its support, to instill a sense of Iraqi nationalism, and to guide the direction of Iraq's domestic and foreign policies. They are dynamic in the sense that they may be modified in response to political pressures from within and outside Iraq. Consequently there are differences between the theoretical formulation and the practical application of Ba'thist ideology, a reformulation of some goals, and a reordering of priorities through time. Such changes do not invalidate their significance when one is seeking to understand the Ba'thists.

The Goals Examined: Unity

The first goal, that of Arab unity, was propounded in the 1940s as the essential solution to the region's problems. Pan-Arabism is the extreme formulation of Arab nationalism, and the Ba'thists at least theoretically were its unswerving supporters. In its ideal form, unity was to be attained in three related realms: the eventual elimination of artificial post–World War I boundaries and the formation of a single Arab state, the sharing of human and material resources belonging to all Arabs, and an agreement among Arabs on the purposes of development and the means to achieve it. The territory considered to belong within the Arab preserve, roughly that comprising the twenty-two states of the Arab League,[26] also included three controversial regions—Cilicia and Alexandretta (now known as Iskandarun) in Turkey, Khuzistan (referred to as Arabistan by the Iraqis) in Iran, and Palestine—historically considered to be part of the Arab nation. Elaborate doctrinal provisions rationalized the inclusion of large concentrations of non-Arab minorities such as the Kurds.

This idealized conception of unity began to diminish in importance during the 1960s for reasons that devolved, ironically, from the growth of the Ba'th party and from the process of state formation. Among them can be included the tensions resulting from the formation of the United Arab Republic in 1958, disagreement between Ba'thists who were pro-Nasirites and those who were not, the split in the Ba'th Party in 1966, the development of regionalism concurrently with these events, and the consequent emphasis placed on practical rather than theoretical problems of governance. Changing circumstances thus have dictated a progressive modification of key aspects of the Iraqi Ba'th's conception of Arab unity.

As a member of Iraq's Revolutionary Command Council confided in 1981, "While [Arab] unity remains an ideal, it is not expected to be implemented either now or possibly ever in the future." It can be argued plausibly that failure of the attempted union between Iraq and Syria in 1979 reflected a deeply ingrained belief in the Iraqi Ba'th elite that pan-Arab unity as then defined was no longer desirable, at least not to the dominant element in the party. Once Arab nationalists had gained control of their respective state governments, the union of even two Arab states would cause these same men to lose the positions they had struggled to attain.

Although Iraq would have benefited in some ways from union with Syria, there were also disadvantages. Iraq's oil wealth would have compelled it to assume additional economic burdens for Syria and, despite Iraqi Ba'th rhetoric regarding Israel, to become a confrontation state in reality. In normal circumstances Iraq's physical distance from Israel was a sufficient excuse to delay the country's involvement in

26. There were twenty-two states until the Arab League suspended Egypt after the Camp David accords were signed in 1978. The members as listed by the Arab League itself are as follows: Algeria, Bahrain, Djibouti, Iraq, Jordan, Kuwait, Lebanon, Libya, Mauritania, Morocco, Oman, Palestine, Qatar, Saudi Arabia, Somalia, Sudan, Syria, Tunisia, United Arab Emirates, Yemen Arab Republic, and the People's Democratic Republic of Yemen.

costly disputes, and its leaders' radical rhetoric protected them on the domestic front from an issue potentially volatile to the average Arab. Francis Fukuyama has pointed out that Iraq showed signs of reluctance to intervene in the October 1973 Arab-Israeli war, and did so three days into the war only after President Brezhnev had asked Iraq to send 500 tanks to Syria to replace Soviet tanks already lost. "Although they did not honor Brezhnev's request in the precise manner suggested," Fukuyama writes, "they did send an armoured division to the Syrian front. Consistent with past policies, however, the Iraqis used their 'rejection' of the ceasefire resolution, 338, as an excuse for withdrawing their forces almost immediately after the end of the fighting." Fukuyama notes that this position was not unlike the one the Ba'thists took in regard to the oil crisis: "Pretending to be yet more radical than other OPEC members, Iraq nationalized some U.S. and Dutch holdings in the Basra Petroleum Company. . . . Claiming that this was a greater 'blow' to the West than the embargo, Iraq then actually *raised* its oil production, profiting handsomely in the process."[27]

It is the idealized conception of unity that has been responsible for the Iraqi Ba'th's position on Israel, which essentially calls for Israel's dismemberment and its replacement by a Palestinian state. Since the first of the three goals of the Ba'th party was to unite the Arabs, it took a strong position on the dangers of Zionist policies even before the first party congress in 1947. In 1948 many Syrian Ba'thists went to fight in Palestine. The issue was felt so strongly that many Arabs, including Iraqis from several political parties and from the Iraqi regular army, joined the struggle. The issue of Arab rights to Arab lands, primarily embodied in the loss of Palestine, has remained an ideal and a pivotal symbol of unity ever since.

There are, however, some surprising aspects to this subject. While the Ba'thists have consistently refused to accept United Nations Resolution 242 and have continued to express hostility toward Israeli policies, ever more sharply since the Israeli bombing of Iraq's nuclear reactor and the Israeli invasion of Lebanon, they have tempered extreme declarations by stating that they would accept whatever agreement the Palestinians might reach in any negotiations. A high-ranking Ba'th official stated off the record in 1981 that such negotiations could be successful

27. Francis Fukuyama, *The Soviet Union and Iraq Since 1968*, N-1524-AF, prepared for the U.S. Air Force (Santa Monica, Calif.: Rand Corp., 1980), p. 41.

only if they were sponsored by the United States. While the Ba'th party appreciated the good will exemplified by the European peace initiative, he did not perceive it as an offer that could be supported substantively. When U.S. Congressman Stephen Solarz visited Iraq in August 1982, President Husain departed from formal doctrine and, making a bid for American support, stated the necessity for Israel to have secure borders. At the Fez Conference in November 1981 the Iraqis remained remarkably quiescent; nor did they oppose President Reagan's peace initiative of September 1982.

Iraq's relationship with the Palestinians is even more complex and enigmatic, revealing the Ba'th's ideological concessions to external political pressures. Three episodes illustrate the underlying conflict between ideology and reality.

The first surrounds the controversy in Jordan in 1970 between King Husain and the Palestinians that brought the country close to civil war.[28] Many, including the Jordanian military, which moved two full divisions into place confronting the Iraqi forces, feared that Iraq might intervene on the side of the Palestinians. In fact they did not, although the reasons have never been clearly understood. After public demonstrations took place against the Iraqi government's failure to intervene, the Iraqi minister of defense, Hardan al-Takriti, was removed from his job. In the controlled political environment of Ba'thist Iraq, however, it is improbable that the defense minister alone could have dictated this policy. Even after Takriti's removal, Iraqi brigades did not assist the Palestinians in fighting later that year. An argument reportedly took place between Michel Aflaq and Saddam Husain. The former wished to intercede on behalf of the Palestinians and the latter did not, which suggests that Takriti might well have been a scapegoat. He eventually went into exile and was assassinated in Kuwait in 1971. The assassination was attributed to the Iraqi Ba'th, but its complicity was never proved. If the Ba'thists did assassinate Takriti, it was almost certainly because he had powerful supporters within the Iraqi military, particularly the air force, who wished to resurrect him politically. Many of these men along with Takriti had also opposed Saddam Husain's plan for Kurdish autonomy.

The second episode occurred after the beginning of the Iran-Iraq war. The Palestine Liberation Organization, resenting the war because it

28. See ibid., pp. 33, 53–54, for another example of Iraq's delayed response to Palestinian needs.

diverted attention from its own political struggles and diminished whatever unanimity of external support might have been crystallizing for its cause, originally adopted a position of neutrality, at least publicly.[29] In the summer of 1981, local Iraqis said that Palestinians had been responsible for blowing up several large ammunition dumps and for other acts of sabotage in Iraq. Security increased noticeably in Baghdad as rumors spread that the government was anticipating a showdown with the Palestinians.[30] Then, just as quickly as the tension appeared, it dissipated with no explanation.

Third, it is noteworthy that between June 1980 and December 15, 1981, Iraq suffered some eleven incidents of sabotage against its embassy staff or property in Beirut,[31] the most severe having been the destruction of the Iraqi embassy on December 15, 1981, with the loss of more than fifty lives. It is unclear whether these acts of terrorism were carried out by Palestinian, Syrian, or pro-Iranian Shi'i groups, or some combination thereof, but they brought about a wholly unexpected alliance. Iraq, an Arab and predominantly Muslim state, took the unprecedented and innovative step of moving its embassy to the safety of Christian-dominated east Beirut—something even Western governments had not done. Foreign embassies in the Middle East then began to report rumors that Iraqi diplomats, under the auspices of RCC member Tariq 'Aziz, were meeting with Christians in Beirut. Members of groups associated with or belonging to Bashir Gemayel's Phalange confirmed in interviews that Iraq had had contacts with them at least since March or April 1982. One informant said that contacts had occurred even in Baghdad with the full knowledge of the upper echelon of the Iraqi Ba'th. Even though

29. Ironically, this may be one case in which Israel and Iraq had an enemy in common. The *Jerusalem Post* published a report on October 31, 1980, that one of Yasser Arafat's main aides—Abu Iyad—was secretly financing Lebanese Shi'i groups against Israel and Kurdish guerrilla activities against Iraq with Libyan money. Abu Iyad's activities were in contradistinction to those of another key aide of Arafat—Abu Jihad—who, feeling that the Palestine Liberation Organization's originally neutral stance in the Iran-Iraq war was counterproductive to its cause, called for support of Iraq and continued ties with moderate political forces, including Jordan. See FBIS, *Daily Report: MEA*, November 3, 1980, p. N3.

30. During an interview in 1982 with Nasif Awad, director of the Palestine Bureau, he estimated that some 20,000 to 25,000 Palestinians had entered Iraq after the 1948 war and that the total number of Palestinian immigrants to Iraq up to 1982 was approximately 100,000. Several residential areas in Baghdad have concentrations of Palestinian populations.

31. *Monday Morning* (Beirut), February 15–21, 1982, p. 24.

some may dismiss this support as simply a demonstration of the government's antipathy toward the Syrian Ba'thists, an Iraqi Ba'th official explained his party's position on Lebanon to me in the summer of 1981 as follows: "While we are against the interference of others with the Palestinians in Lebanon, we are also against the interference of the Palestinians with every issue in Lebanon."

Therefore, although the conflict between Palestine and Israel is undeniably a deeply felt issue among Iraqi Ba'thists, as is evident in their diplomatic, financial,[32] and military support of the Palestinians, their sympathies are tempered by Iraq's extenuating political and geographic circumstances. This constraint was partially confirmed during interviews in 1981 with members of Palestinian groups, including the Iraqi-supported Arab Liberation Front. Started by the Iraqi Regional Command in April 1969 in the occupied West Bank, this group in 1972 became one of several groups composing the Palestine Liberation Organization. Baghdad is considered a policy office, but the front also has operated offices in Jordan, Syria, and Lebanon. Palestinian members of the front said that their interests overlapped with those of the Iraqi Ba'th to the extent that they agreed to struggle for Arab goals of liberation and internal social change in the Middle East generally, but tensions frequently arose when the Palestinians were thought to be exercising too much initiative in working toward their own more narrowly defined goals.

There have been rumors that Iraq has taken punitive measures against Palestinian groups, such as the People's Front for the Liberation of Palestine and the People's Democratic Front for the Liberation of Palestine. In an unattributed commentary on the clandestine Voice of

32. Saudi Arabia, Iraq, Kuwait, the United Arab Emirates, Libya, Algeria, and Qatar agreed at the Baghdad summit conference of November 1978 to contribute some $3.6 billion to Arab "front-line" states facing Israel. Of this total, approximately $1.85 billion was designated for Syria, $1.25 billion for Jordan, $350 million for the Palestine Liberation Organization, and $150 million for the inhabitants of the occupied territories of Gaza and the West Bank. Jordan was to assist in the distribution of this last amount. Baghad itself committed approximately $520 million of the total annually; it completed payments for 1979 and had paid at least one installment of about $172 million by May 1980. Iraq stopped payments to Syria after it gave support to Iran in the war, but payments to Jordan did continue amid rumors that Iraq had also replaced funds promised to Jordan by Algeria and Libya that were not forthcoming. Iraq has contributed other funds to the PLO through the years, the total amount being unknown. Iraq also has aided the Palestinians by agreeing to supply oil to certain countries—Spain, for example—in return for their recognition of the PLO.

the Iraqi Revolution on March 14, 1981, Iraqi leaders were accused of turning Palestinian resistance groups against one another, of assassinating Palestinian leaders in London and Kuwait who opposed Iraqi policies, and of strengthening relations with reactionary Arab regimes such as Saudi Arabia. It is notable that the broadcast also accused the Iraqi Ba'thists of opposing the establishment of a Palestinian state because they believed that it would be secular and pro-Soviet.[33] Iraqi Ba'thists denied these charges in subsequent interviews, but it is significant that they have decided to dismantle the party's Palestine Bureau, which began functioning in 1969, and to submerge it within a comprehensive bureau of revolutionary movements.[34]

A more observable gap between ideological commitments and practical policies was demonstrated on September 8, 1982, when Saddam Husain made a definitive declaration regarding Arab unity. Remarkable for its frankness and its pragmatic acceptance of the current Arab political milieu, his statement was the first in which the Iraqi Ba'thists publicly discarded with absolute clarity the notion of a single Arab state.

The Iraqis are now of the opinion that Arab unity can only take place after a clear demarcation of borders between all countries. We further believe that Arab unity must not take place through the elimination of the local and national characteristics of any Arab country. If the people in the PDRY [People's Democratic Republic of Yemen] and President 'Ali Nasir Muhammad wish to establish unity with Iraq today on the basis of dissolving the Iraqi and Yemeni personalities, I, Saddam Husayn, will personally object to such unity. I will say: Let the two personalities coexist with one another.

The question of linking unity to the removal of boundaries is no longer acceptable to present Arab mentality. It could have been acceptable 10 or 20 years ago. We have to take into consideration the change which the Arab mind and psyche have undergone. We must see the world as it is. Any Arab would have wished to see the Arab nation as one state. . . . But these are sheer dreams. The Arab reality is that the Arabs are now 22 states, and we have to behave accordingly. Therefore, unity must not be imposed, but must be achieved

33. FBIS, *Daily Report: MEA*, March 20, 1981, p. E5.
34. Nasif Awad, its most recent director, is being sent to Paris to be the editor of *The Arab Vanguard*, a new magazine on Arab and world affairs. Consonant with Ba'th doctrine, it was not a requirement that the director of the Palestine Bureau be a Palestinian although Nasif Awad happens to be one. He left Ramalla in 1965 and became a member of the Ba'th as early as 1954. He was the editor-in-chief of *al-Thawra* for two years before becoming the vice-deputy director of the Palestine Bureau for another two years under the directorship of Naim Haddad. Awad was appointed its head in the late 1970s and continued in that position until 1982 when his new post was assigned.

through common fraternal opinion. Unity must give strength to its partners, not cancel their national identity.[35]

Iraq's Ba'thist authorities clearly have progressed beyond their earlier manifestation as a revolutionary government. Indeed, members of the party's upper echelon acknowledge that they have matured a great deal since taking power in 1968. What Iraq could not obtain by threat or by appealing to the ideal of unity it has begun to seek by more pragmatic means. As was pointed out in chapter 3, Iraq made a deliberate attempt just before and early in the war to settle outstanding boundary disputes with neighboring countries. After 1975 it contributed to the Arab Fund for Economic and Social Development, the Arab Fund for the Development of Africa, the Islamic Bank for Development, and the United Nations Relief and Works Agency. It also had its own bilateral aid program called the National Fund for External Development, which by 1980 had provided grants, low-interest loans, and aid for the financing of oil imports to more than twenty-seven developing countries in Africa, Asia, and the Middle East. The Fund's capital in the late 1970s was said to be $680 million and its commitments $1.25 billion.

Iraq does not share its records with international financial institutions, so it is difficult to verify Iraqi claims of financial commitments and disbursements. During the mid-1970s, however, Egypt was the largest recipient of Iraqi aid in the form of support for Egypt's balance of payments. Iraq's aid quintupled from 1978 to 1979, reaching roughly $860 million, or nearly 3 percent of its gross national product. Twelve countries under long-term contracts to buy Iraqi oil—Bangladesh, India, Madagascar, Morocco, Mozambique, Pakistan, the Philippines, Senegal, Somalia, Sri Lanka, Tanzania, and Vietnam—received in the last half of 1979 long-term interest-free loans totaling some $200 million to be applied against future oil increases. It is safe to assume that once the war began, Iraq's disbursements dropped considerably despite its announced financial commitments.[36] Nevertheless, Iraq's emphasis after 1975 on joint financial and commercial projects as well as on political

35. FBIS, *Daily Report: MEA*, September 14, 1982, p. E5, excerpt from a press statement and interview given by Saddam Husain to chief editors of Kuwaiti newspapers in Morocco on September 8, 1982, as read on the Baghdad Voice of the Masses on September 10, 1982.

36. Information from yearly reviews of Organization for Economic Cooperation and Development, *Development Co-operation* (Paris: OECD, various years).

and military consultations among Arab countries was an indicator that the concept of pan-Arabism as originally defined was no longer practicable.

Wartime exigencies probably were the impetus behind Saddam Husain's public reformulation of the concept of Arab unity in 1982. Other Arab states, whether Jordan, Saudi Arabia, or the smaller Gulf states, understandably perceived the war in the context of their own internal needs. In calling for fraternal Arab assistance in the war, Iraqi leaders could legitimately appeal to those needs and thereby encourage a form of Arab unity without undermining the nationalism or traditional rulers of other states.

Freedom

The second of the three Ba'th goals—freedom—may be interpreted in two ways: as internal democracy, and as freedom in the sense of independence from external domination. Neither should be considered an absolute or immutable concept, nor should they necessarily be equated with Western definitions of the same terms, though their origin was Western.[37] In Iraq they have evolved and been applied in a wholly different social context. In the sense of "democracy," Ba'thists refer to the right of Arabs to participate in decisions affecting their own welfare or the welfare of their countries. Party members therefore point to the party's own electoral process, to the establishment of the Kurdish Autonomous Region and the National Assembly, to greater freedom for women, and to the legalization of at least some political groups within the National Front.

This democracy, however, functions only through the controlled agency of the party, which ironically may serve as an incentive for recruitment to the party. The exercise of centralized control over the Iraqi state by a strong power elite is not unique to the Ba'thists, but has characterized every Iraqi government of this century regardless of its political inclinations. A sudden and unqualified granting of democracy to all of Iraq's diverse and numerous interest groups has been perceived by all of them, without exception, as more likely to result in chaos than

37. It will be recalled that many early Ba'thists were educated in the West. During an interview in 1981, an Iraqi Ba'thist commented on democracy by stating that "this term is not so different from what early Americans in 1776 thought about: equality and the pursuit of happiness. They [are ideas] similar to those of your Thomas Jefferson, Paine, George Washington, and Abraham Lincoln."

in the achievement of an ideal, however desirable the intent. The Ba'th, having broadened the base of popular support for its policies since 1975, actually has liberalized its domestic policies, if only by incremental steps. It must be expected, however, that these advances might be undermined or delayed by repercussions from the Iran-Iraq war.

In its second sense, independence from external domination, the Ba'thist concept of freedom is derived, like the concept of unity, from an essentially negative reaction to Western interference in the Middle East and to control of the state's wealth by indigenous privileged groups, generally those supported by Western powers. In Iraq, it is also a by-product of the leaders' sense of the state's vulnerability arising from geographic constraints, such as the fact that Iraq is virtually landlocked, has few port facilities, contains geographic and climatic features that inhibit development in both south and north, and is adjoined by two large non-Arab nation-states—Turkey and Iran.

The concept of freedom as defined by the Ba'thists is not unique to them, although they have refined it considerably. It has been argued elsewhere that an Iraqi alliance with a superpower is essential in order to guarantee Iraq's independence.[38] Be that as it may, more than one Iraqi government has found itself weakened domestically by such alliances or even overthrown. Perhaps not without reason, the policy of neutralism or positive neutralism already was developing in Iraq shortly after the revolution of 1958. Later, with the growth of regionalism in the 1960s, neutralism evolved for the Ba'thists into the concept of nonalignment: the avoidance or diversification of dependence on any external source, whether great power or neighboring state, in all spheres of politics, economics, and more recently, technology.[39] In an interview on July 9, 1981, Tariq 'Aziz expressed the basic dictates of nonalignment as follows:

We have worked hard to maintain our independence. . . . Independence means not only the absence of foreign troops, but also the freedom of choice, movement, and relations with big powers. It also means economic independence. Oil is important, but what is more important is to build our economy without connecting our destiny in this field with that of other countries. We sell to many buyers and, therefore, we face no major problems. We also have diversified our technology,

---

38. Khadduri, *Socialist Iraq*, p. 143.

39. Therefore the Israeli bombing of the Iraqi nuclear facilities on June 7, 1981, was described as a Western attempt to deny a country's right to modernization. Members of Iraq's government described this as "technological imperialism."

seeking cooperation with all East, West, and Third World countries. We also seek many sources for our purchases, such as arms. In 1968 perhaps 98 percent of our arms came from the Soviet Union. Now they come from many sources: France, the Eastern bloc, Brazil, and so forth.

The political importance of nonalignment gained poignant significance for the Ba'thists during the first half of the 1970s, when the shah asked the United States to supply weapons through Iran to the Kurds for their use in guerrilla activities against the Iraqi government. Much of the Iraqi government's bitterness and distrust of the two superpowers can be traced to this period. Accounts of this episode can be found elsewhere; briefly stated, the Iraqi government was forced to wage a costly human and material war within its own borders. Because of Iraq's geographic features and the location of its resources, state authorities are acutely sensitive to any pressure applied on either their northern or southern sectors, both of which are essential to the national economy. It has been estimated that in 1974 and 1975, some 60,000 civilians and military personnel were killed or wounded in this conflict in the north with the Kurds. Saddam Husain later attributed the Iraqi government's decision to sign the Algiers Declaration of 1975 to the fact that Iraq was not being resupplied by its Soviet allies. This decision was hotly debated and left bitterness in many Iraqi quarters, particularly the military, which believed it was close to victory. In any event the Kurdish conflict badly bruised Iraq's Achilles' heel, reinforcing Ba'thist inclinations against entering into an exclusive alliance with either superpower.

Iraq's pursuit of practical forms of independence is apparent in its economic development policies, which have attempted to reduce the country's dependence on foreign expertise. To begin with, considerable emphasis is placed on the eradication of illiteracy through the government-sponsored literacy campaign for Iraqis between the ages of fourteen and forty-five and through the expansion of educational facilities at all levels. In a related policy, no foreign enclaves of skilled labor are allowed to develop in Iraq as they have in Saudi Arabia with the Arabian American Oil Company (ARAMCO). Rather, the government has insisted that all contracts with foreign companies include training clauses so that Iraqis eventually can replace foreign workers, who as individuals are not permitted to remain in the country more than two years in normal circumstances. Second, Iraq is developing a multifaceted rather than an oil-dependent economy. In 1974 oil accounted for 60 percent of the gross national product, but Iraqis told me they hoped to reduce this figure to

50 percent by concentrating on the development of other export commodities: fertilizers (phosphate, urea), steel, and sponge iron. Third, Iraq is diversifying its sources of imports. After 1973 the predominant trading pattern shifted from the Soviet Union and Eastern bloc countries to the West, specifically Western Europe and Japan. Iraq's import and export trade with Europe is further diversified.[40] To a certain extent this may have been a result of the petrodollar surpluses accumulated after 1973 in all oil-producing countries, which simply allowed them to spend more than they had previously and in different ways. Iraqis also said, however, that the shift was justified not only because Western countries offered better technology, thereby reducing numerical demands on the labor force, but also because they represented an alternative to membership in one of the two superpower camps and hence less vulnerability to the pressures associated with such a relationship. By 1981 approximately 78 percent of Iraq's imports, totaling $20 billion, came from countries in the Organization for Economic Cooperation and Development, 12 percent from Eastern Europe and the Soviet Union, 8 percent from developing countries, and 2 percent from the Arab world.[41] Imports from the United States accounted for 1.5 to 5 percent, the exact figure usually being disguised within other categories.

Socialism

The Ba'th's concept of socialism, the third and least defined goal of the party, has two complementary aspects—material and social. Mate-

40. In 1980 oil accounted for 90 percent of Iraq's total export earnings. The Iraqi oil minister claimed in 1981 that Iraq did not sell oil on the spot market but offered only three- to ten-month contracts. Iraqis deny that either an equilibrium of trade or a trade ceiling is specified for individual countries, but they say that oil production levels are linked to the needs of the infrastructure, development plans, and foreign aid programs. Therefore they give preferential treatment to some countries and are not averse to pressuring others that are not buying enough to reduce trade imbalances. Claudia Wright, in "Whom Iraq Will Buy From and Why," *Middle East Executive Reports,* vol. 3 (October 1980), pp. 27–30, has emphasized Iraq's desire to balance import and export trade. She notes that the Federal Republic of Germany exported to Iraq four to six times the value of goods that it purchased; when Iraq threatened to stop further trade, Germany agreed to new oil purchases. Wright also notes that Sweden, Canada, and Australia had a similar imbalance of trade that Iraq was seeking to alter before the Iran-Iraq war. Imbalances with France, Italy, and Brazil, however, were tolerated because those countries had important contracts relating to military supplies and training.

41. Interview with Farouk D. Salman, director-general of foreign economic relations, Ministry of Trade, June 21, 1981.

rially, it refers simply to economic development through the allocation of Iraq's resources to public service projects. The government assumes direct responsibility for providing, among other things, free health and educational services and for developing communication and transportation facilities, introducing water purification, water storage, and land reclamation projects, and constructing new housing. Perhaps because of their earlier failures, the Ba'thists have established planning and research bureaus as adjuncts to government ministries. In addition to training clauses, contracts with foreign companies may also call for the establishment of research projects. First Deputy Prime Minister Ramadhan said in an interview on June 21, 1981, that he ranked research and development as the most important aspect of economic development, followed by transport and communications, housing, industrial projects of strategic importance, such as electronics and engineering, and then agriculture. It should be noted that in 1979 the Ministry of Planning was downgraded to become more a coordinator than an initiator of policy. Presumably planning became more directly controlled by the Revolutionary Command Council.

The second aspect of socialism is social advancement. This goal arose from awareness that economic development could not be successful if it were considered in isolation from social factors. Many Iraqis talk of a "critical balance" between the two, noting that in most third-world countries the gap cannot be bridged. To a large extent the emphasis placed on education, on the rights and responsibilities of citizens of both sexes, and on attitudes toward corruption in government and business, among many other subjects, is derived from a Ba'thist construction—literally the "new Iraqi man."

In this abstract construction, education is the primary element in the path to socioeconomic development. Ba'thists continually encourage the people to remember this idea through publicly displayed slogans, such as "Teaching the woman means teaching the family," "Knowledge is light, ignorance is darkness," and "The Campaign for Literacy is a holy *jihad*." A concerted effort has been made to instill in the public the idea that functional education—the ability to read a health pamphlet, or an instruction on a fertilizer bag or a piece of machinery—is of benefit to everyone.

Iraq has two needs: more people, which is unusual among third-world countries, and more trained people. An official estimated in 1981 that approximately 3.5 million Iraqis are in the labor force out of a total population of 14 million. It was anticipated that the government's emphasis on development would lead to increasing shortages of skilled manpower. The 1976–80 National Development Plan sought to enlarge the Iraqi labor force by 18.48 percent (from 2,962,400 in 1976 to 3,510,000 in 1980) and to increase the ratio of labor to the total population from 25.7 percent in 1976 to 27 percent in 1980.[42] The authorities therefore have concentrated on four tasks: incorporating training and research programs in foreign contracts, bringing women into the labor force, increasing the birthrate, and importing foreign labor. To encourage large families, the government pays a subsidy for each child; couples marrying before the age of twenty-two are granted $2,500 and are eligible for additional loans. Foreign labor now totals approximately 2 million workers from the People's Republic of China, Yugoslavia, Morocco, Syria, Palestine, Lebanon, India, Pakistan, the Philippines, Sudan, and Egypt, the last of which contributed about 1.5 million workers before the war and no fewer than 750,000 during the first year of the war.

Even though the Ba'th constitution recognized women's rights as early as the 1940s, simple demographic facts have forced the government to take a particularly pragmatic approach to the potential economic contributions of women, an approach more progressive than is found in the other Arab Gulf countries. Housewives and professional women are not regarded as being in exclusive categories, both occupations being considered valuable. Families in the rural areas who opposed sending women to literacy schools were liable to have their public utilities temporarily suspended. In the early 1970s the police subjected men seen bothering women to public humiliation by shaving their heads or by similar actions, with the result that women are now more independent in their movements to work, school, or stores and are slowly becoming an asset to the economy. In certain fields, such as textiles or electronics, the government has decided that women are better suited for the work than men. Women also have been encouraged to study traditionally male-dominated subjects such as law, petrochemical engineering, journalism, and architecture. Although women in Iraq have a long heritage of professional career achievements dating to at least the 1930s, it is

---

42. "Figures and Indicators: Manpower in the Development Plan," article by Lahay 'Abd al-Husain in *al-Thawra*, November 10, 1978, as translated and reprinted in JPRS 72681, *NE/NA Report*, no. 1898 (January 23, 1979), pp. 34–35. Several other Iraqis noted that manpower shortages were so acute that it was difficult even to obtain household servants or individuals for more menial tasks.

evident that they are receiving fresh encouragement today. Their efforts are rewarded with "equal pay for equal work" in the marketplace. They are active in the Popular Army and are also included in the regular military, where two women have become air force pilots.

The concepts of the "new Iraqi man" and of the "nation" are also demonstrated in the government's ambitious drive against crime and against the use and distribution of drugs other than alcohol, which is legal although its sale is restricted during some religious holidays. Although Iraq does not administer the kind of penalties meted out in Saudi Arabia, such as beheading or public whipping, those found engaging in criminal acts nonetheless receive swift punishment. Because anyone caught dealing in drugs is immediately executed, this problem reportedly has been nonexistent since the mid-1970s. During interviews conducted in Iraq, whether they were with Ba'thists or even with Iraqis critical of the Ba'thists, there was consistent praise for this aspect of government policy. Crimes against persons are seemingly infrequent, as are crimes against personal property. One non-Ba'thist, while critical of some government policies, said that he frequently left his home unlocked and felt safe in doing so. Crimes such as drunken or careless driving that result in the injury or death of others or in the destruction of property are also beginning to receive new and harsh attention from government authorities.

The underlying rationale for socioeconomic development, however idealistic, is the belief that the government exists to serve the people and not the ruling elite. From this follow several generalizations. First, Ba'thists, who prefer to think of their party as a popular political movement, traditionally regard conservative monarchical regimes as reactionary systems that exist for the privileged few and fritter away their countries' wealth on status projects. Thus a well-known Ba'thist writer, though not an Iraqi by birth, metaphorically described the Saudis as "white shrouds of walking death." Iraqis are not immune to the glamour of status projects, as exemplified by the Baghdad subway, but they appear far less susceptible to the glitter than the other oil-producing countries of the Gulf. Second, the Ba'thists regard corruption as an inevitable spinoff of an oil-based economy that is potentially destabilizing for the government. Although it is not clear to what extent corruption does exist, it is discouraged by heavy penalties. In 1978 two directors-general of major ministries were arrested for accepting bribes and immediately executed; a British businessman received a life sentence.

The Ba'thist attitude toward bribery was explained by Ramadhan when he said that "if we allow them to take $30,000 and $40,000 bribes this year, then next year they will be taking $1 million bribes. We do not like to make public examples, but emotions are less important than the sound mental health of the people."[43] Several executives of European companies confirmed independently that inducements commonly regarded as part of contractual relationships in Saudi Arabia and the Gulf did not have to be costed into their calculations in Iraq.[44] There are reports, however, that 10 to 15 percent commissions have been added to contracts since 1982 because of uncertainties related to the Iran-Iraq war.

The Iraqi Ba'th is frequently asked whether the third goal of the party—socialism—contradicts the second—freedom with democracy. Ba'thists unequivocally answer no. Ramadhan offered the following explanation:

If there is no freedom of will, there can be no socialism. We want to develop a form of socialism to respond to the aspirations of the people. Therefore, the detailed application of socialism is subject to discussion by the party leadership. We do not take Marxism as a basis of socialism. We look at our own needs— equality, justice, end of exploitation, and enough guarantees to all people. Our thought is "Whoever does more, eats more, but there will never be a hungry person."[45]

Several paradoxes support Ramadhan. The state's collective farms, first instituted in 1964, were dismantled in 1980. As one Iraqi said in June 1981, it was felt that they were "not part of the Arab experience because he [the farmer] always felt that he worked for someone else." Thus the farmer was reluctant to put forth the necessary effort and farms were inefficient. More surprising, there has been a continuous if slow expansion of the private sector since 1978, when private owners assumed

43. Interview with Taha Yasin Ramadhan, June 22, 1981.
44. Both the receipt and the donation of gifts in Iraq are highly curtailed, particularly in government ministries, and the acceptance of bribes is a crime that receives immediate and harsh punishment. Once when I was waiting in the office of a departmental director of a major ministry in the summer of 1981, two Lebanese journalists each tried to offer the director a gift. Although he accepted a small book written by one of the journalists, he refused a larger unidentified gift from them, saying that the government forbade its acceptance. A European businessman working on a military contract in Iraq related a similar story. He bought a small book in Europe on beekeeping, which was a hobby of one of the Iraqis with whom he worked, intending it as a gift. The Iraqi was appreciative but insisted on reimbursing the businessman. Before the war, the only commercial projects that inspired rumors of corruption were those related to construction of Iraq's nuclear reactor. Military-related contracts are highly regulated and reputedly correct.
45. Inteview with Taha Yasin Ramadhan, June 22, 1981.

control of approximately 3 percent of Iraq's import trade, particularly
that related to industry and construction, and another 1 percent in the
mixed sector. Farouk D. Salman at the Ministry of Trade said that state
enterprises cannot do everything, and "as long as the private sector
operates within the priorities of the government, then it can be expected
to increase." Sabah Kachachi, a consultant to the Ministry of Planning,
added that the authorities were beginning to realize that decentralization
of some aspects of government was more efficient than central control
because the bureaucracy was unable to keep pace with development.
Therefore, he observed, "We have no fixed development model. It is a
corridor in which we are trying to find our way; it is not a narrow line."[46]
While it is as yet unclear to what extent private ownership may expand,
some forms of private ownership indeed are protected by the Ba'th
constitution.

Ramadhan said later in the interview quoted above that all developing
countries are afflicted with economic and social maladies that neither
Saudi Arabia nor any other country of the Middle East would find easy
to cure. The Ba'th party had hoped by 1985 to have completed the basic
economic foundations of the country, such as the extension of water
purification systems and electricity to even the most remote rural areas,
so that these investments would then yield practical gains. "Practical
gains" in the context of the conversation referred to greater internal
stability brought about by increased confidence in the central government, which in turn would gain flexibility in its conduct of foreign affairs.

Despite the gaps between theory and practice, the party's ideological
goals—unity, freedom, and socialism—will continue to be the basic
framework guiding the domestic and foreign policies of the government
as long as the Ba'thists are in power. None of the three will remain static
but will be adapted to changing political, social, and economic circum-

46. Interview with Farouk D. Salman, director-general of foreign economic relations,
Ministry of Trade, June 21, 1981; interview with Sabah Kachachi, industrial planning
adviser, Ministry of Planning, June 23, 1981. It is notable that Iraqi imports rose from
$1 billion in 1975 to almost $20 billion in 1981. Of this latter figure 20 to 25 percent of
Iraq's imports were consumer goods, specifically food and health-related imports, while
the remainder were industry and investment related. Salman stated that until the
beginning of the Iran-Iraq war, import priorities in descending order of importance went
to consumer goods, development and industry, and the social sector, subject to the
need to protect local industries, balance of payments considerations, and the requirements
of cooperative commercial or technical projects with other countries. Since the war
began, the government has continued to replenish local consumer markets but has also
devoted many of its imports to the army's needs and to the repair of damaged projects.

stances, if only by incremental steps. Prolongation of the Iran-Iraq war may of course bring more dramatic realignments and reformulations of Ba'thist ideals than have been customary in the past.

Six Problems

At least six problems will continue to confront the Ba'th party—problems that will be of critical importance to any future governing elite in Iraq regardless of its base of political support or its ideological inclinations. Many of them reflect the recurring themes in Iraqi history that have often served to constrain the central government. A few are unique or made more critical by events of the twentieth century.

First, there is a critical and evolving relationship between the cities and the rural areas. More than 60 percent of the Iraqi population is urban, with some 23 percent of the total concentrated in Baghdad alone. Rural areas have experienced little or no population growth because the towns and cities offer quicker avenues to success, whether illusory or not. The last several years have brought movement toward greater autonomy for rural areas in matters directly affecting them; collective farms, considered innovative in the mid-1970s, were abandoned by 1980 as unproductive. Officials from Baghdad increasingly tend to be technocrats rather than loyal party workers rewarded with government posts; they have increased the number of investigative trips into the countryside, but it will take time to ameliorate distant and unfamiliar problems, particularly those related to agriculture[47] and irrigation, that went unrecognized in the past and only recently have gained the attention of central government authorities. Certainly the administrative relationship between urban and rural districts remains fraught with difficulties.

A second problem for the Ba'th is the lack of an efficient bureaucracy, most often manifest in the government's inability to translate large oil revenues into workable economic development projects. Sabah Kachachi told me on June 23, 1981, that "it is not difficult to obtain a 12

47. Problems and prospects in the agricultural sector are touched on in Robert Springborg, "Baathism in Practice: Agriculture, Politics, and Political Culture in Syria and Iraq," pp. 191–209, in *Middle Eastern Studies, 17* (London: Frank Cass, 1981); and U.S. Department of Agriculture, Economic Research Service, *Agricultural Situation: Africa and Middle East,* Review of 1980 and Outlook for 1981, Supplement 7 to WAS-24 (Washington, D.C.: USDA, 1981).

percent growth rate in industry whereas in the agricultural sector it is difficult to obtain a 3 to 5 percent growth rate." While a developing country whose economy relies primarily on oil revenues can obtain large growth figures in industry, the agricultural sector is frequently burdened by an outmoded bureaucracy that is slow to respond to new problems with new solutions. Failures in that sector are often attributable to a lack of sufficiently skilled individuals and to their inability to communicate or meet basic requirements with accuracy or speed—though some individuals and ministries, such as the Ministry of Irrigation, are well organized and have sufficient initiative to be innovative and responsible.

Another aspect of this problem is that the parallel state and party structures may be a hindrance to economic development. There is a dearth of people who on their own initiative will take responsibility for a given action, particularly if they may be punished for a failure. The bureaucracy and the Ba'th have so many systems of checks and balances that even the smallest task may take half a day.[48] Efficiency is encouraged and at times materially rewarded, however, by the upper echelon of the Ba'th. On certain projects like the Hamrin dam, monetary gifts were distributed to the workers when a stage in the construction was completed on time. Ba'th officials have frequently asked that civil servants cut the red tape in their ministries and that cabinet ministers themselves assume greater responsibility for the internal functioning of their organizations. European firms have been hired to increase the productivity of middle-level bureaucrats. But though the Ba'th is well aware that the competence of the civil service will be a critical factor in future development plans, more thought and effort will be required to make the bureaucracy responsive to party political control.

Third, the Ba'th party will continue to have a problem of image—of attaining the legitimacy that has eluded all Iraqi governments. It must try to portray itself as a protector of all the diverse Muslim and non-Muslim, Arab and non-Arab groups in the population by emphasizing Iraqi nationalist sentiments. It must also balance the often conflicting

---

48. A letter of permission for me to travel outside Baghdad in the summer of 1981 took several hours to be typed and signed, then had to be registered in two separate log books and photocopied for distribution to appropriate authorities. Mileage on cars traveling in the Kurdish region must be recorded. Similarly, a West German businessman said that work had been delayed on one of his projects because the authorization of any payment or release of funds required four signatures and it was not easy to get everyone together at the same time.

demands of various segments of the Iraqi population and even within the Ba'th party against the need for internal security and maintenance of the central government. There remains much room for progress in the latter regard, but it would be unrealistic to suppose that replacement of the Ba'thist government by either an Islamic or a military government would result in greater leniency. Indeed, it would almost certainly lead to the implementation of similar internal security measures as the new government consolidated its power.

Another aspect of the image problem is the question of who controls the party. Political parties during the twentieth century have created opportunities for individuals in the Middle East to participate in the political life of their countries instead of remaining subject to powerful landowning families, to tribes in which membership conferred inherent rights, or to military rulers. Larger social groups bonded by common traditions and aspirations not unnaturally seek to use the party mechanisms to acquire or reacquire political power. Thus it is not surprising to find that 'Alawis dominate the Syrian Ba'th, or that Christians and during one period Jews have been particularly active in the Iraqi Communist party, or that both the Shi'i and Sunni Muslims have dominated the Iraqi Ba'th party at different times.

The Arab Ba'th Socialist party in Iraq is not an inflexible monolithic structure, either in its component groups or in their aspirations. Ba'thists themselves admit that distinctions exist between longtime party members and the newly joined, between the young and the old, between civilians and the military, and between the technocrats and the politicians. There may also be distinctions, though they are not openly discussed, between Shi'is and Sunnis, within regions, and among the right, the left, and the moderates in the party.

Nevertheless the Iraqi Ba'th party in the 1970s was frequently accused of being a Sunni ruling elite that came primarily from Tikrit, a town northwest of Baghdad, and from other Sunni towns like 'Ana,[49] even though the party continued to stress competence and party loyalty rather

49. A number of writers refer to various aspects of this question. Peter Sluglett and Marion Farouk-Sluglett, "Some Reflections on the Sunni/Shi'i Question in Iraq," in *British Middle Eastern Studies Bulletin*, vol. 5, no. 2 (1978), pp. 79–87; Nikolaos van Dam, "Middle Eastern Political Clichés: 'Takriti', and 'Sunni Rule' in Iraq; 'Alawi' Rule in Syria," *Orient* (January 1980), pp. 42–57; and Phebe Marr, "Saddam Husain and the Iraqi Ba'th: The Question of Legitimacy," draft paper submitted to the seminar on the Persian Gulf Project, Georgetown University, April 1982.

than religious or ethnic backgrounds as qualifications for promotion. Some Western observers accuse the Ba'th of being a Sunni ruling elite from Tikrit and other Sunni towns. It is true that Sunnis compose 50 to 60 percent of the upper elite and that sometime during 1977 Ba'th party members began to omit public use of their last names, which in the Middle East often indicate a person's geographic or family origin. Saddam Husain al-Takriti became Saddam Husain, 'Izzat Ibrahim al-Duri became 'Izzat Ibrahim, Taha Yasin Ramadhan al-Jazrawi became Taha Yasin Ramadhan, and so forth.

While statistics regarding the composition of the party have not been released officially, there are a number of reasons why this accusation should be noted but regarded with caution. Within Ba'th party organs such as the Revolutionary Command Council and the Regional Command, all members should not be considered equal in strength. Of the five most influential men in Iraq as of 1984 who alone shared positions in the National Command, the Revolutionary Command Council, and the Regional Command, one was Christian (Tariq 'Aziz), one Shi'i (Naim Haddad), one Sunni (Saddam Husain), one Sunni rumored to have Sabean origins ('Izzat Ibrahim), and another Sunni who has some distant Kurdish ancestry on his maternal side (Taha Yasin Ramadhan).[50] Obviously Saddam Husain is on a different level than the other four, though it would be a mistake to assume that the power of the other four is necessarily derived from or contingent on Husain. Some have exceptional political skills and others possess political influence that is independent of Husain.

Moreover, Takritis closely related to Husain who are in government have occupied primarily security-related positions. 'Adnan Khairallah, a cousin, is the minister of defense and Barzan Ibrahim al-Takriti, a half-brother, was the chief of intelligence until he and two other relatives who had been appointed to government posts were dismissed in October 1983. These men seemingly have acted as a protective apparatus for Saddam Husain. There is little evidence that they have played a significant part in policy formulation generally, none has had a particularly visible public role, and none appears to have developed his own strong cadre. While Khairallah is on the Revolutionary Command Council, Barzan Ibrahim never attained that position. Saddam Husain, perhaps

50. Ramadhan confirmed this but deemphasized its importance during an interview on August 12, 1982.

more clearly than any, realizes that a display of excessive dependence on relatives would undermine the raison d'être of the party; once that occurred, he would be in an extremely vulnerable position. Thus Husain must publicly emphasize and demonstrate to his fellow Ba'thists that the leadership is collective even though one man may figure usefully as a prominent symbol of unity.

Demographic data in any case shed insufficient light on Iraqi politics when it is recognized that "power resides where political decisions are taken, in the towns, especially Baghdad."[51] The problem of determining political legitimacy is further complicated by the growing number of intermarriages between young Shi'is and Sunnis, Palestinians and Iraqis, and persons from different urban areas in Iraq. Dating at least to the 1950s, this phenomenon may be a consequence of social engineering or simply the result of higher levels of education or career moves to new areas. It has accelerated in recent decades and will be of major significance if it continues unabated.

The fourth problem confronting the Ba'th party, not unrelated to the third, is its quest to establish the stability of the central government. Ba'thists have sought to do so in part by extending the appeal and hence the legitimacy of their party, particularly into segments of the population that were previously excluded. This strategy has created a dilemma that has persistently plagued the party's leadership, especially during the 1960s: should the party expand its membership if doing so would reduce the quality of individual Ba'thists and their dedication to the party? Saddam Husain alluded to this in his opening address to the ninth regional congress of the Ba'th party on June 27, 1982:

[There is a] problem posed by the choice between a desire to expand the Party's base, and a fear that the expansion might turn into a burden for the Party and into a field for infiltration aimed at killing it from inside. . . . particularly in the last few years, the Party faced a very serious state; either to keep itself small . . . isolating it from the people . . . which is suicidal . . . [and excludes] the continuous human need for innovation which requires enlargement of the Party— or to open itself to the people . . . [which creates] a special kind of suicide.[52]

Husain went on to say that the Iran-Iraq war was a most difficult

51. Sluglett and Farouk-Sluglett, "Some Reflections on the Sunni/Shi'i Question," p. 80.
52. Iraqi Ba'th Party Congress Statement by Saddam Husain on June 27, 1982, reprinted by the British Broadcasting Corporation, *Summary of World Broadcasts*, ME/7066/A/1–4, July 1, 1982.

challenge for the party, but that it provided the means to build a greater Iraq, to expand the party's base, and to deepen the awareness of historical responsibilities in the people. It is not clear whether expansion of the party referred to its 25,000 full members, to persons in the earlier stages of supporter or sympathizer, or simply to the Popular Army. Husain may also have been referring figuratively to the potential for creating a greater awareness of Iraqi nationalism. If indeed the party has expanded as a result of the war, the Ba'th's leaders understand the problems they will confront in the future, especially in the aftermath of the war. Trendsetters who are perceived to threaten the party apparatus thus may expect the same fate as those who were executed in 1979 on grounds of treason and those in 1982 who simply lost their party positions because of their bureaucratic inefficiencies or because they engaged in activities considered detrimental to the party as a whole.

Fifth, Ba'th members share one characteristic that limits their appeal in the short term. They are a group of elites, not in the sense of wealth, but rather in education. The party's founders came from diverse backgrounds united only in their intellectual belief in the strength of Arab unity. Acceptance of the party's ideals naturally meant the sublimation of other associations, which initially limited the party's appeal because the ideals were relatively abstract and remote. Ba'thism was not a popularly based movement, nor one whose ideas were easily expounded in rural areas or among illiterates. One could not be uneducated and yet fully indoctrinated into Ba'thist goals, the more so as the party and its ideology grew and became more structured. Party membership was a key to upward career mobility, and education was clearly a key to being a good Ba'thi. It has been noted that of 122 Ba'thists who held National or Regional Command positions from 1947 to 1965, there was only 1 who was not a white-collar professional; of the entire group, at least 24 held advanced degrees in law, medicine, and similar fields.[53] It is therefore easy to understand the seriousness with which the party approached the Campaign for Literacy.

The sixth problem confronting the Ba'th—its relations with the military—is the most serious of all. The Iraqi military has been involved in every successful coup during this century. Qasim, the 'Arif brothers, and Ahmad Hasan al-Bakr were all military officers by training and occupation when they took and consolidated control of the government.

53. Devlin, *The Ba'th Party*, p. 39.

Their takeovers in part reflected the fact that Arab militaries in general have provided a means of upward career mobility for members of less fortunate socioeconomic groups. They also reflected the nature of the Iraqi army itself, with a long history of professionalsim embodied in its own staff and training college. Because Iraqi political life has seldom allowed freedom to any political movement in opposition to the government, however benign,[54] the military has been the organized group most capable of effecting radical political change. A high-ranking Ba'th official remarked to me that "the military loves to meddle in politics, and therefore the party has to be ever watchful."

The gradual strengthening of the civilian wing of the Ba'th during the 1970s under the direction of Saddam Husain has led to the first durable nonmilitary government in Iraq since the revolution of 1958. As noted earlier, the Ba'thists have discouraged the presence of any large number of military careerists in governmental organs, such as the National Assembly. The military structure itself is permeated with monitoring units of the Ba'th, and military personnel are strictly forbidden to belong to any political party other than the Ba'th. It is perhaps not surprising to find that Iraqi military officers meticulously avoid discussion of political subjects.

The relationship between the civilians and the military will be particularly critical in the aftermath of the Iran-Iraq war. If the military does succeed in taking control of the government, the difficulties of consolidating its power in Iraq will be no less problematic, indeed may be more so, than those that confronted the Ba'th party.

54. Devlin, *The Ba'th Party*, p. 232, notes that Qasim himself said that in the three and one-half years since he had assumed power, he had knowledge of twenty-nine coup attempts against his government.

PART THREE

Iraq Goes to War

CHAPTER FIVE

Sources of Conflict

THE length and severity of the Iran-Iraq war not only have direct implications for the durability of Iraq's Ba'thist leadership, but also affect the range of domestic and foreign policy options available to future Iraqi governments. One possible approach to a study of the war is to examine military effectiveness and specific military achievements according to criteria such as logistics, command and control, and combat success. A great deal is known about this by foreign governments, some of which is publicly available.

Another analytical approach is to examine the causes and foreseeable consequences of the war. Iraqis themselves have repeatedly stressed that it is not simply "a war over borders." Indeed, its causes and consequences are varied and far-reaching. There are, however, difficulties in this approach. Knowledge of Iraqi decisionmaking in the war has been sharply limited by the secretiveness of the Iraqi military, which in the early stages carefully shielded officers' identities, their personal opinions, and military intelligence affairs generally. It also has been limited by both governing regimes in the disputed area: Iraq is characterized by the secrecy and discipline of the Ba'th party, Iran by the intra- and interfactional rivalries and turmoil of a social revolution. Neither from the war front itself nor from the capital cities of Baghdad or Tehran has there been consistent or substantiated reporting on the war. Moreover, both disputants occupy strategic positions that contain valuable reserves of oil and thus engage the competitive interests of both superpowers, whose government agencies are naturally reluctant to discuss the information they have obtained.

While it incorporates available military data wherever relevant, the following analysis focuses on those factors that influenced the initiation and early military strategy of the war. As will become evident, it is precisely those factors that were discussed earlier that best explain the genesis of the war. Some are endemic, having recurred throughout the past four thousand years as variations on a theme with which successive leaders have had to contend as they attempted to reinforce a central state apparatus. In this respect the current Ba'thist government in Iraq resembles former Mesopotamian empires despite their distance in time and the territorial extent of the state, as Georges Roux, a historian of Iraq, has trenchantly remarked:

The rise and fall of the Akkadian empire [c. 2334 to 2193 B.C.] offers a perfect preview of all subsequent Mesopotamian empires: rapid expansion followed by ceaseless rebellions, palace revolutions, constant wars on the frontiers, and in the end, the *coup de grace* given by the highlanders. . . . Iraq required, to be viable, two conditions: perfect cooperation between the various ethnic and socio-political units within the country itself, and a friendly or at least a neutral attitude from its neighbours. Unfortunately, neither one nor the other ever lasted for any length of time.[1]

The two preconditions for a viable Iraqi state fundamentally remain a minimum level of "cooperation between the various ethnic and sociopolitical units" and "a friendly or at least a neutral attitude from its neighbours." The central predicament facing all Iraqi governments— past, present, and future—is that neither of these conditions has ever prevailed for very long.

All the other factors pertaining to this analysis of the Iran-Iraq war are unique to the twentieth century. Among the most significant are the structure and decisionmaking procedures of the Arab Ba'th Socialist party, within which the assumptions about Iran's domestic affairs prior to the war and Iraq's objectives once it decided to go to war were largely determined. Another is the complex relationship between the civilians who dominate the Ba'th party and the Iraqi military command, a relationship that has influenced the conduct of the war and undoubtedly has changed during its course.

The consequences of the war, some of which may be only dimly perceived at present, will affect not only the internal political environment of Iraq but also the content of future negotiations between Iran and Iraq, as well as diplomatic relations in the region generally. These consequences devolve from two fundamental challenges posed by the war. The first is a systemic threat to the stability of the respective governments of Iran and Iraq. To Iraq in particular the war is a challenge

1. Georges Roux, *Ancient Iraq* (Penguin, 1980), p. 152.

to the practical and conceptual nature of the Iraqi nation-state and to the Ba'th party, which has striven over the last decade to consolidate diverse interests within Iraq and to raise economic and social welfare standards throughout the country.

The second and broader challenge of the war tests two diametrically opposed and competing ideologies—Arab nationalism and Islamic conservatism—which not only seek legitimacy in Iraq and Iran, respectively, but also transcend state boundaries to challenge Arabs and Muslims wherever they live. This issue is significant for both American and Soviet policy in the Middle East, yet it remains little understood and appreciated.

Turning Inward

A pivotal point in Iraqis' perceptions of their domestic and foreign policy interests can be discerned in the issues that culminated in the revolution of 1958. Before that event both the leaders and the people of Iraq were oriented toward the so-called Fertile Crescent region and toward the West. As recently as 1955 Iraq's government had joined the Western-supported security treaty known as the Baghdad Pact, in the face of strong opposition by Arab nationalists in Iraq and elsewhere who harshly criticized it as a pro-Western, hence anti-Arab alliance extending from Turkey and across Iraq and Iran to Pakistan. Their opposition was a fundamental cause of the overthrow of the royal Hashimite family, which had ruled Iraq until the revolution of 1958, ending Iraq's alliance with the West. The Hashimites not only owed their throne to the West, but they and their colineal Hashimite family in Jordan together opposed their historic southern rivals, the Sa'udi family of Arabia.[2] Similarly, most of the Iraqi population, particularly those of the central and northern sections, felt greater socioeconomic identification with Syrian and even

2. The Hashimite family, the official guardians of Mecca and al-Madina under the Ottoman Khalifa, were forced into exile by the Al Sa'ud, who successfully invaded al-Hijaz in 1924 and assumed total administrative and religious control of the region by 1926. The Al Sa'ud also attempted to extend their authority into Transjordan, Iraq, and Kuwait until physically prevented from doing so by Great Britain. Eventually in 1932 'Abd al-'Aziz bin 'Abd al-Rahman Al Sa'ud named himself king of Saudi Arabia, which included al-Hijaz, Najd, and the eastern provinces around al-Qatif. It was natural that the Hashimites bitterly resented these events. Christine Moss Helms, *The Cohesion of Saudi Arabia* (Johns Hopkins University Press, 1981), pp. 181–249.

with Turkish populations and institutions than with those of the Saudi south or Persian east.

Iraq's westward orientation has been further substantially altered by successive governments since 1960 for strategic and ideological reasons. Iraqis began to seek greater independence in their relations with countries outside the third world; in regional affairs, they shifted their focus from pro-Nasir ideals and involvement in the Fertile Crescent to Iraqi and southeastern Arabian Gulf concerns. A number of political and economic factors account for these changes of the 1960s. The royal link between the Hashimites in Iraq and Jordan was severed with the elimination of the Iraqi monarchy. The association of the West with what Iraqis perceived as wrongs committed against the country by the pro-Western Hashimites led to an almost immediate cessation of former policies by the new government. Moreover, formerly clandestine political parties, such as the Arab Ba'th Socialist party and the Iraqi Communist party, were deliberately allowed to surface under 'Abd al-Karim Qasim, who led Iraq between the revolution of 1958 and 1963. Because these parties attributed the decline of the importance of the Arab world to foreign interference, and especially Western interference, they were increasingly attractive to the young students, workers, and intellectuals who were to become active participants in Iraq's future political life. Their anti-Western attitudes were heightened when, just as Great Britain was preparing to withdraw from the Gulf, the United States became more openly associated with the region's conservative and hereditary regimes.

The most tangible reason for the shift in Iraq's interest from the West toward the Gulf arose from the country's oil resources. The government wanted greater control over the exploitation and marketing of oil, which even in 1953 contributed nearly 40 percent of the gross domestic product.[3] It entered into negotiations with the Western-dominated Iraq Petroleum Company, which with its affiliates controlled all the concessionary areas of Iraq. When the negotiations proved unsuccessful, the government in 1961 imposed additional charges on oil shipments and expropriated all

3. The oil industry contributed 39.9 percent of the gross domestic product of Iraq in 1953. This figure rose to 53.4 percent in 1976 while that of agriculture dropped from 22.1 percent in 1953 to 7.6 percent in 1976. These figures can be expected to grow even more disproportionate unless the government, as it was attempting to do before the start of the war in 1980, can limit the sectoral share of the oil industry to no more than 50 percent in the future. Kadhim A. Al-Eyd, *Oil Revenues and Accelerated Growth: Absorptive Capacity in Iraq* (Praeger, 1979), p. 29, and interviews in Iraq during 1981 and 1982.

of the company's unexploited concessions, amounting to 99.5 percent of the concession area.

The expansion of port and oil facilities in southern Iraq and Iraq's reiteration of its historical claims to Kuwait also may be understood within the context of Iraq's turning toward the Gulf. The interest in Kuwait, dating at least from the days of the Ottoman empire, has if anything grown more acute, although that interest is now expressed in different forms. 'Abd al-Karim Qasim made a verbal claim to Kuwait in 1961, but the British and then a multilateral peacekeeping force from the Arab League composed of Egyptians, Jordanians, Saudis, and Sudanese came to Kuwait's assistance and the episode ended. After Qasim was overthrown in 1963, the short-lived Iraqi Ba'th government negotiated an agreement in October of that year to acknowledge Kuwait's sovereignty. During tension between Iran and Iraq in 1969, Iraq was allowed to station troops on the Kuwaiti side of the border, but in March 1973 Iraqi troops seized the Kuwaiti border post of al-Samita and fired on another, claiming the Kuwaiti islands of Warba and Bubiyan. The Arab League again intervened and Iraq withdrew the following month. Another clash occurred in 1976. Early in the Iran-Iraq war, the Iraqi government attempted to lease the two islands on a long-term basis, which Kuwait refused to do. Shortly after this approach Iran bombed northern Kuwait, an act the Iraqis did not criticize.

Yet a third motive for Iraq's shift in interests from the West toward the Gulf arose from the coupling of two events during the latter half of the 1960s. The first was the split in 1966 in the national leadership of the Ba'th party, which had been headquartered in Syria; the second was the reassertion in 1968 of Ba'th control in Iraq, whose government had been largely dominated by the military since the revolution of 1958. In consequence of regional differences, the now autonomous national Ba'th commands in Syria and Iraq gradually began to pursue interests in what they hoped would become their respective and independent spheres of influence, Syria in the west and Iraq in the east.

During the succeeding decade of the 1970s, Iraq was no less concerned with its interests in the Gulf, although it was primarily a respondent to rather than an initiator of international events. Rhetorical pronouncements were rarely substantiated by parallel actions because the ruling Ba'th elite, which had not reacquired political control until 1968, was almost solely preoccupied with pressing domestic concerns until the start of the Iran-Iraq war. Civilian rather than military Ba'thists had succeeded in dominating the Ba'th party structure, but their control both within and outside the party remained tenuous. It was necessary for them to muster broader support for Ba'th policies generally.

Throughout the 1970s the Ba'thists therefore gave priority to four domestic political goals: internal consolidation of the party, the acquisition by party members of the skills required to run a government, establishment of the party as preeminent within the Iraqi state through extensions of the party apparatus, and greater cooperation among Iraq's numerous particularistic groups. These closely related objectives were gradually translated into concrete actions, among which were the establishment of the Kurdish Autonomous Region in 1970, the promulgation in 1971 of a National Action Charter that allowed opposition movements to participate in politics so long as they stayed within proscriptive guidelines, the establishment of a National Assembly in 1980, and internal development programs. Oil revenues were used to expand the agricultural and industrial sectors and to broaden existing educational and welfare programs. Kurdish areas in the north and Shi'i areas in the south were notable beneficiaries of these policies.

By 1970, however, the Ba'th's domestic priorities began to be overshadowed by a foreign policy concern that had started to crystallize among Iraq's non-Ba'thist leaders almost a decade earlier: the increasing economic, political, and social influence of Iran. As early as the Ba'thists' accession to power in 1968, Iran and the shah's ambitions became major determinants of Iraqi policies toward the Gulf and Arab states, the United States and Israel, and the Soviet Union, and even of Iraqi domestic policies. The Iranian factor became no less salient following the Ayatullah Khomeini's rise to power in Tehran.

Iran, among all the other states in the area, posed the most direct threat to the Iraqi oil industry, for reasons that were social and political as well as military. In the northern Kurdish region, which at the time accounted for almost 65 percent of Iraq's annual oil production, Iraq was vulnerable to internal political unrest fomented by outside powers and to direct bombing in wartime; in the south, through which one-half to two-thirds of all Iraqi oil was transshipped, it was exposed to foreign agitation, direct attack, and blockade. In both cases Iran was well positioned to exploit these vulnerabilities. Iranian Kurds were in regular contact with Kurds in northeastern Iraq, and in the south a number of urban areas and economic facilities were in close proximity to Iran and to an Iranian military installation at Khosrowabad on the Shatt al-'Arab. Indeed, most of Iraq's urbanized areas, whether considered numerically or by population size, lay to the east of or along the Tigris River. Additionally, the marshes of Misan province provided an ideal avenue for smuggling arms or other support from Iran to political opposition groups in Iraq.

Beginning with the military regimes of the 1960s, many Iraqi actions can be viewed as indicators of the government's sense of the oil industry's vulnerability. The anticipated expansion and use of Iraq's oil wealth were essential to the ambitious social and economic development programs of the Ba'th. Concern for the safety of the industry increased during the 1970s: Iraq nationalized the northern oilfields in 1972,[4] the reversible "strategic pipeline" was completed between Haditha near the Turkish border and the Gulf in 1975, and additional oil facilities were built in the south around Basra. Iraq renewed its claims, albeit diminished in scope, to the Kuwaiti islands of Warba and Bubiyan that dominate the estuary of the Iraqi port of Umm Qasr.

Faced with growing Iranian ambitions, Iraqi leaders in the late 1960s and throughout the 1970s felt increasingly isolated politically among the conservative and hereditary regimes in the Gulf. Their sense of isolation was heightened when in late 1972 the United States declared that it would depend on regional allies, especially Iran and Saudi Arabia, to act as political stabilizers—the so-called two-pillar policy. The concern of Iraqi leaders became even sharper after Iran became a major buyer of American military hardware and the de facto guardian of the Gulf. American military equipment had begun to flow in significant quantities after 1955; between 1973–74 and 1976–77 more than one-third of all American foreign military sales were made to Iran. Total U.S. arms sales to Iran between 1972 and 1976 amounted to $10.6 billion.[5]

Iran and Iraq: Wary Neighbors

Significant though they were, the tensions and anxieties arising from Iraq's strategic exposure were manifestations of an older and deeper

4. The role of the oil sector in Iraq's economy before and during nationalization is discussed in Al-Eyd, *Oil Revenues*; Adil Hussein, *Iraq: The Eternal Fire, 1972 Iraqi Oil Nationalization in Perspective* (London: Third World Centre for Research and Publishing, 1981); Michael E. Brown, "The Nationalization of the Iraqi Petroleum Company," *International Journal of Middle East Studies*, vol. 10 (1979), pp. 107–24; and Edith and E. F. Penrose, *Iraq: International Relations and National Development* (Westview Press, 1978).

5. Barry Rubin, *Paved with Good Intentions: The American Experience and Iran* (Penguin, 1981), p. 158; and Alvin J. Cottrell, *Iran's Quest for Security: U.S. Arms Transfers and the Nuclear Option* (Institute for Foreign Policy Analysis, 1977), p. 40.

malaise. The outbreak of war between Iraq and Iran in September 1980 was the result of conflicts that are rooted in history and ever-present, if at times quiescent.

Ancient Enmities

The earliest of these conflicts arose from the differentiation between Shi'i and Sunni Muslims. This division, dating from the early days of Islam in the seventh century, has been exacerbated at various times during the last several hundred years, as when the Ottomans or the British favored one social group over another for their own political ends. Then the origins and doctrinal differences of Shi'i and Sunni Islam became politically significant once again.

Iraq perhaps more than any other Arab country is directly affected by this ancient schism and its modern political ramifications. It was within the present geographical limits of the Iraqi state, predominantly in or around the southern cities of Basra, Samarra, al-Kufa, al-Najaf, and Karbala, that the original differentiation between Sunni and Shi'i Islam was made. This history of bloody battles, intrigue, and calculated murder has become part of the hagiology of Islam, particularly among the Shi'a. Of the twelve Imams in Shi'i Islam, six are enshrined in Iraq, one died while traveling toward Iraq, and the twelfth or "hidden Imam" went into concealment there. Moreover, some Shi'is consider the pilgrimage to al-Najaf and Karbala to be as essential as that to Mecca and al-Madina because they are the places of martyrdom of two of the first three Shi'i Imans—'Ali and his second son, Husain—and the sites of their shrines.

The Iraqi government is well aware that there are more than 7 million Shi'is in Iraq's total population of 14 million. Some 1 or 2 million of them are concentrated around al-Najaf and Karbala, a significant but undisclosed percentage of whom are of Persian origin. At al-Najaf itself is an impressive Shi'i cemetery that encircles the city. Over the centuries hundreds of thousands, some say millions, of people have brought their dead for one last circumambulation of the shrine of Imam 'Ali, followed by burial. By 1978 an estimated 30,000 Iranian Shi'is were performing the pilgrimage to Shi'i holy places in Iraq each year—a number that the Iraqi government had carefully curtailed because of its fear that pilgrims might be used for subversive purposes. After the improvement of relations between Iraq and Iran in 1975, their numbers were gradually allowed to increase until 1979, when Khomeini's return to Iran renewed that fear.

Another focus of hostility is the Persian-Arab conflict that dates from the clashes between the Persian and Ottoman empires. Although their frontiers roughly approximated the present boundaries of Iran and Iraq, since the sixteenth century innumerable conferences, surveys, and treaties have failed to determine a permanent and mutually satisfactory boundary. A treaty dated at Zuhab in 1639 was one of the earliest agreements between the two empires that dealt with frontier demarcation, allocation of the Kurdish population, provision for Persian Shi'is to perform the pilgrimage to shrines in Iraq, and seasonal grazing rights. A boundary survey conducted between 1843 and 1847 resulted in a treaty dated at Erzurum in 1847, but subsequent conflicting claims led to yet another survey between 1857 and 1865. Although the Persian-Arab conflict is most clearly manifest by the boundary disputes, the undertone of racial prejudice can clearly be discerned. Significantly, when the Iran-Iraq war began, Iraqis referred to it as "Qadisiya Saddam" or "a second al-Qadisiya," a reference to a battle at the town of that name in the early history of Islam when Arabs drove Persians out of what is now modern Iraq. At the site of Ctesiphon in Iraq an elaborate museum was erected to portray the details of this battle.

In the early 1900s a new political situation began to emerge. The Ottoman empire and Russia began to encroach militarily on northwestern Persia, factional strife continued among the Kurds, and the Shaikh of al-Muhammara sought to assert his independence in the south. The Tehran protocol of 1911 provided a basis for negotiations and established a boundary commission. In 1913 a delegation of British, Russian, Persian, and Ottoman representatives met and delineated the boundary from the Gulf to Mount Ararat and redefined navigational rights on the Shatt al-'Arab in what became known as the Constantinople protocol or Turko-Persian delimitation of 1913 and proceedings of the commission on delimitation of frontiers of 1914. The Ottoman government retained control over the Shatt al-'Arab, but Persia received the eastern bank and certain rights of navigation on the river from the juncture of the land frontiers of the respective empires to the head of the Gulf. Persia, or modern Iran, was also assigned sovereignty over the city and port of al-Muhammara and some islands in the Shatt al-'Arab.

After World War I, yet another dispensation was made in which Britain turned the Basra Port Authority over to what became modern

Iraq. Refusing to recognize Iraqi control, Iran persisted in the use of Iranian pilots and navigational signals and claimed that the 1913 agreement had recognized the thalweg as the boundary. Tension grew between the two states when trouble again broke out in the northern Kurdish areas from 1924 to 1926 and in the central border area around Khanaqin and Qasr-i Shirin in 1926. Additional negotiations took place in 1929, but no agreement was reached. Iraq appealed in 1934 to the League of Nations, where a settlement eventually was reached in 1937. It recognized the land boundary as defined in 1913–14, but provided that between 'Abadan and the Gulf—a distance of some 6.5 kilometers—the boundary in the Shatt al-'Arab would be the thalweg.

In 1954 Iran protested the collection of tolls, claiming that the Basra Port Authority was improperly distributing funds for operations and improvements. In 1959 Iran also questioned the validity of the 1937 treaty and established a military facility on the Shatt al-'Arab. The dispute simmered until 1969, when Iran abrogated the 1937 treaty and sent gunboats up the Shatt al-'Arab, effectively taking possession up to the thalweg, a claim that was not legitimate until it was recognized in an agreement between Iran and Iraq in 1975.

Contemporary Frictions

It is not the purpose of this study to argue the relative merits of the actions taken by Iraq and by Iran against each other during this period. To do so would be futile, for the underlying and less tangible points of discord have been obscured by time and transcend legalistic interpretations of existing treaties. Justifications were arguable on both sides.

Iranian actions during the early years of the new Ba'thist government were not calculated to dispel Iraqi fears. Among them were the shah's claims to Bahrain, initiated by his father in 1937 and not renounced until 1969; his subsequent abrogation of the treaty regarding the Shatt al-'Arab waterway in April 1969; his attempts to form a cooperative relationship with Iraq's southern neighbor, Saudi Arabia, during 1969 and 1970 coincident with American military assistance to Saudi Arabia; his alleged involvement in a conspiracy to overthrow the Ba'thist regime in Baghdad in 1970;[6] his military occupation of three strategic islands in

6. On January 21, 1970, the Ba'th government announced that it had crushed a coup attempt ostensibly organized under the direction of military officers who had received weapons from Iran and had transmitted messages through the Iranian embassy in Baghdad. Tape recordings of conversations between the conspirators and Iranian

the Strait of Hormuz in 1971; his economic and military assistance to Kurdish rebels in northern Iraq beginning in 1972 and not ending until 1975; the activities of his secret police (SAVAK) in Iraq;[7] and finally his continued economic, political, and military links with Israel.[8]

Iraq retaliated against Iran by boycotting Iranian goods and lending support to nationalist movements in Baluchistan and Khuzistan (Arabistan) in Iran. After Iran abrogated in 1969 the treaty of 1937 concerning the Shatt al-'Arab and annexed the three Gulf islands in 1971, Iraq expelled first 20,000 and then some 70,000 Shi'is of Iranian origin. The Iraqi government claimed that these were illegal aliens who only recently had come on the pilgrimage to al-Najaf and Karbala and then settled

---

representatives were presented as evidence in a trial that lasted from January 21 to 24 under the direction of Taha Yasin Ramadhan. Forty-four persons were found guilty and executed, almost three-quarters of them from the military. Another fifteen were imprisoned and some twenty were released. One of the two organizers of the conspiracy, General 'Abd al-Ghani al-Rawi, took refuge in Iran, where he reportedly was still living in 1978. Soon after this episode, Iranian troops massed at Iraq's border while Iraq appealed to the United Nations on February 2 to prevent an escalation of the conflict and then sought Turkish support. War was averted when Iran proposed the withdrawal of both Iraqi and Iranian border troops. See Majid Khadduri, *Socialist Iraq: A Study in Iraqi Politics since 1968* (Washington, DC: Middle East Institute, 1978), pp. 53–56, for a detailed description of these events. When Nazim Kzar, Iraq's chief of security police, led an unsuccessful coup attempt against the Iraqi government in June 1973, he fled in the direction of Iran before being caught. It is not known whether Kzar had received support from Iran or simply believed he would obtain a sympathetic reception.

7. One of the most daring and public examples of this activity was the assassination of Taimur Bakhtiar, a former Iranian general who had fallen into disfavor with the shah and gone to Beirut. During the mid-1970s, while ostensibly on a hunting trip in Iraq, he was assassinated by SAVAK agents.

8. It is difficult to interpret the financial links between Iran and Israel because of large discrepancies in the trade statistics provided by each country. These discrepancies may result from the fact that the data are politically sensitive: they exclude trade in oil and armaments, which presumably was significant, and they also exclude Iranian investments, made privately or by the Iranian government, in Israel. Trade, however, did begin on a small scale during the 1950s and gradually increased until 1973, when it dropped slightly because of the Arab-Israeli war. It resumed in 1975 at more than double its former peak. In 1976 Israel estimated that its imports from Iran were $3.4 million while its exports to Iran were $120.6 million. After the Islamic revolution the National Iranian Oil Company claimed that Israel owed Iran some $700 million to $800 million, half for crude oil deliveries and half for Iran's investments in the construction of a crude oil pipeline between Eilat on the Red Sea and Ashkelan on the Mediterranean. Opened in 1970, the pipeline had a capacity of 300,000 bpd and was in use until the overthrow of the shah in February 1979, when Iranian oil shipments were halted. Israel claims that its debt is only $300 million. See *Middle East Economic Survey,* vol. 22 (May 21, 1979), p. 11; *Middle East Economic Digest* (hereafter *MEED*), vol. 25 (August 21, 1981), p. 14; *MEED,* vol. 24 (January 4, 1980), p. 27; and *Direction of Trade Yearbook, 1980* (Washington, D.C.: IMF, 1980).

permanently. Because it was difficult to control pilgrims, they could avoid naturalization, the otherwise obligatory service in the armed forces, and the payment of taxes. They were also considered a potential security risk. Competition between Iraq and Iran also occurred elsewhere. Iraq, for example, aided the revolutionary Dhofar Liberation Front in Oman while the shah assisted the Omani sultan.[9]

Superpower involvement further polarized the Iranian and Iraqi regimes, propelling the conflict onto a higher plateau of intransigence. Pressed beyond their capacity by their rivalry with Iran, by their lack of governmental experience, by the need to establish their legitimacy among disparate interest groups, and by the anticipated nationalization of their oil industry, the Iraqi Ba'thists sent a delegation to Moscow in July 1970 to seek weapons. In April 1972 they signed a fifteen-year treaty of friendship with the Soviet Union. Henry Kissinger, President Richard M. Nixon's assistant for national security affairs, visited Tehran at the end of the following month and undoubtedly discussed the shah's future assistance to the Kurds.[10]

The disputes capable of negotiated settlement between Iran and Iraq in 1974 formed three discernible issues: the Shatt al-'Arab, the central sector of the Iran-Iraq border, and Iraq's Kurds in the north. Since detailed accounts of these disputes, their formal negotiation, and the resulting treaties can be found in other sources,[11] only a brief review of their significance is presented here.

9. The province of Dhofar periodically had rebelled against politically dominant groups centered toward the north in Muscat and Oman. By the mid-1960s the Dhofar Liberation Front, a force estimated at between 700 and 1,000 men, actively began to engage the army of the sultanate of Oman. Originally a contained dispute, these guerrillas began to receive assistance from the People's Democratic Republic of Yemen by 1967 as well as from nationalist movements, such as the Communist party in China and the Ba'th party in Iraq. The Omani government, for its part, received military assistance from the British and financial aid from the more conservative regimes in Arabia, including the United Arab Emirates and Saudi Arabia. The shah of Iran also sent the Omani Sultan, Qabus bin Sa'id, 1,200 troops in late 1973, a number that had expanded to 2,000 by 1975. The rebellion collapsed in 1976, and most of the Iranian forces returned home by the following year.

10. See Henry A. Kissinger, *The White House Years* (Little, Brown and Company, 1979), pp. 1263–65. Later, less than six months after the conclusion of the Algiers agreement of 1975, the Iraqis cannot have failed to notice that the Kurdish guerrilla leader Mullah Mustafa Barzani went to the United States for a lengthy visit from his reputed residence near Tehran. Barzani subsequently was in and out of the United States before dying of natural causes in Washington, D.C., in 1979.

11. See Robert D. Tomasek, "The Resolution of Major Controversies between Iran and Iraq," *World Affairs*, vol. 139 (1976–77), pp. 206–30; and Tareq Y. Ismael, *Iraq and Iran: Roots of Conflict* (Syracuse University Press, 1982).

The Shatt al-'Arab dispute, predating the Iraqi Ba'thists, was predetermined by the physical complexity of the waterway and the proximity of Iranian and Iraqi interests there. Despite frequent adjudication over the centuries, it has remained a constant source of friction. Iraq demanded in April 1969 that rights and obligations established in the 1937 treaty be enforced, including the collection of tolls from Iranian ships traversing the Shatt al-'Arab, the lowering of Iranian flags in the waterway, and the prohibition of naval personnel unless prior permission had been granted. Subsidiary complaints were that Iranian mariners practiced unsafe seasmanship and disregarded Basra port rules. Iran responded by unilaterally abrogating the treaty and sending armed boats up the waterway. An uneasy status quo ensued, with both sides of the river remaining heavily fortified.

Despite the standoff, both states continued to have large unsatisfied interests in the Shatt al-'Arab. Iraq believed that its own needs were acute: its coastline is restricted to approximately fifteen kilometers; the Shatt al-'Arab is Iraq's sole means of egress to the Gulf; the port city of Basra is some ninety kilometers from the river's mouth; the river must be dredged frequently in order to be navigable. Moreover, the importance of the waterway and its surrounding region continued to increase in proportion to the role of oil in Iraq's economy. The Iraqi government argued that Iran's 2,300-kilometer coastline made possible numerous ports, among them Chah Bahar, Bandar Abbas, and Bushire. Iraq already had consented to placing the boundary opposite the Iranian cities of 'Abadan and Khorramshahr in mid-channel rather than on the eastern bank. Iran countered that it too had vital strategic interests in proximity to the waterway: Kharg Island, Iran's major oil terminal and shipping facility, lay only forty-eight kilometers offshore; 'Abadan was the site of a major oil refinery; and Khosrowabad, some twenty-five kilometers south of 'Abadan on the Shatt al-'Arab, contained a naval base.

The second controversy between the two states, their central border region, also predated the Ba'thist government in Iraq. Although geographically confined, this issue became inextricably linked with the other two disputes. The contested region is some 210 kilometers long, bounded by Khanaqin and Qasr-i Shirin in the north and Badra and Mehran in the south, varying in width from 3 to 16 kilometers. Sporadic shooting incidents occurred in April 1972 and again from December 1973 to February 1974. After one confrontation in which some eighty-one Iranians and twenty-four Iraqis sustained injuries, half of them resulting in death, Iraq appealed to the UN Security Council, which arranged a ceasefire on March 17, 1974. Subsequent negotiations collapsed when the Kurdish issue erupted again in August 1974.

Dating from the early days of the Hashimite monarchy, this third source of conflict arose from the nationalism of the Iraqi Kurds, some 2.5 to 3 million of whom are concentrated in northeastern Iraq, where adequate rainfall and fertile grazing land afford them greater economic autonomy and social independence than the rest of the Iraqi population. Since the inception of the Iraqi state the Kurds had agitated for a larger share of national revenue, greater representation in the central government, and more political autonomy or complete independence. Four military campaigns launched by the central government against the Kurds in the 1960s were costly in both men and matériel. Kurdish guerrillas had several advantages: operating in their own rugged terrain and numbering by their own account between 50,000 and 60,000 during the first half of the 1970s, they occupied the high ground and could isolate police and military garrisons, cut supply lines, and control the rural areas.

Most of Iraq's neighbors, recognizing the volatility of Kurdish nationalist fervor and its potential to spread, had little desire to worsen this dispute, as they could easily have done. Estimates of the Kurdish population in these countries vary widely. Turkey, for example, is estimated to have from 7 million to 12 million Kurds, Syria 400,000 to 800,000, the Soviet Union approximately 100,000 to 300,000, and Iran 3 million to 5 million. Within the context of Iran-Iraq tensions, however, the shah of Iran with American agreement chose to give limited support to the Iraqi Kurds beginning in 1972. Iranian support gradually increased prior to Iraq's 1975 settlement with Iran, contributing to heavy losses on both sides. Saddam Husain said that the Iraqis lost 16,000 army personnel and suffered more than 60,000 casualties among civilians and the armed forces during hostilities with the well-armed Kurds. Estimates on the Kurdish side, which remain in doubt, vary from 2,000 to more than 7,000 dead.[12]

President Houari Boumedienne of Algeria intervened in the conflict and negotiated the Algiers Declaration of March 6, 1975, a joint com-

---

12. FBIS, *Daily Report: MEA*, December 29, 1980, statement by Saddam Husain in a speech to a cabinet meeting on December 24, 1980, p. E2. See also Gerard Chaliand, ed., *People without a Country: The Kurds and Kurdistan* (London: Zed Press, 1980); and Edmund Ghareeb, *The Kurdish Question in Iraq* (Syracuse University Press, 1981), p. 174.

muniqué between Iran and Iraq. On June 13 representatives of the two countries signed an additional agreement known as the Treaty of International Boundaries and Good Neighborliness, which contained three protocols and annexes. It was designed to settle disputes over the land and riverine boundaries, territorial waters, and internal security issues. The basic agreement involved one major exchange. In return for Iraq's acceptance of the thalweg as the southern boundary with Iran rather than the eastern bank of the Shatt al-'Arab, each country agreed to the principle of noninterference in the internal affairs of the other country. It was an integral agreement: violation of one part of the treaty invalidated it entirely. This meant in this instance that Iran would cease to aid Kurdish guerrillas in Iraq.

A number of constraints on the two governments prompted the agreement. Both knew that the central border issue had become increasingly volatile as a consequence of the Kurdish violence in the north. They also foresaw that an escalation of hostilities would not only make their oil industries primary and indefensible targets, but also invite further superpower entanglement.

On the Iranian side, at least two other considerations came into play. Neither was insignificant. In addition to the possibility that Iran would eventually alienate the other regional states and politically isolate itself, there was the risk that a major Iraqi offensive during the spring of 1975 would succeed unless the shah substantially increased his support of the guerrillas. In retrospect it is notable that Iraq's last offensive against the Kurds, begun only six hours after the communiqué announcing the agreement was issued, eliminated Kurdish resistance in only two weeks, an indicator of the level of the shah's support during the preceding two years.

On the Iraqi side, the Kurdish dispute had been a financial and political drain, inhibiting flexibility in both domestic and foreign affairs. Until an agreement could be reached, the young Ba'thist government would continue to be distracted from its program of domestic development, which was linked to the long-term stability of the Ba'th party in Iraq. Problematic situations were also brewing in Iraq's foreign relations. Tension between Syria and Iraq, starting in 1974 when the Syrians began filling the Tabqa reservoir, intensified and culminated in May 1975 in the massing of troops along the border after no agreement was reached on sharing the water of the Euphrates. Syrian news media broadcast stories of internal Iraqi discontent throughout April and May 1975, reporting the execution of persons who opposed the Algiers Declaration and the subsequent treaty, most of whom were in the military. The additional Syrian accusation that Iraq had ceded fourteen Iraqi villages to Iran, essentially forfeiting "national rights," clearly was not intended to harmonize relations between the two countries or between the Iraqi government and its people.[13]

The most cogent reason propelling the settlement with Iran, however, was that by mid-1975 the Soviet Union had so curtailed its arms shipments that Iraq's military stores were being rapidly depleted. Saddam Husain stated in 1980 that the Algiers initiative had come at a time when "there were only three heavy missiles left in the air force and very few artillery shells."[14] This period, characterized by the slowing of Soviet aid and by American support of the Kurdish guerrillas, had a profound effect on the dominant civilian wing of the Ba'th. Many came to the belief that heavy political or military dependence on a superpower reduced Iraq's maneuverability and jeopardized the security of the state. The communiqué at Algiers and the subsequent treaty of June 1975 thus presented Iraq with diverse and sorely needed policy options. Soon Baghdad began to pursue nonalignment in Iraqi economic and political life. In September 1975, less than three months after the treaty, Saddam Husain, then the right-hand man of President Ahmad Hasan al-Bakr, went to Paris to seek closer economic ties with France and to investigate the possibility of purchasing Mirage F-1 fighters, Jaguar fighter-bombers, and Alpha jet trainers. By 1978 countries belonging to the Organization for Economic Cooperation and Development, primarily France, West Germany, and Italy, accounted for almost 78 percent of Iraq's foreign trade.

Between 1975 and the start of the Iran-Iraq war, the Ba'th also increased its efforts to extend the party's credibility throughout Iraq. Domestic development programs continued with renewed vigor. The government even maintained a cordial, albeit cool, relationship with the

13. *Arab Report and Record*, May 16–31, 1975, p. 308.

14. FBIS, *Daily Report: MEA*, December 29, 1980, p. E2. It is uncertain what prompted the Soviets to reduce their supplies to Iraq. If they foresaw the future direction of Saddam Husain's policy of nonalignment, they may have wished to encourage a change in Iraq's leadership by exploiting reported discontent among members of the Iraqi political-military establishment who felt they were close to victory over the Kurds and resented the Algiers Declaration. The Soviets may also have been worried about the growing rift between Syria and Iraq and about the increasing level of hostilities in the Kurdish region, particularly since they had Kurdish and other ethnic minorities in their own southern regions.

shah. An Iraqi delegation visited Tehran in July 1977 and held talks with the shah and other high Iranian officials; joint Iranian-Iraqi committees discussed a wide range of affairs, including consular matters, trade, energy and oil, agriculture, fisheries, and tourism. The shah was shown full respect by Iraqis when they addressed him in public announcements as the shahanshah, or king of kings, and messages were exchanged between the shah and Iraq's President Bakr.

If any period in recent Iraqi history might facetiously be described as quiescent, this was it, though it was not destined to last long. The disclosure of an alleged plot to overthrow the government by some of its own members in mid-1979 led to ruthless elimination of the plotters. Soon the Islamic revolution on Iraq's eastern flank began to press in upon the Iraqi government.

From the Islamic Revolution to the Outbreak of War

In retrospect, the animosity displayed between the governing regimes in Iraq and Iran after the success of the Islamic revolution in Iran went one step beyond their rivalry in the shah's time. It reflected a fundamental incompatibility between Arab nationalism and Islamic conservatism, between the regimes' political credentials, and between their ambitions. While hostility was not inevitable, the underlying differences would have been difficult to reconcile.

When demonstrations against the shah erupted in Iran in early 1978, Iraqi officials were as apprehensive as those in Iran. Ayatullah Khomeini, an important Shi'i religious leader, had resided in al-Najaf since his expulsion from Iran in 1964; several Iraqis related that he had remained primarily in the company of Persian Shi'is, residing several blocks from the mosque of Imam 'Ali. Before the Iran-Iraq settlement in 1975, Khomeini was asked to contribute to Iraqi propaganda against the shah. Khomeini refused, and apparently remained unknown to, or at least was kept from the attention of, the great majority of Iraq's population. Sa'dun Hammadi, a Shi'i by birth and a former Iraqi foreign minister, said in August 1982 that he personally had not known of Khomeini's political significance or even that he was in al-Najaf until several months before the religious leader was expelled from Iraq. While this may simply reflect the personal interests of Hammadi or the controlled, segmental nature of the Iraqi government, Khomeini nevertheless seems to have been isolated during his stay in Iraq. He is said to know only Qur'anic or classical literary Arabic rather than colloquial Arabic. Since Iraqis speak a unique and difficult Arabic dialect containing many loan words from Kurdish and Turkish as well as from Farsi, Khomeini's contacts within Iraq may well have been limited. This would not necessarily have limited his prestige and appeal, however, given the high esteem in which scholars of literary Arabic are held.

When Khomeini refused several years later to restrain what had now become open attacks on the shah, the Iraqis placed him under house arrest in September 1978 or shortly before, and soon thereafter expelled him from Iraq. (Some say that the shah requested Khomeini's explusion, others that the shah implored Iraq to keep him. In either case the Iraqi government must have been increasingly concerned about Khomeini's potential influence within Iraq as the Islamic revolution gained strength.)[15] Kuwait, Khomeini's next choice of residence, denied him entry and he proceeded to France, where unencumbered he expanded his political circle and became the focus of opposition to the shah. On January 16, 1979, the shah was forced to leave Iran, and on February 1, 1979, Ayatullah Khomeini returned to his homeland.

At first the Iraqi media adopted a pragmatic "wait-and-see" position, neither condemning the shah nor welcoming the Iranian revolution. Privately, Iraqi officials seemed more concerned about the nature of the new government. In late January 1979, Tariq 'Aziz gave an interview in which he acknowledged Shahpour Bakhtiar, who had been appointed by the shah, as the legitimate head of government in Iran. In the first week of February, an unidentified high-ranking Iraqi official said in

---

15. Significantly, there was civil unrest on February 5 and 6, 1977, in the Sh'i-revered cities of Karbala and al-Najaf, the latter of which was then Khomeini's residence. Very little information about the trouble is known except that it specifically concerned a Shi'i festival and that the government closed its border posts in consequence. Syrian propaganda broadcasts accused the Iraqis of widespread arrests in the cities of al-Najaf, Karbala, al-Samawah, and al-Hilla and the district of al-Thawra in Baghdad, notably all areas inhabited predominately by Shi'is. Iran's General Toufanian stated to General Ezer Weizman, the Israeli minister of defense, on July 18, 1977, only five months after the Shi'i disturbances, "Lately some people from Iraq were in Tehran. We made some type of agreement together." Toufanian did not offer any further clarification of this "agreement." The timing of this statement is significant, suggesting that both Iranian and Iraqi officials may have identified a common thread of concern as early as 1977. FBIS, *Daily Report: MEA*, February 25, 1977, pp. E-1–E-2; and *Documents from the Nest of Espionage*, vol. 19: *America, the Protector of Israel*, Asnad Lanah-i Jasusi (Spy-nest Documents) (Tehran: Danishijuyan-i Musalmanam Pirut Khatt Imam, 1982).

another published interview that "the entire situation awaits the emergence of another General Zahedi [leader of the countercoup in 1953 against Musaddiq] who can quickly solve the issue." After listing many of the reasons for the shah's alienation from his people, the official went on to ask some surprising and revealing questions: "Does this mean that the only way to punish the Shah is by dethroning him, that the regime can only be improved by a coup d'état. . . . Why don't they amend the Iranian Constitution. . . . Why doesn't the Shah turn into a mere sovereign who reigns but does not rule and thus returns to the country?"[16] Unlike Iraqi statements made after the war began, which complained of inequities in the 1975 agreement between Iran and Iraq, both interviews stressed the treaty's positive aspects and the fact that outstanding problems between the two countries had been resolved, and reminded the Iranians of the legal provisions for noninterference in each other's internal affairs.

Events, however, moved rapidly. On February 9, 1979, Iraq issued a statement requesting closer ties with Iran even though the Iraqi media avoided discussion of the Iranian religious leaders. Khomeini apparently was not mentioned until February 13, when Iraq congratulated the Iranian people on their victory and reiterated the importance of noninterference in the internal affairs of their neighboring state. Iraq sent to Khomeini a congratulatory cable on the proclamation of the Islamic Republic of Iran on April 5, 1979, but their relations had already begun to sour. Throughout the summer, inflammatory events and unproved allegations by both Iran and Iraq began to occur with increasing regularity. Perhaps the most significant event was Iran's appointment of a Shi'i religious leader, Hojat al-Islam Dua'ai, as its new ambassador to Iraq. As a Hojat al-Islam, Dua'ai was only one administrative grade below an Ayatullah.

Propaganda and Subversion

Iran's anti-Iraqi propaganda during this period illustrates the attitude of the new Iranian government toward its western neighbor, particularly the Ba'thists themselves, and also sheds light on those political areas in which the Iraqi governing elite might be most sensitive and vulnerable.

16. See these interviews respectively reprinted from *Monday Morning,* January 22–28, 1979, and from *al-Mustaqbal,* February 2, 1979, in FBIS, *Daily Report: MEA,* February 2, 1979, pp. E1–E7, and FBIS, *Daily Report: MEA,* February 9, 1979, p. E6.

In June 1979 an anti-Iraqi government demonstration was permitted in Tehran, during which calls were made for the institution of an Islamic republic in Iraq under the leadership of Khomeini and for the deaths of Iraqi President Ahmad Hasan al-Bakr and Vice-President Saddam Husain.[17] Demonstrations against the Iraqi government in which Iranian Kurds were identified took place along the border in June and July. Talabani, a Kurdish-Iraqi guerrilla leader, was reported to have taken refuge in Iran. Tehran radio, broadcasting in Arabic, sought to discredit the Iraqi Ba'thist leaders with accusations that they had disgracefully banished Khomeini from Iraq, arrested Iranian revolutionaries, aided the shah's secret police, remained silent about the shah's crimes when he ruled, received the shah's wife in Baghdad during the Iranian revolution, gave refuge to Iranians fleeing after the revolution, incited Iranian minorities, and broadcast against both Khomeini and the revolution.[18]

In another Arabic-language broadcast, Iran radio focused on the internal Iraqi situation, stating that a schism was developing between the Iraqi people and their government; that a public uprising against Iraq's Takriti leaders was imminent; and that there was distrust between the Ba'th party and the Popular Army, which had been disarmed, and between the Ba'th party and the regular army, which sided with the Iraqi people.[19] The suggestion that Iraqi soldiers were brothers of the Iraqi people and therefore could be separated from the government was, of course, the same tactic Khomeini had used when he urged the Iranian people to greet the Iranian army not with violence but with flowers because they were allies.[20] Iran also announced that the Iraqi Shi'i leader

17. A popular rally was organized in Baghdad the following month on July 3, 1979, in which the "aggressive, racist policy" of the new Iranian regime was denounced. See FBIS, *Daily Report: MEA*, July 3, 1979, p. E1.

18. FBIS, *Daily Report: MEA*, July 3, 1979, pp. R5–R6, excerpts from the Tehran international service in Arabic on July 2, 1979.

19. FBIS, *Daily Report: MEA*, July 2, 1979, pp. R9–R10, Tehran international service in Arabic on June 29, 1979.

20. Mohamed Heikal, *Iran: The Untold Story* (Pantheon Books, 1982), pp. 142–46, has noted that Khomeini's assessment of the ability of the opposition to overthrow the shah was heavily centered on the response of Iran's military. Because of the relevance of similar propaganda being used against Iraq, it is important to digress momentarily. Since direct confrontation with the Iranian army was unthinkable, the army would have to be undermined. Soldiers had to be made to question their loyalty to their officer elites. Many of Khomeini's tapes smuggled into Iran after 1977 were directed to the army, urging soldiers to desert in small numbers with their weapons. Desertions began to be reported that same year and were occurring in ever increasing numbers by 1978.

Khatam Yazdi and some fifteen clergymen from al-Najaf seminary had been expelled from Iraq and were given refuge by Imam Khomeini in Qum.[21] When Iranian Prime Minister Shahpour Bakhtiar escaped to Europe, it was further claimed that Iraq had sheltered him.

Diplomatic contacts continued despite the war of words. At least one meeting took place between Iranian and Iraqi officials during August 1979, and at the Conference of Nonaligned Nations in Cuba in September, Foreign Minister Ibrahim Yazdi of Iran met Saddam Husain. Meanwhile, in response to renewed Iraqi demands that Iran recognize Arab rights in the Shatt al-'Arab and the three islands in the Strait of Hormuz, Iranian officials in September 1979 called for the annexation of Bahrain. In support of this position at least one Shi'i leader in Iran, Sadiq Rohani, called upon Bahrainis to revolt against their Sunni ruler, Shaikh 'Isa bin Salman Al Khalifa, if he persisted in anti-Islamic practices. Rohani claimed that 85 percent of Bahrainis were Shi'i and opposed to their corrupt ruler, that he had already sent envoys to supervise the struggle, and that he volunteered to oversee the revolution from Iran if the Bahrainis requested him to do so.[22]

Iran's propaganda campaign took a new twist in November 1979 when demonstrators in several Iranian cities produced concerted charges that officials in Baghdad were puppets of the United States and that Iraq was a secret participant in the Camp David agreement.[23] This explained, it was said, why the Ba'thists were allied with the shah, why American

---

Under no circumstances, Khomeini advised the Iranian people, should they oppose the soldiers even if the army was forced to fire on them, but rather people should prove they were all brothers by welcoming their fate as martyrs. In this way, the inner consciousness of each soldier would be touched. This, of course, was the reason that the Iranians put flowers in the gun barrels of the soldiers in Tehran, as was seen in the Western media.

21. FBIS, *Daily Report: MEA,* July 2, 1979, p. R9, report on Tehran domestic service in Farsi, June 29, 1979.

22. FBIS, *Daily Report: MEA,* September 25, 1979, p. R8.

23. See FBIS, *Daily Report: MEA,* November 2, 1979, pp. R2–R3, excerpt from Tehran international service in Arabic on November 1, 1979; FBIS, *Daily Report: MEA,* November 5, 1979, pp. R24–R25, excerpt from Tehran domestic service in Farsi of Ayatullah Muntazari's remarks at the University of Tehran on November 2, 1979; and FBIS, *Daily Report: MEA,* November 5, 1979, p. R25, Tehran international service in Arabic on November 2, 1979. During an interview with Ramadhan in August 1982, as I was preparing to visit the war front, he jokingly referred to Iran's continued charges of American complicity with Iraq. "If you are captured on your visit to the south by Iran," he said, "the Iranians will say that this proves the United States has relations with Iraq."

agents in Baghdad were trying to incite a conflict with Iran and deflect attention from the real enemy of the Islamic revolution (Israel), and why Iraqi leaders were guilty of the same crimes as the shah. These charges were followed by armed attacks on Iraqi consulates in Iran and the takeover of the one in Kermanshah by a group publicly acknowledged to be following Khomeini. Although the Iranian governor of Kermanshah denied in a public statement that Iran had instigated Kurdish-related border incidents during this period, he added that "since Iraq is a neighboring Moslem country, we seek good neighborly relations and hope that finally one day that country will proceed along the path of Islam."[24] In any case, Iraq expelled some twenty Iranian residents of Iraq who were thought to be responsible for border violence.

From the beginning of 1980 until the start of the war in September, relations between the two countries deteriorated to such an extent that it is difficult to affix responsibility or evaluate the claims and counter-claims. In late March, for example, President Abul Hasan Bani Sadr of Iran made a bitter attack against President Saddam Husain. Iraq accused Iran of seizing one of its diplomatic pouches. Radio transmissions that were pro-Soviet, pro-Kurdish, and anti-Saddam Husain were first monitored in that month and believed to have originated in Kurdish Iran. Other radio stations broadcast anti-Saddam Husain messages, but their point of origin was not determined. Iraq, for its part, broadcast pro-Bakhtiar, pro-Oveissi, and anti-Khomeini messages on two new stations first monitored during May and June.[25]

A more concrete source of Iraqi concern was the increasing number of incidents of internal subversion. A member of Fedaye Islam, a militant right-wing Islamic movement associated with Sadigh Khalkhali, the head of Iran's revolutionary courts, claimed in Iran that the movement was responsible for the attempted assassination in Baghdad on April 1, 1980, of Tariq 'Aziz, a deputy prime minister and member of Iraq's Revolutionary Command Council. Whatever the validity of that claim, Iraq attributed the assassination attempt to the Islamic revolutionary movement al-Da'wa, which in Iraq was believed to have links with Iran and was becoming a more active force. Its acts of sabotage included the

24. *Keyhan* (Tehran) in Farsi on November 22, 1979, as translated and reprinted in JPRS 74787, *NE/NA Report*, no. 2059 (December 18, 1979), p. 65.

25. They were identified as Iraqi broadcasts because one station accidentally played a few bars of the Iraqi national anthem before realizing the error. British Broadcasting Corporation, *Summary of World Broadcasts*, ME/67A/1–2, July 10, 1981.

cutting of telephone lines, destruction of ammunition dumps, and at least one other assassination attempt against a Ba'th official,[26] to all of which Iraq responded swiftly. Later in April the most prominent Shi'i leader in Iraq, Muhammad Baqir al-Sadr, was executed by the Iraqi government, which publicly accused al-Da'wa of exploiting sectarianism in the country, of receiving aid from Iran, and of trying to establish a purely religious government.

Sadr's execution received attention at the highest levels in Iran, where Khomeini proclaimed a three-day period of national mourning in Iran for Islam's most recent martyr. Then, as he had done under the shah, Khomeini appealed to the Iraqi military:

I have given up hope on the upper echelons of the Iraqi law enforcement forces. But I have not given up hope in the officers, NCOs and soldiers and I expect them either to rise heroically and to destroy the foundations of oppression just as happened in Iran, or to desert their garrisons and barracks so that they will not bear the shame of the Ba'th Party's oppression.[27]

An extremist Shi'i leader, Husain 'Ali Muntazari, made a statement on the same occasion in which he declared that the regime of "butcher Saddam Husain" was opposed to Islam:

I am confident that the noble blood of the martyrs of Islam will boil in the Islamic Iraqi people and in those of the Islamic countries. This blood will continue to boil until Saddam Husain's regime is completely overthrown and until the Islamic republic is established, as happened when the noble blood of the Iranian martyrs initiated the Islamic revolution in Iran and wrecked the regime of the shedder of blood [the shah].[28]

Ideologies Collide

The potential for controversy was heightened by the fact that the Iraqi leaders based their rule on the premise of Arab nationalism. Therefore they rejected the notion that unity should be achieved through the common denominator of Islam irrespective of one's ethnic origins. Rather they believed that Arabism should be the shared ideal whether

26. See FBIS, *Daily Report: MEA*, January 12, 1982, pp. E3–E4, for a personal account by an al-Da'wa member, Abu Nasir Said, of his party's subversive activities in Iraq.

27. FBIS, *Daily Report: South Asia*, April 23, 1980, pp. I15–I16, text of Khomeini's message on April 22, 1980, on the Tehran domestic service in Farsi. (Hereafter FBIS, *Daily Report: SA*.)

28. FBIS, *Daily Report: SA*, April 23, 1980, p. I16–I17, text of Muntazari's message on April 22, 1980, on the Tehran international service in Arabic.

one was a Muslim or a Christian. The Iraqi Ba'thists, as distinct from other Arab nationalists in the Middle East, had gone one cautious step further by trying to rationalize the inclusion of Kurds and by propounding "Iraqi nationalism." Therefore, when Iranian statements as early as March 1979 asked that Arab and state nationalism be submerged or eliminated, wherever Muslims resided, for the greater unity of the Islamic revolution, serious concerns began to arise in Iraq about the possibility of sectarian strife.

Saddam Husain emphasized the potential consequences and his fear of this fundamental disagreement between the two ideologies as early as October 1979. He described the "Arab revolution" as a "qualitative transformation" that derived its values from history and religion, but went on to say that "in order for the Islamic revolution [or] any [other] revolution to be Islamic, it must be a friend of the Arab revolution. Any contradiction between a revolution which calls itself Islamic and the Arab revolution means that that revolution is not Islamic. As an Arab revolutionary, I understand the matter as such . . . because a true Islamic revolution should absorb the Arab ideology . . . and remove any contradiction between it and this ideology.[29]

On February 8, 1980, Husain made a significant declaration of pan-Arabism that became known as the Eight-Point Pan-Arab National Charter. In one sense, the charter itself produced no surprises. It can be summarized as a call for all Arab states to reject the presence of any foreign army and the use of armed force against countries bordering the Arab homeland except in self-defense, to join as one Arab bloc in the defense of any Arab state that is invaded, to affirm international laws relating to the use of waters and airspace and land unless a state of war exists, to commit themselves to nonalignment in international conflicts, and to establish constructive economic relations among themselves.[30] Husain's emphasis on Arab unity, on the protection of Arab rights to land, and on Arabness generally was to be expected, but his appeal was significant at a time when the Ba'thists anticipated the installation on Iraq's flank of a conservative Islamic government in Iran.

Even more revealing of Iraqi concerns was the introduction to the charter, a terse exposition against the Iraqi Communist party in which Husain described in some detail how the Communists had exploited

29. FBIS, *Daily Report: MEA,* October 17, 1979, p. E4.
30. FBIS, *Daily Report: MEA,* February 11, 1980, pp. E1–E4.

sectarian strife in Iraq under Qasim. Husain reminded young Iraqis that they were not old enough to remember the horrors, which had included torture and burying people alive, and that only the Ba'th party had been able to suppress those evils and overcome differences within the country. Husain scoffed at those who said there is a difference between Sunni and Shi'i, Arab and Kurd: "We in Iraq are one united people." He warned them, however, that there might be a new attempt to divide the Arab homeland.

Khomeini's attitude toward the Iraqi leaders and the inherent conflict between Arab nationalism and Islamic fundamentalism now deserve attention. In France during 1978, between his expulsion from Iraq and his return to Iran, Khomeini was asked to list his enemies. He replied, "First, the Shah, then the American Satan, then Saddam Hussein and his infidel Baath Party".[31] As the source of this quotation noted, Khomeini by 1980 had defeated the first, had humiliated the Americans by seizing their embassy, and had turned his attention to the third remaining enemy—Saddam Husain and the Ba'thists.[32] Aside from ideology, Khomeini might have had personal reasons to harbor a grudge against Iraq. After the Iran-Iraq agreements in 1975, Iraq had attempted to improve relations with the shah, which required clamping down on Khomeini's activities in al-Najaf and eventually placing him under house arrest before actually expelling him. Sometime during the fall of 1977, one of Khomeini's two sons died in an unexplained and sudden manner in al-Najaf. Although Khomeini accused the shah, one must wonder whether Khomeini also felt bitterness against Iraq either for the lapse of security (if indeed he believed his son was assassinated) or for what he saw as cooperation after 1975 between the shah and the Ba'th party in Iraq.

On the ideological level, there was an unbridgeable gap between the

31. *Time,* July 26, 1982, p. 25.

32. Khomeini never differentiated on the theoretical level between Husain as an individual, Ba'thists, and other Arab nationalists. In a number of misinformation leaflets and propaganda broadcasts by Iran after Khomeini's return, the Iraqi regime often was referred to as that of "Saddam Aflaqi" or "the tyrannical Aflaqi regime," a reference to Michel Aflaq, one of the founders of the Ba'th party, discussed in part 2. Supporters of Khomeini published biographical sketches of Aflaq that were intended to discredit him and, hence, all Ba'thists. Aflaq was accused of being a classmate of Menachem Begin, a spy for Israel, a freemason, and a Communist at heart. Notably, his greatest crime, it was said, was "the racist ideology of Arabism." See "Know the Enemies of Islam: Michael Aflaq," in *Islamic Republican Party Weekly Bulletin,* vol. 1 (January 30, 1981), pp. 15–17.

men who now controlled the governments of the two countries—in fact, between Khomeini and all Arab nationalists. Although Khomeini's ethnic background is Persian, it would not diminish his appeal to devout Muslim Arabs. Khomeini believed that the ultimate aim of Islam was "to abolish nationality," and therefore Arab nationalism was "fundamentally opposed to Islam" because it hindered the ability of Islam to act as a uniting force, religiously and politically.[33] As Mohamed Heikal observed, "When I had conversations with Khomeini I discovered that Khomeini did not believe . . . in Arab nationalism. I said this to Khomeini and I told him that as long as he opposed Arab nationalism it means he wants to fragment the *umma* [Islamic community] . . . without a doubt this threatens the Arab *umma.*"[34]

To the hardline Islamic revolutionaries in Iran, Arab nationalism not only in Iraq but in any other country was a negative and obstructionist philosophy that would have to be eliminated before the Islamic revolution could proceed. Iranian Prime Minister Mohammad 'Ali Raja'i reiterated this view in the UN Security Council on October 18, 1980, shortly after the Iran-Iraq war began. After extolling Nasirism for its anti-Western stance, Raja'i went on to portray "seemingly 'leftist' " regimes as creations of the West that were intent on destroying Nasirism. He asked whether the United States was "trying to establish yet another Israel under the guise of Arab nationalism." The Ba'thists in particular, Raja'i said, were followers of Michel Aflaq, "Zionist freemason who created a so-called 'nationalist-socialist' organization with . . . racist ideologies in order to corrupt the anti-colonialist and anti-Zionist struggles of the oppressed Muslim Arab peoples."[35] Raja'i's use of terms such as "racist," by which he presumably meant anti-Persian, was intended to discredit the Iraqi Ba'th and its leaders, and with them Arab nationalism.

The Arab states, particularly those whose leaders were perceived as moderates or had ties to the West, anticipated significant political repercussions from an extremist interpretation of Islamic revolutionary ideology in their own countries after the successful establishment of an Islamic government in Iran. Khomeini had proclaimed the revolution to be antiracist, anti-shah, anticorruption, anticolonialist, anti-United States,

33. Interview with Khomeini on December 29, 1979, in Hamid Algar, ed. and trans., *Islam and Revolution: Writings and Declarations of Imam Khomeini* (Berkeley: Mizan Press, 1981), p. 332.

34. *Al-Majallah,* March 6–12, 1982, pp. 1, 3–6.

35. FBIS, *Daily Report: SA*, October 20, 1980, pp. I4–I10.

and anti-Zionist. Moreover, he had won. A number of young Arabs began to doubt the efficacy of the Arab nationalist philosophy and to question the authority of their governments, which had failed to prevent, for example, more Israeli settlements on the West Bank or the Israeli invasion of Lebanon. Religion, they said, was the only defense against a state (Israel) founded on religious principles or against corruption in their own societies. After the outbreak of war, Tehran broadcasts defined the full extent of the conflict by declaring that it was "a war against all the tyrants of the region. It is a war against the Camp David policy, against traitorous treaties and capitulatory plans. It is a war against . . . Israel."[36] Afghan refugees reportedly were recruited to fight on the Iranian front against Iraq because that was the real Islamic war. They were told that one's first duty was to eradicate corrupt elements in one's own Islamic community rather than to fight in Afghanistan against the Soviets.

The influence of religion on events before the war is clear. In August 1980, for example, an Iraqi Shi'i leader, Yusuf Sayid Muhsin Tabataba'i, rejected a call by Khomeini to move the Shi'i seminary at al-Najaf to Qum. Iraqi authorities later alleged that Khomeini claimed that Imam 'Ali's body had been secretly removed to Qum centuries ago from the shrine in Iraq.[37] While the validity of the Iraqi position remains uncertain, the fact that Iraq asserted it in its own propaganda war pointed to those areas where the government might receive the most public support.

A review of public pronouncements made by Khomeini before his return to Iran discloses little confidence that the Islamic revolution would spread to other countries of the region, for most of them were dominated by Sunni governments. In 1978, for example, Khomeini pointed to communal differences and the obeisant Sunni clergy in Iraq as obstacles to the realization of an Islamic government.[38] Once Khomeini returned victorious to Iran, however, he refrained from making public distinctions between Sunni and Shi'i Islam and by March 1979 began to talk of exporting the Islamic revolution to other countries. This was not defined as overt invasion; rather, the pro-Khomeini media implied that govern-

36. BBC, *Summary of World Broadcasts*, ME/7037/A/1, May 27, 1982, an excerpt from Tehran in Arabic for abroad on May 24, 1982.

37. FBIS, *Daily Report: MEA*, August 13, 1980, p. E3; and *Baghdad Observer*, June 6, 1981.

38. See two interviews with Khomeini by Hamid Algar on December 29, 1978, and December 29, 1979, published in Algar, *Islam and Revolution*.

ments that were considered corrupt by the new Iranian regime would be overthrown through active subversion by their own people. Sunnis and Shi'is, Persians and Arabs would join together against established authorities that had been labeled corrupt and non-Islamic. Moderate Arab nationalist governments, many caught between the disparities of new oil riches and poverty and promises to their people that remained unfulfilled, understood the consequences of these words.[39]

A new political configuration emerged from the victory of Iran's Islamic revolution as Khomeini and his followers publicly singled out those leaders who were not destined to remain. They included President Mubarak of Egypt, Sultan Qabus of Oman, King Fahd and the other Al Sa'uds of Saudi Arabia, King Hasan of Morocco, King Husain the "Shah of Jordan," and President Numairi of Sudan. Later, any of the Gulf states that helped Iraq during the war could also expect retribution, although Khomeini already had included conservative hereditary regimes on his list because they were not truly Islamic. Only Libya, Algeria, and Syria seemed absolved.

The stage setting for the Iran-Iraq war therefore was complete long before the hostilities began. After Khomeini returned to Iran, his Islamic revolution became an issue of growing concern to Iraqi leaders and to Arab moderates throughout the Middle East. The conflict between the two ideologies was a war for minds, fought at least initially with the symbols of identification—whether ethnic, religious, or nationalistic— that were readily available to all participants.

39. Shahpour Bakhtiar, the last Iranian prime minister under the shah, told the author that in discussions with Saddam Husain in 1979, Husain clearly revealed his fear that the Islamic revolution would have dire consequences for Iraq, whose domestic affairs were already being affected.

CHAPTER SIX

The War and Its Consequences

ON September 10, 1980, the Iraqi foreign minister, Dr. Sa'dun Hammadi, declared that Iranian troops had not withdrawn from certain territories, including the Zain al-Qais and Saif Sa'd regions on the Iraq-Iran border, as stipulated by the Iran-Iraq treaty of 1975. Notes of protest had been sent to Iran's representative in Baghdad, stating that in the absence of a response Iraq would be forced to expel the offending troops. Hammadi advised the Iranian government to consult the agreements between the two countries, to return other areas affected by the treaty, and to refrain from escalating the crisis. On September 14, however, the acting chief of staff of the Iranian army, General Fallahi, stated in an interview that Iran would not honor the agreement, implying that it had been foisted upon his country by foreign powers.

Three days later the Iraqi Revolutionary Command Council formally abrogated the treaty, citing Iran's failure to return Iraqi territory and its interference in Iraqi domestic affairs. It will be recalled that violation of one part of the treaty would abrogate it in its entirety. Cross-border hostilities initiated by both sides had continued with mounting intensity throughout August and September, and on September 22 Iraqi infantry units invaded Iran and the Iraqi air force bombed ten Iranian military installations. The war had now begun.

Iraqi Goals and Assumptions

Whether candidly expressed or not, the Iraqi Ba'thists' objectives in the war were territorially limited although critically important from a

163

political standpoint. One was a recognition of Iraq's legal claims over the Shatt al-'Arab, and perhaps what might be termed a defensive perimeter for ports and other economic facilities in the south. After the onset of hostilities, Iraqi authorities emphasized that the causes could be traced to the unsatisfactory settlement regarding the waterway and the status of the three islands in the Strait of Hormuz, which Khomeini had refused to renegotiate after his return to Iran.

As the war continued and became protracted, statements related strictly to Iraq's territorial claims receded and a deeper concern—intimated by Iraqi officials in January and early February 1979—came to the surface and became paramount: the specter of an Islamic government dominated by Khomeini and other extremist Shi'i conservatives in Iran. The heterogeneous nature of Iraqi society, the concentrations of its Shi'i population, and the presence of important Shi'i shrines in Iraq made religion a potentially divisive force that had been exploited in the past by internal political opposition groups and by foreign countries for their own purposes. Official Iranian broadcasts during the war exhorted both Iraqis and Iranians to liberate the sacred cities of Karbala, al-Najaf, al-Kazimain, and Samarra and their territories; Iranian tanks had the words "to al-Najaf" written on them. In going to war, the Iraqi Ba'thists sought to discredit or encourage the overthrow of the Islamic revolutionaries in Iran and thus lessen the political threat posed by their ideology. An important related objective was to deliver a blow sufficient to dissuade Iran from interfering in internal Iraqi affairs. In the course of attaining these goals, Saddam Husain and the Ba'th party may have hoped to assert themselves as preeminent Gulf and Arab leaders, but that could be only a by-product of the war and was not its primary motive.

Iraq's inability to bring the war to a swift conclusion is a reflection of Iraqi assumptions regarding Iran's domestic affairs before the war and of the objectives with which the Iraqi Ba'thist leaders entered the war, which they seemingly have been loath or unable to reevaluate during its course. What were those assumptions and what part did they play in Iraqi calculations before the war? How did those calculations affect Iraq's overall military strategy? After nearly four years of war, what are the challenges that remain for Iraq and for its leaders?

The Iraqi analysis of social and political conditions in Iran by midsummer 1980 was not dissimilar to and may actually have been based on political assessments made elsewhere, including the West. There has been speculation both in the Arabic press and by Arab officials that Iraqi leaders were provided information by exiled Iranian officials such as former Prime Minister Shahpour Bakhtiar during 1979 and 1980, although such assertions remain unverified by the Iraqis. In any case, the general turmoil apparent in Tehran at that time was summarized by Baghdadis, both Ba'thist and non-Ba'thist, in the oft-repeated statement, "There is a government on every street corner in Iran." Later, as the war continued seemingly without end, Iraqis attributed the failure of intermediaries to negotiate an end to the hostilities to that same logic.

Five fundamental assumptions flowed from this general Iraqi assessment of domestic Iranian affairs and were responsible for the determination of Iraq's objectives in the war.[1] First, the Iranian military had been substantially weakened after the shah's exile. The Imperial Guard was dismembered, officers above the rank of lieutenant-colonel were subjected to purges, and a militarily untrained religious guard was instituted that functioned alongside or instead of the professional military. It was uncertain whether enough trained technicians remained to repair sophisticated weapon systems or whether stockpiled matériel was still usable and, if so, could be located and organized.

Second, it was assumed that the Iranian leaders were so divided among themselves and lacking in unity of purpose that a concerted response by the government would be unlikely in the event of a major escalation of the conflict. The existence of competing centers of influence was evident in the sudden emergence of Qum as equal in importance to the capital city of Tehran. Subsidiary centers of power gained new relevance from the presence of influential religious leaders. Tabriz in northwestern Iran, for example, acquired new significance because Ayatullah Kazim Shariat-Madari, renowned for his moderating views, was associated with it.

The Iraqi leaders' third assumption was that the Islamic revolution was not wholly supported by Iran's civilian population, or at least that certain parts of it had become disillusioned and might deliberately undermine Khomeini. Such elements might include members of educated elites, military officers, minority populations such as Arabs in Khuzistan or Baluchis in Baluchistan, or even comparatively moderate religious leaders such as Shariat-Madari. Reported incidents of widespread unrest

---

1. See, for example, Tariq 'Aziz, "On Arab-Iranian Relations," published in the summer of 1980 by the Iraqi Ministry of Culture and Information, pp. 44–45.

might indicate not only a lack of centralized control, but even a rejection of it. Rising unemployment, shortages of previously available consumer goods, and other evidence of disarray in the economic sector could logically be expected to provoke disaffection with the new Iranian government.

Fourth, there was the assumption that repeated Iranian statements calling for export of the Islamic revolution to other Muslim-dominated states would alienate those states, particularly in the Gulf. The Gulf regimes were not only Arab but hereditary, legitimizing their rule by right of birth and not by criteria based on Muslim piety or popular choice.

The fifth assumption was that Iran would become isolated from the superpowers and receive little assistance from them in the immediate future, given the Islamic revolution's strong anti-imperialist stance resulting primarily from U.S. involvement with the shah and the Soviet Union's invasion of Afghanistan. In any case, the Iranian students' seizure of American embassy personnel as hostages probably led the Iraqis to conclude that public opinion in the United States would rule out American assistance to Iran.

Military Strategy

What was the relationship between Iraqi assumptions about Iran before the war and the objectives Iraq sought once the decision was made to go to war? There must have been two considerations: the sacrifices required to attain Iraq's objectives, and whether the outcome would justify the predicted costs. In examining these questions and seeking to understand the link between assumptions and objectives, it is important to look at what outside observers considered an anomaly in Iraqi strategy in the early stages of the war. The Iraqis pursued only limited military objectives. Instead of moving their forces rapidly north and east toward the mountains in September 1980, Western observers noted that Iraqi troops in the initial days of the war attacked only military targets, then took only a few small towns in the northern sector of the border. Saddam Husain issued public statements warning Iran to confine its own military operations and to avoid bombing civilian and economic facilities. When Iran did bomb them, Iraq responded in kind.

Later, even as the war dragged on, the Iraqis avoided bombing strategic roads, supply depots, and troop reinforcements. They used artillery bombardment to stop resistance in urban centers rather than actually entering the towns. Their failure to bomb oil-related facilities, particularly in 1982 and early 1983, raised additional questions about Iraq's military objectives and its ability to achieve them. It was not clear whether the Arab Gulf states had asked Iraq to spare oil installations because they wished to avoid Iranian retaliation for their aid to Iraq.

Western analysts had expected Iraq to move aggressively to exploit the internal difficulties that characterized Iran in mid-1980 and quickly consolidate its gains. The first phase of the war, however, ended in December 1980 because of winter. When hostilities resumed in May 1981, the Iranians had had time to assemble needed men and supplies and to plan counteroffensive moves that continued until 1982. A lull in the fighting ensued during which the Iraqis built defensive fortifications. In July 1982 the Iranians began to invade Iraqi territory at selected points.[2] That the Iraqis did not make better use of this initial period has been attributed either to the incompetence of the Iraqis or to the Western training and armaments of Iran.

Saddam Husain's own assessment of the relative military strengths of both countries in the initial stages of the war and why Iraq was then at a disadvantage is noteworthy.[3] Husain said that Iraq's original lines of communications were too long, leading to problems in repositioning troops between operational sectors, to a neglect of defensive positions in Iranian territory, and to difficulties in the placement of artillery. These handicaps were compounded by the dispersal of some Iraqi forces, the inexperience of reservists, the problems of fighting a protracted war, and the possibility that Iraqi units might be isolated by the Iranians. Moreover, the Iranians had fought more aggressively when defending their own homeland, had better intelligence at the start of the war, and had exploited knowledge of their own terrain. This situation, Husain

2. See Stephen R. Grummon, *The Iran-Iraq War: Islam Embattled* (Praeger, 1982); Anthony H. Cordesman, "Lessons of the Iran-Iraq War: The First Round," *Armed Forces Journal International*, vol. 119 (April 1982), pp. 32–47, and Cordesman, "Lessons of the Iran-Iraq War: Tactics, Technology, and Training," *Armed Forces Journal International*, vol. 119 (June 1982), pp. 68–85; William O. Staudenmaier, "A Strategic Analysis," in Shirin Tahir-Kheli and Shaheen Ayubi, eds., *The Iran-Iraq War: New Weapons, Old Conflicts* (Praeger, 1983); John W. Amos II, "The Iraq-Iran War: Calculus of Regional Conflict," in David H. Partington, ed., *Middle East Annual: Issues and Events*, vol. 1 (G. K. Hall, 1982), pp. 133–60; and Anthony H. Cordesman, "The Iran-Iraq War: Attrition Now, Chaos Later," *Armed Forces Journal International*, vol. 120 (May 1983), pp. 36ff.

3. BBC, *Summary of World Broadcasts*, ME/7252/A/5–9, February 8, 1983.

added, was not reversed until Iraq adopted defensive positions on its own territory in early 1982. Iraqi military officers also remarked to me in interviews that Iraq's heavy reliance on tank warfare placed its forces at a disadvantage because the Iranians often attacked at night, or in pre-dawn hours, when tanks are unable to maneuver.

Political Considerations

Purely military explanations for the conduct of the war have their limitations. A number of other possible explanations, individually or in some combination, can also account for the determination of Iraq's military strategy and shed light on questions regarding its efficacy.

One explanation is that the restraint of the Iraqi military was intentional, indicative of an overall military strategy that was constrained by the political objectives of the Ba'th party. If this was so, what were those objectives? Tariq 'Aziz, an influential member of the Revolutionary Command Council, told a French journalist that "our military strategy reflects our political objectives. We want neither to destroy Iran nor occupy it permanently because that country is a neighbor with which we will remain linked by geographical and historical bonds and common interests. Therefore, we are determined to avoid taking any irrevocable steps."[4] President Husain referred to "the defense" of Iraq without specifying the intent or object of Iranian aggression.[5] Here he may have alluded to Iraq's chronic vulnerability to internal dissension that could be easily fomented from abroad. In this case Iraq's indigenous Shi'i population or the thousands of Iranian Shi'is who annually make the pilgrimage to the holy shrines in southern Iraq were particularly suspect. It was unthinkable that the Ba'th or any other Iraqi government could control this influx of people and ideas, let alone stop it entirely. Massive destruction or large numbers of civilian casualties in Iranian cities such as 'Abadan would jeopardize future relations with Iran and its people, perhaps causing unforeseeable consequences among Iraq's own Shi'i population. As noted earlier, the most esteemed shrines in

4. FBIS, *Daily Report: MEA,* August 28, 1981, p. E4, excerpt from interview with Tariq 'Aziz, deputy prime minister of Iraq, by Eric Rouleau in Paris, published in *Le Monde* on August 22, 1981.

5. FBIS, *Daily Report: MEA,* September 11, 1981, p. E2, excerpt from an interview with Saddam Husain by Radio Monte Carlo correspondents Antoine Nawfal and Nabil Darwish, broadcast on September 9, 1981.

Shi'i Islam are in southern Iraq at al-Najaf, Karbala, and al-Kufa, and in central Iraq at Samarra and at al-Kazimain in Baghdad. Iranian Shi'is annually had made the pilgrimage to these shrines for centuries, a pilgrimage considered by many Shi'is to be as essential as that to Mecca or al-Madina.

This last point suggests another possible explanation for Iraq's initial restraint in the war. To what extent did political concern for the internal dynamics of Iraqi society determine tactics and strategy? One of Iraq's aims clearly was to minimize its own casualties, as was apparent in its tactics toward urban areas. Iraq could afford neither to lose large numbers of men nor to suffer significant percentage losses within any of its sectarian groups. This was especially so because of its losses during the Kurdish campaigns of the 1960s and the 1970s, because the population of Iraq was only one-third the size of Iran's, and because southern Iraq was predominantly Shi'a.

Another possibility is that military strategy was deliberately constrained by the civilian Ba'thists who were the primary policymakers in decisions related to the war. Several facts support this conjecture. The Revolutionary Command Council, composed of a limited number of men led by Saddam Husain, dominates the Ba'th party and guides all decisions of the Iraqi government. Of the five men who simultaneously hold positions on the Revolutionary Command Council and in the Ba'th's Regional and National Commands, all but one have purely civilian backgrounds, as was noted in chapter 4. The only one with military experience had been a lieutenant in 1959 and eventually had risen to the rank of captain.

The Ba'th party structure itself may have been detrimental to the kind of decisionmaking necessary in planning and conducting a war. The party's organizational apparatus is ideal for attaining domestic political objectives—to coordinate action among government ministries, to foster an Iraqi nationalism among particularistic groups, and to maintain a government in power so that the goals of economic and social development are kept constant. In another sense, however, the degree of centralization, regimentation, and obedience required by a party whose structure was originally designed for clandestine purposes may have superseded the independence, creativity, and professional skills that are indispensable to military strategists. Could the party leaders alter the course of the war or redefine their objectives and the means to attain them? Did Ba'th units or individuals monitor the professional military officers, as occurred between Revolutionary Guard units and the professional military in Iran? If so, what was the effect on the officers' performance? Were decisions related to the conduct of the war controlled directly from Baghdad and to what extent? When Iraq's regular army retreated during Iran's offensives in mid-1982, particularly from Khorramshahr, it showed a high level of professional expertise not displayed by the Popular Army. It demonstrated the same expertise in classic emplacements of defensive positions within Iraq's borders that same year. Could both phenomena be explained by circumstances in which the Iraqi regular military were in command or given greater scope in decisionmaking?

Yet another explanation is that Husain himself, who had urged restraint frequently in the past, was primarily responsible for decisions relating to the war. It is said that he personally had been responsible for the decision in 1969 not to confront the shah, in 1970 not to intervene militarily on behalf of the Palestinians in Jordan, in the early 1970s to find a conciliatory solution to the Kurdish question before it became clear that the existing policy was not working, in 1975 to negotiate a settlement with the shah, and in 1979 to aid North Yemen.[6] He also had been a primary instigator of the effort in the early 1970s to make civilians dominant in the bureaucracy and the Ba'th party, reputedly executing military officers or transferring them either to strictly military or to ambassadorial posts.[7]

Husain's role in wartime policymaking is partially confirmed by an interview in 1981 with an Iraqi Ba'thist who said that there were rumors in Baghdad that Saddam Husain alone had insisted on limiting Iraq's military objectives against the advice of other high-ranking civilian Ba'thists and military officers. Such rumors, of course, might simply be a preliminary effort by an opposition group to find a scapegoat in the

6. In late February and early March 1979, Iraq and Syria dispatched envoys to mediate in the border war between the Yemen Arab Republic and the Peoples' Democratic Republic of Yemen. This diplomacy followed a period of improved relations between Iraq and Syria, demonstrated in an agreement in February of that year to allow Iraq to resume oil shipments through Syria. The Iraqi and Syrian envoys played a major role in arranging a cease-fire on March 2. They stressed neutrality in mediation between the two Yemens in the hope of averting the further polarization of those countries, which, it was felt, might have led to outside intervention.

7. Saddam Husain won his first victory in this regard by exiling General Hardan al-Takriti, a man respected by the military. He was killed in 1971 by unknown assailants, presumably Iraqis, in Kuwait. Another influential general, Salih Mahdi 'Ammash, had political ambitions and was simply neutralized by being transferred to a diplomatic post.

aftermath of the war. If, however, the policy of restraint had yielded low casualty figures as well as the attainment of Iraq's political objectives, Husain might have been considered a hero for having displayed moderation in the context of volatile Iraqi politics.

Whether appropriate or not, Iraq's military strategy bears the signature of Iraqi politics of the 1970s, a signature for which Saddam Husain was largely responsible. It is enlightening in this regard to contrast the political decisions of Husain and his predecessor, Bakr, with those of the Ba'thist Nazim Kzar, who unsuccessfully attempted to overthrow the Ba'th government in 1973. Kzar had advocated active military engagement with Israel, harsh repression of Kurdish nationalists and Communist party members, and increased support for the Palestinian resistance movement, as well as more active manipulation of Ba'th party members.[8]

Miscalculations

Foremost among the many possible explanations for Iraq's strategy in the war must be included the fact the Iraq apparently entered the war without having a plan to bring it to a conclusion, by either military or diplomatic means.[9] Even if Iraq's objectives changed during the war, the government, perhaps having expected a quick victory, may simply have been unable to extricate itself once hostilities began.[10] That Iran might demonstrate persistent intransigence in third-party mediation attempts seems not to have been anticipated, a miscalculation that was to have profound consequences. Protracted warfare involved at least three dire possibilities for the Iraqi government: that reconciliation would become more difficult, that the chance of losing would increase, and that it would be increasingly hard to justify the costs of the war within the government and to the Iraqi people.

8. Khadduri, *Socialist Iraq*, pp. 64–66.
9. Significantly, one Iraqi official commented to the author that when the war started, the government was unable to find Persian-Arabic translators that could be trusted. This fact alone had created great consternation in the Iraqi bureaucracy.
10. When, after a discussion of the Iran-Iraq war, I asked Taha Yasin Ramadhan what he thought of the failed American attempt to rescue the hostages in Tehran, Ramadhan paused, looked out the window, and said reflectively, "You know, all things which are planned well on paper, do not always have the intended outcome." He made no criticism of the U.S. raid and seemed to have some empathy for America's frustration in its outcome.

What the Iraqis presumably hoped would be the swift attainment of their goals with minimal casualties became an exhausting, costly, and prolonged war. As early as 1981 Iraqis identified this kind of conflict as *harb al-istinzaf*, a war of attrition (from the Arabic root "to be drained" or "to be drawn off"), which was precisely the kind of war that was ultimately to the advantage of Iran. From the early days of fighting it had also become evident that in order to take Iranian cities, Iraq would have to engage in costly tactics of house-to-house combat or massive artillery bombardment.

The seriousness of such a war for Iraq becomes clear when one recalls that Iraq's total population is approximately 14 million while that of Iran is more than 40 million. The combined forces of Iraq's military services were estimated at the start of the war to number some 222,000 while those of Iran numbered approximately 415,000. Comparative numbers for the armies alone were 190,000[11] and 285,000, respectively. The International Institute for Strategic Studies has estimated that some 60 percent of the Iranian military had deserted after the shah's departure, although many of these men returned to their services.[12] In actual combat the Iranian regular forces were joined by the Revolutionary Guards as well as by volunteers or recruits, including children and older men. In Iran's debilitating human wave assaults during 1982–84, these groups suffered the greatest exposure and hence casualties, while Iran's professional military remained relatively protected. By contrast, every eight regular soldiers in Iraq were usually assigned one member of the Popular Army to provide noncombat support, though members of the Popular Army were later used as the occupying force in Khorramshahr.[13] It was

---

11. My own interviews suggest that the composition of Iraqi forces is approximately as follows: a battalion, or *katiba*, is the equivalent of 600 to 700 men; a brigade, or *liwa* has 2,700 to 3,500 men; a division, or *firqa*, has 11,000 to 12,000 men; and three divisions form a *failaq*, or corps, of roughly 36,000 men. There are some five to eight corps, three of which were stationed around Basra in August 1982 during Iranian counter-offensives. The Iraqis may have altered some of these groupings during the war.

12. See International Institute for Strategic Studies, *The Military Balance, 1979–1980* (London: IISS, 1979), pp. 39–40, which also gives an estimated breakdown of divisions and available military equipment.

13. Iraq also accepted Arab volunteers from other countries, though it seems implausible that they numbered a significant percentage of Iraq's forces. A statement by Taha Yasin Ramadhan carried by the Iraqi News Agency on February 4, 1981, in BBC, *Summary of World Broadcasts*, ME/6642/A/7, February 6, 1981, indicated that there were some 5,000 other Arab participants, mostly Palestinians in the Popular Army, but it is not known whether they were Palestinians who already had been living in Iraq

the Iraqi professional military that bore the brunt of fighting and sustained the highest losses.

Having expected a quick victory, the Iraqis were unprepared for the Iranian ability to regroup and for the war of attrition that followed. This was another grave miscalculation, for there were no internal constraints on the time horizon of the Iranian government. If two potentially disaffected groups—a growing number of unemployed and the military, which had sustained several purges since Khomeini's return to Iran— could be kept preoccupied by the war, it was to the advantage of the new Iranian leaders to prolong the fighting. Moreover, the Iranians had a stiff resolve to resist the invasion at almost any human cost. Many factors contributed to this phenomenon, among which were that Persians and Arabs were historically antipathetic to each other; that the Iranians were fighting on their own soil; that the Arabs who lived in Khuzistan where the fighting occurred had been "Persianized" after long years of residence there; and that the Revolutionary Guards and the regular military eventually were able to coordinate their efforts.

Perhaps the most important contributor to the Iranians' stiff resolve was the nature of the Islamic revolution itself. Various expressions of so-called Islamic conservatism have appeared in the Middle East throughout history, each internally rational in the formulation of its doctrine. Although Western understanding of them at present is restricted to their outward manifestations, theoretically no aspect of the life of the individual or of a society remains unaltered. Even though all these movements eventually deviated from their original doctrines, they could not readily do so without undermining the justification for their existence or rationalizing the deviation.

Because of the unique historical development of Shi'ism, martyrdom carries a special significance as the outward manifestation of self-sacrifice for Islam, representative of an inner and ultimately successful struggle. The Iranians, many recruited off the streets into what became known as the Army of Twenty Million, launched attacks against Iraqi positions with little regard for their lives preliminary to attacks by the regular Iranian military. As early as the summer of 1981, Iraqis who had been at the war front related their personal experiences of these attacks, which were later referred to in the West as "human wave assaults." By early 1984

for some time. On February 6, 1983, Ramadhan said that Arab volunteers numbered 14,000 and came from countries as distant as Sudan and North Yemen. See BBC, *Summary of World Broadcasts*, ME/7253/A/1, February 9, 1983.

the war had claimed the lives of 65,000 Iraqi troops and more than 300,000 Iranians and left much higher percentages of wounded. Only 5,000 Iranians were reported captured as against 50,000 Iraqis.

A number of other factors may have had a negative effect on Iraqi morale, civilian as well as military. The sporadic bombing and shelling of Basra, Khanaqin, and other border cities brought the war home to Iraqi civilians, though its influence on their morale cannot be judged. What is clear is that the government attempted to insulate the population from physical evidence of the conflict and from the sacrifices usually associated with war. Markets were kept stocked with fresh food and consumer items, and construction projects continued throughout Iraq until mid-1982 as if the country were still at peace. Baghdad itself underwent extensive renovation and expansion during the first two years of the war in preparation for a conference of nonaligned nations. Although the conference later was moved to India, Baghdad appeared to be anything but the capital city of a country at war. Did this "all systems normal" approach lull people into believing that their best efforts need not be expended? Iraqi claims of victory must have seemed hollow once it became clear that there was as yet no end to the war and its economic costs became more visible to the general public.

There is also speculation that Iraqi troops became demoralized as the war continued. As early as 1981 and certainly by 1982 the Iraqis were settling into defensive positions, a situation that can have a slowly eroding effect on morale. Iraqi solidiers commented that it was depressing to see so many people die in "human wave assaults" even if they were the enemy. They said the Iranian losses in those attacks were numbing and indescribable. On the other hand, Iraqi troops were frequently rotated, received new weapons, and had time to build strong defenses. They often expressed the feeling that, in any case, they had no other options. Soldiers at the front, compared with those at checkpoints, appeared to be older and militarily more experienced men in their late twenties and early thirties.

More problematic are the training and discipline of the Popular Army. Its size more than doubled after the war began and by 1982 numbered 400,000 or more including many office workers with little or no military experience.[14] In some small villages, police and teachers volunteered

14. The Iraqi News Agency stated on November 17, 1980, that the number of volunteers was increasing at such a rapid rate that there were difficulties in training. FBIS, *Daily Report: MEA*, November 18, 1980, p. E6.

with their career groups to fight at the front; they were frequently assigned to the same unit and suffered heavy casualties in some of the offensives. About 10,000 members of the Popular Army were captured by the Iranians in Khorramshahr while the Iraqi regular army made an orderly retreat, a difficult maneuver that required a great deal of discipline, training, and organization. If heavy losses in the Popular Army indicate the depletion of a significant percentage of the young male population of small communities, they could have important social, economic, and political consequences in the future. Moreover, it is plausible to speculate that the Iraqi regular military may have resented the presence of the Popular Army as an ineffective, perhaps even cumbersome force.

After the Iranian counteroffensives began in September 1981, both the regular military and the Popular Army began to sustain heavy casualties. Funerals became a more common sight, as were women wearing black dresses in mourning. It was said that hardly any family had not experienced the death of at least one member or friend in the hostilities. Moreover, large numbers of Iraqi prisoners of war, many from the Popular Army, reportedly have been executed in Iran by the Revolutionary Guard. Among the reports is one by an Iranian air force officer who defected in October 1982 and asked for political asylum in Great Britain. He stated that he personally had witnessed the execution of some 400 Iraqi prisoners of war only an hour after they had been captured near 'Abadan.[15] It was in these circumstances that Iraq in early 1984 was accused of using chemical weapons against Iran. It cannot be doubted that Iraq resorted to such a measure, risking international censure, for its regular army could not continue to sustain the heavy casualties inflicted by Iran's successive and massive human wave attacks.

External Responses to the War

Factors external to the conflict have a bearing on the success or failure of Iraqi strategy and on the fortunes of Iran. Among them are the

15. See *The Times* (London), January 24, 1983; *Time*, October 11, 1982, p. 31; and *Washington Post*, April 12, 1983.

positions adopted by the United States, the Soviet Union, and other countries during various stages of the hostilities.

The Superpowers and Western Europe

In the West there had been initial worries about the possible disruption of oil supplies and the spread of the Islamic revolution, but policymakers seemed to conclude that little could be done to change the content or direction of Islamic movements, which in any case were not well understood. Both superpowers apparently believed that neither side would win and that the conflict would end in a stalemate. They may also have hoped that the war would offer an opportunity to establish ties with revolutionary Iran, which in purely strategic terms was then considered to be the more valuable of the two Gulf states.

Iran consequently received new armaments in the early part of the war from a variety of sources, including the Soviet Union, though it is not fully known in what quantity. A steady flow of arms to Iran from North Korea was valued in 1982 at between $800 million and $2 billion. Libya and Syria are said to have provided Iran with Soviet military equipment, and Syria may have sent advisers and military intelligence as well. Starting in early 1981, Israel arranged to purchase or supply $50 million to $100 million in spare parts and ammunition for Iran from Western Europe, and itself shipped $50 million to $70 million worth of arms to Iran.[16] Pakistanis and other third party intermediaries sought in Europe and the United States to purchase and transfer, sometimes illegally, spare parts for Iran's predominantly American-equipped military.

By 1983 the situation had changed. The Soviet Union, whose influence in Iran had been sharply curtailed, slowed or halted its arms deliveries to Iran. The crisis in Lebanon also deflected the attention not only of the Soviets but also of the Syrians, who were showing signs of annoyance with their Iranian ally. Israel, fearful of the long-term consequences of Islamic conservatism, is believed to have halted or reduced its aid. The United States began to focus on stopping arms shipments destined for Iran through intermediaries and sought to persuade other countries to stop direct sales to Iran; in one case involving Italy, it reportedly

16. *Defense and Foreign Affairs Daily*, January 20, 1983, pp. 1–2; *New York Times*, March 8, 1982, and *Time*, July 25, 1983, pp. 26–28.

attempted to buy the weapons itself. Although Iran's ties with Pakistan increased and China reportedly sent significant quantities of weapons to Tehran through North Korea, Iran's overall procurement program seemed much less effective than before. To a certain extent this was confirmed by Iran's inability to maintain its air force and by the observation that some of the Iranians killed in their offensives in early 1984 had no weapons.

The Soviet invasion of Afghanistan, Communist subversion in Iran, the American hostage crisis, the Israeli invasion of Lebanon, and consolidation of the Islamic revolution all tended to limit the depth and duration of international feelers toward Iran. Neither superpower had close links to Iran or to Iraq; neither saw much opportunity to end the hostilities nor did they claim to have sufficient leverage to do so. Both ostensibly remained neutral while leaving their options open. Not until later in the war, as they witnessed increasing numbers of arrests of leftist leaders in Iran, did the Soviets apparently decide that relations with Iraq even under the leadership of Saddam Husain were preferable to relations with neither of the countries. Direct shipments of Soviet military supplies to Iraq thus began during 1982.

Before then Iraqi-Soviet relations were far from cordial, even though the Soviet Union had become the major supplier of Iraqi arms after the 1958 revolution. Despite a $1 billion arms agreement between the two countries in 1976, the Iraqi Ba'thists had deliberately sought to diversify their arms suppliers after the rapprochement between Iran and Iraq in 1975. By 1978 Iraq was receiving arms from France, Brazil, Spain, West Germany, Belgium, and Italy; and by 1982 France had become Iraq's second-largest supplier of arms. The harsh Ba'thist suppression of the Iraqi Communist party that began in 1977 hastened the deterioration of relations with the Soviet Union, resulting in a sharp cutback in Soviet military assistance. After the war began, Iraq received Soviet military equipment through third parties, primarily Eastern European countries such as Poland, which then was transferred through countries such as Saudi Arabia.

Since the Iranian government's crackdown on Communists and left-wing sympathizers in 1982, there had been a greater motive for the Soviet Union to resume direct arms shipments to Iraq and for the Iraqis to accept them, particularly since diplomatic overtures to the United States in 1982 and 1983 did not begin to bear fruit until the fall of 1983. While the Iraqi government has publicly welcomed its renewed relationship with Moscow, it is by no means certain that it signifies a renewal of trust or understanding between the two countries or between the Communist party and the Ba'th party.[17]

By early 1984 Iraq's ability to procure weapons had improved considerably. Soviet shipments had resumed in growing quantities. The United States, though officially neutral, was actively discouraging arms shipments to Iran while privately encouraging others to share intelligence with Iraq and provide it with military equipment. The United States, in fact, became increasingly discouraged with Iran after the pro-Iranian terrorist incidents directed at American interests in Lebanon in 1983, including the attack on the marine headquarters, similar terrorist incidents in the Gulf, and Iran's threat to shut the Strait of Hormuz to international shipping in 1984. While professing neutrality, the United States therefore began a gradual "tilt" toward Iraq in late 1983, a tilt that Iraqi officials had been hoping for.

Meanwhile, Iraq has continued its assiduous courtship of Western European countries, particularly France, with which it has discussed or negotiated the purchase of equipment that includes wire-guided missiles and Gazelle and Puma helicopter gunships, Super-Etandard jets, and Exocet air-to-surface missiles. France in fact has taken the lead by capturing half the defense market of the Arab Gulf states, which have applauded its Arab policy and its military, economic, and diplomatic support of Iraq in the war.

The Arab States

The actions of Syria were a major factor in the direction the war took in its early stages. If Iraqi leaders made a full range of contingency plans, they presumably also made some assumptions about Iraq's relations with Syria. The rival Syrian Ba'thist leader, President Hafiz al-Asad,

17. Even the present dominant wing of the Ba'th party had no desire to further alienate the Soviets. A Ba'th official said in an interview in 1981 that when Iraq tried to buy artillery shells in Europe that year, the deal was called off because the United States, which was the real supplier, had insisted on the transfer of an advanced Soviet tank, whose model the official did not specify. Whatever Iraq's relations with the Soviet Union, the official said, it was not feasible to be engaged in such a trade. Information could be deliberately leaked after the transfer that would impugn the trustworthiness of Iraq's leaders and perhaps further isolate Iraq from outside sources of assistance. No evidence exists that any deal was made between the two countries or, indeed, that any agency of the United States was authorized to offer such a deal.

was the first Arab head of state invited to visit Tehran after Khomeini's return. Although he did not go, the invitation was particularly significant in that Asad is a member of an extremist Shi'i sect. Saddam Husain went to Damascus for unannounced reasons on January 30, 1979, and it is tempting to assume that he tried to find a basis for personal concord between himself and Asad. For Iraq, the worst-case scenario would have included Syrian acquiescence in an Iranian victory that might lead either to the formation of a single political bloc between Iraq and Iran, with a combined population of more than 50 million and a potential capacity to produce some 8 million bpd of oil, or to the formation of a land corridor through northern Iraq between Iran and Syria. Even if the Iraqi leaders did not consider these outcomes remotely plausible, it would be surprising if they did not recognize the possible lesser consequences devolving from a Syrian-Iranian alliance. That Husain, in fact, had seen this as a concern is evident from an October 1979 statement in which he said, "If the Iranian revolution had stated that it is against all corrupt Arab elements, then we would have said this revolution is an Islamic one." The Iranians, he went on to say, hypocritically selected some Arab nations as allies and rejected the others as corrupt.[18]

Syria, the country most similar to Iraq in its economic, political, and social life, could have offered critical support but did not do so. That Syrian President Hafiz al-Asad and his immediate supporters formally sided with Iran was to a great extent a consequence of the rivalry between the Ba'th regimes, a rivalry that reached serious proportions in 1979 when Iraq, under the guidance of Saddam Husain, withdrew from a planned union of the two countries and subsequently announced the discovery of an abortive coup attempt ostensibly aided by the Syrians. Earlier, Iraq alleged that Syria was partly responsible for instigating civil unrest in al-Najaf and Karbala in 1977; and when the Iraqi embassy in Beirut was destroyed in December 1981, Syria again was considered partly responsible. During the war, Syria has openly assisted Iraqi dissident groups, arranging meetings in Damascus and making daily propaganda broadcasts. As noted, Syria also is reported to have sent military equipment and perhaps even advisers to Iran.

More important, Iraqi shipments of oil through Syria after the war had started were substantially reduced, frequently sabotaged on or close to Syrian territory, and entirely halted by the Syrians in 1982, thereby

18. FBIS, *Daily Report: MEA*, October 17, 1979, p. E4.

facilitating an Iranian attempt to place an economic stranglehold on Iraq. Iranian bombing in the early months of the war resulted in extensive damage to Iraqi oil installations, many of which have been repaired, although the proximity of the southern oilfields to the fighting is believed to have caused them to remain idle. As a result, oil production and exports have shifted once again to northern Iraq. Total oil production in the early stage of the war was less than one-fifth of Iraq's prewar production of approximately 3.5 million bpd, and had risen to only one-third of production by 1984. In the summer of 1983 Iranian officials, including Hashemi Rafsanjani, speaker of the Iranian parliament, began to claim that their offensives in the Kurdish region were a preliminary to cutting off Iraq's sole remaining outlet for oil shipments, the Iraqi pipeline through Turkey.[19]

To what extent could Iraq depend on assistance from other Arab states once the war had begun? It was said in the United Arab Emirates, for example, that the war was unfortunate because "it is a war between a brother and a friend." Many of the Arab governing elites nevertheless were sympathetic to Iraq, perhaps even more so because they feared domestic repercussions from the Islamic revolution in their own countries—especially the Gulf states, several of which had large percentages or concentrated groups of Shi'is. Of an estimated 750 million Muslims in the world, some 85 million are Shi'is, or 11 percent of the total. Estimates of the number of Shi'is in the Gulf vary widely because of political sensitivities, but the best approximations are as follows: Iraq, about 50 to 55 percent; Bahrain, 50 to 60 percent; Kuwait, 15 to 30 percent; Qatar, 10 to 20 percent; and the United Arab Emirates, anywhere from 3 to 15 percent. Although Saudi Arabia's Shi'is number only 5 to 10 percent of the population, they comprise more than 98 percent of al-Qatif and an estimated 50 percent of the population around al-Ahsa in eastern Arabia. Some states, such as Kuwait, have in their labor force a large number of Shi'is of Persian descent who have lived there for decades as well as many Iranian citizens. The merchants of Dubai in the United Arab Emirates also have had a long history of profitable trade and, one presumes, associated personal ties with merchants in the Iranian ports.

19. See John Rossant, "Iraqi Oil in the 1980s," *Petroleum Information International Special Report* (Houston, 1983); BBC, *Summary of World Broadcasts*, ME/7399/i, July 30, 1983; and *Wall Street Journal*, August 24, 1983. Turkey reportedly told Iran that it would oppose an attempt to interrupt the flow of oil in this pipeline because it relied on Iraqi oil for part of its own needs, some 115,000 bpd in March 1984.

Whether the Arab governing elites, all Sunni, who supported Iraq in the war were disturbed by the Islamic revolution or simply relieved that their sometimes threatening neighbor, Iraq, had turned its attentions elsewhere, there is speculation that at least some of the Arab states were aware of the approaching war and may actually have given Iraq encouragement. From the time Saddam Husain took the reins of the Iraqi government in July 1979, he was in frequent contact with all the major states—Saudi Arabia, Kuwait, Morocco, Jordan, the United Arab Emirates, Oman, the Yemen Arab Republic, Sudan, and Bahrain—that were to offer verbal if not material support to Iraq in the war. A chronological review of visits and messages exchanged between the heads of state or their emissaries and Saddam Husain during the last two months before the war shows that King Husain of Jordan sent a message on July 1, 1980, and made several personal trips to Baghdad during 1980; Shaikh Surur bin Al Nahayan arrived on July 28 as a special envoy of Shaikh Zaid, the ruler of the United Arab Emirates; Saddam Husain made an unprecedented two-day trip to Saudi Arabia starting on August 4, the first visit by an Iraqi head of state to Saudi Arabia in twenty-two years; a message was delivered from the shaikh of Kuwait on August 10; Shaikh Surur returned with a personal message from Shaikh Zaid on August 23; and on September 2 the Bahraini prime minister arrived in Baghdad. Neither Saudi Arabia nor Jordan had been particularly friendly toward the Iraqi Ba'thists, yet Saddam Husain maintained almost monthly contacts with the leaders of both these countries after late 1979.

Additional contacts were made in the military sphere. Iraqi Defense Minister 'Adnan Khairallah went to Kuwait and Bahrain in September 1979 to discuss freedom of navigation in the Gulf and the importance of noninterference in the internal affairs of Gulf states. There were also exchanges of information between Iraqi commanders of border troops and their counterparts from Romania in October 1979, from Turkey in November, from East Berlin in February 1980, and from Yugoslavia in March and April. The Bahraini heir apparent and defense minister arrived to talk with Iraq's defense minister on February 17, 1980, Jordan's chief of staff arrived on April 10 for talks with Saddam Husain, and during Shaikh Surur's visit on July 28 he was greeted by an Iraqi staff general.

Between 1979 and 1984 a number of actions were taken against the so-called moderate Arab governments that were attributable to Iranians or to supporters of Khomeini and the Islamic revolution. Demonstrations and smaller disturbances took place in Mecca and al-Madina in which the Saudi authorities arrested a number of Iranians and other supporters of Khomeini, and there were demonstrations among the Shi'is of Saudi Arabia's eastern province in November 1979 and early 1980. Broadcasts from Tehran declared that the corrupt Sa'udi government would fall next after that of Saddam Husain. The United Arab Emirates arrested Iranians trying to enter the country illegally for unknown purposes. In Kuwait, whose population is estimated to be from 15 to 30 percent Shi'a and includes 60,000 Iranian nationals in the labor force, there were pro-Khomeini demonstrations. There were also calls for segregation of the sexes in the university, and women began to wear the veil in public. Alarmed by these trends, the Kuwaiti government—which had refused Khomeini a permit to enter the country in 1978—expelled a prominent Shi'i prayer leader in 1983 for his inflammatory support of the Islamic revolution. During the ensuing demonstrations, several Iranians were arrested and arms caches were found. In Qatar, pro-Khomeini demonstrations were sparked by the death of a Shi'i. In Lebanon there were incidents pitting pro-Khomeini Iranian Shi'is against the Lebanese army. They posted pictures of Khomeini on many buildings around their headquarters in Baalbek, and they tried to hold pro-Khomeini demonstrations in Syria. Even in Pakistan, Iranians belonging to an Islamic organization were arrested for possessing explosives believed to be destined for the French embassy because of France's commercial ties to Iraq.

The most dramatic act undertaken by pro-Khomeini revolutionaries against an established government, however, was the coup attempt in mid-December 1981 in Bahrain, a country whose population of some 360,000 is 50 to 60 percent Shi'a. The attempt was led by a Shi'i religious leader whom the Bahraini authorities had expelled in 1979 for expounding radical views and who had previously been arrested in the United Arab Emirates. The coup group consisted of sixty guerrillas, all under thirty, furnished with arms and money; most were Bahrainis, but they also included a dozen Saudis, a Yemeni, and an Omani. Another twelve Bahrainis who were implicated in the plot are reported to have traveled in Iran before the coup attempt or to have sought refuge there afterward. Under questioning, some of the guerrillas said that the Iranian navy had been expected to help consolidate the coup. According to subsequent reports, corps of revolutionaries were being trained in South Yemen, Libya, and Iran. Significantly, although the Ba'th ideology of pan-Arabism led to the unique policy of admitting Arabs into Iraq without visas, in late December 1980 Iraq imposed visa requirements for citizens of Bahrain. Hence it is not surprising that the Gulf Cooperation Council, representing Bahrain, Qatar, Saudi Arabia, Kuwait, the United Arab Emirates, and Oman, joined together in early February 1982 to denounce acts of sabotage by Iran aimed at destablilizing the countries of the Gulf.

Later that month, King Husain of Jordan summarized the underlying cause of the Iran-Iraq war and the reason most of the "moderate" Arab states supported Iraq:

I am worried of what I believe is a very sinister, almost criminal attempt to create a rift between Muslims, between Shi'ites and Sunnis. This we saw fairly obviously at the very beginnings [of the Islamic revolution] and then obviously Iraq was a target. Fortunately Iraq and the area has withstood this attempt and I hope that it will not result in any success because it would be devastating. It would cause disintegration and far greater tragedy than this area has seen than any other. . . . Fortunately Iraq held as one nation and to my way of thinking—and that is an idea and opinion shared by many in the area—Iraq is a front line, not only for us in Jordan but for the entire area, for the Gulf, Saudi Arabia, and Oman as well.[20]

If any doubt remained about the position of those countries toward Iran and Iraq, whatever their misgivings about the war or their ability or willingness to change the course of events, it was dispelled by Crown Prince 'Abdullah bin 'Abd al-'Aziz Al Sa'ud of Saudi Arabia, who said in March 1983, "Iran cannot enter Baghdad because that would mean an all-out Arab war with Iran."[21]

Iraq well may have expected a more public display of support by the Arab states, such as open transfers of military supplies, although Oman and Saudi Arabia reportedly did store some Iraqi planes in the early days of the war. Some Arabs in fact complained privately in 1981 that their offers of support were constrained by pressure from the United States, whose government foresaw a spread of the war if the Arab states intervened in a direct and significant manner. Therefore, Arab support was generally limited to financial aid from the Gulf states and to facilitation of the shipment of both military and consumer goods, particularly by Jordan, Saudi Arabia, and Kuwait. While there was no explicitly stated effort to hide this cooperation, all the concerned parties tried to deemphasize its significance. Although a Western businessman with long working experience in Saudi Arabia confided that the Saudis "are busting their guts to help Iraq and in ways you cannot even guess," consistent public pronouncements of support came only from Jordan. News of other aid, including financial assistance, leaked out only gradually. During interviews in Iraq between May and July 1981, some Iraqi officials denied that there were monetary loans, and those few officials who acknowledged their existence did so without further discussion. Iraq apparently was concerned to keep its record of financial solvency intact as well as to avoid further entangling its new Arab friends in the event of retaliation by Iran.

Despite criticism by some elements in the Gulf countries, the size of the financial assistance extended to Iraq by the Gulf states as the war continued reflected the depth of their governments' concern that the consequences of the war would not remain territorially or politically confined. They, like the Iraqis, may not have foreseen the length or the cost of the war, but having become involved, found it difficult to extricate themselves and by 1984 saw that the outcome would deeply affect their own interests. It has been estimated in the press that the war cost Iraq approximately $1 billion a month, substantially depleting by late 1982 Iraqi reserves estimated before the war to be $35 billion. By March 1982 the members of the Gulf Cooperation Council were reported to have extended interest-free loans and grants to Iraq amounting to $25 billion, though an American official stated off the record that the figure was closer to $10 billion.[22] In addition, Saudi Arabia and Kuwait apparently agreed to sell some 300,000 bpd of their own oil on Iraq's account, an act to be reciprocated later.

Construction projects in Iraq could thus continue with no noticeable slowdown until mid-1982, when compromises were made in ambitious social and economic development projects. An increasing reluctance on the part of the other Gulf states to continue their monetary support at its previous level at that time may have been a result of the weakening oil market, which caused them to postpone or cancel some of their own projects. Moreover, it is unclear whether Iraq used the Gulf funds solely to support its military effort or diverted them to economic projects in order to diminish internal criticism of the costs of war. If the latter is so,

22. The secrecy with which Iraq generally has surrounded its financial affairs makes any figure difficult to confirm. Nevertheless, during an off-the-record interview with someone familiar with Kuwait, it was stated that by 1982 Kuwait alone had lent Iraq some $8 billion. One would expect Saudi support at least to equal that amount. This still excludes Qatar and the United Arab Emirates, which also have contributed to Iraq.

it may have been an irritant to the other states and a factor leading to reduction of their support, particularly in light of their own austerity moves. By the fall of 1983, however, fears of Iranian breakthrough and increased pro-Iranian terrorist activity caused Gulf financial aid to resume at reportedly high levels. Arab verbal support of Iraq also grew.

Despite their initial hesitance and the subsequent fluctuations in their aid, Iraq has sought to maintain good relations with Saudi Arabia, Kuwait, Jordan, and Egypt, all of which have furnished military and consumer goods during the war. When Iraqis in 1982 were asked, for example, what they thought of Saudi Arabia's refusal to accept a number of Iranians, including at least one military pilot, who had tried to defect in a commandeered aircraft, they were surprisingly uncritical: "They [the Saudis] have their own problems and this we can understand." In the case of Jordan, Iraq tried to strengthen its relations by making a gift of some thirty American tanks captured from Iran early in the conflict.

Egypt's support of Iraq may reflect some of its own domestic concerns, such as the presence in Egypt of numerous extreme Islamic movements, as well as the changing political configuration among Arab states in the wake of the Camp David agreement. Signs of an emerging relationship with Iraq began under President Anwar Sadat with the sale to Iraq of ammunition valued at $500 million. Military-related sales by Egypt to Iraq have continued under President Hosni Mubarak, who also has given Iraq strong verbal support. These military sales are thought to have totaled some $2.7 billion since 1981. Egyptian pilots have even been rumored to have participated in the war, although this has never been confirmed. Iraq for its part has shown willingness to resume full diplomatic relations. Since January 1983, when Tariq 'Aziz met Egypt's minister of state for foreign affairs, Butros Ghali, there have been steady diplomatic and trade contacts between the two countries, including a meeting between President Mubarak and Tariq 'Aziz in July 1983 in Cairo. In January 1984 Iraq sponsored the initiative to invite Egypt to rejoin the Islamic Conference Organization, and in March 1984 Iraqi officials announced that they were preparing a formula for Egypt's readmission to the Arab League.

The War Becomes Intractable

Nations presumably initiate hostilities because they calculate that a successful outcome will achieve a more lasting state of security. Security, however, depends on reconciliation, which may prove elusive if the justification for a war changes during its course, if the stakes for settlement increase as the war continues, or if negotiation or compromise would undermine the raisons d'être of the contending parties.

For both Iran and Iraq it is difficult either to capitulate or to compromise because of the ideological premises of the ruling elites and because of the social and political implications of the war. The idealism, rhetoric, and philosophy of both regimes have not only inhibited negotiations but also polarized a dispute that might otherwise have been more amenable to settlement. Neither Saddam Husain and the Ba'th party nor Ayatullah Khomeini and the Islamic republicans could readily negotiate their own demise or easily abandon the principles for which they fought because of the ever-growing need to justify the sacrifices made in the war.

Numerous peace initiatives have come to nought, among them those of the Islamic Conference, Algeria, Pakistan, the Gulf Cooperation Council, the United Nations, the nonaligned movement, the Palestine Liberation Organization, Kuwait, and the Organization of Petroleum Exporting Countries. The Algerian initiative expired in the crash of the Algerian negotiating team's plane on May 3, 1982, a tragedy for which Iraq has been generally assumed to be responsible. Iraqi proposals for a truce were rebuffed by Iran, which declared that it would not negotiate until the government of Saddam Husain had fallen and Iraq admitted its responsibility for the war. Iranian officials said this would be the prelude to the establishment of an Islamic government in Iraq, then in Kuwait and the other Arab Gulf countries.[23] When Iraq later agreed to a commission of inquiry, Iran refused to accept it; and when Iraq sought to arrange for the families of Iranian prisoners of war to visit them in Iraq, this too was rejected.[24] Exchanges of prisoners, such as one in May 1983, have been extremely limited. After the disastrous Gulf oil spill in early March 1983, whose origins have been attributed variously to a storm, a tanker accident, or Iraqi bombing, the Iraqis proposed a ceasefire, provided that it extended the length of the war front. Iran, apparently wishing to place maximum domestic strain on the Iraqi government, rebuffed the initiative and launched another offensive.

23. For an example of such statements, see *Wall Street Journal*, December 9, 1983.
24. To accommodate the visiting Iranian families, the Iraqi government in 1982 apparently vacated a new hotel in Samarra of its residents, mostly foreign businessmen and their families. The businessmen rented lodgings elsewhere, and when the Iranian visitors failed to appear the immediate loss to the hotel was 17,000 Iraqi dinars (about $85,000 at the time), which the government reimbursed.

Although a formal set of Iranian demands had not emerged by the summer of 1983, the conditions for settlement most frequently mentioned were the return of occupied Iranian territory, the withdrawal of Iraqi troops, the payment of war reparations ranging from $50 billion to $150 billion, the return to Iraq of Persian Shi'is who had been expelled, and the establishment of an international—some have said Islamic—tribunal to try Saddam Husain as a war criminal.

From Iraq's perspective, these were not realistic preconditions for negotiations. Not only did the Iraqis doubt that the contending factions in Iran could unite in support of a firm negotiating position, but they also questioned whether the superpowers wanted an end to the war, particularly after Israel began sending armaments to Iran whether or not they were in sufficient quantities to influence the course of the war. For Iraq to accept the 40,000 to 120,000 Persian Shi'is who had been expelled from Iraq was completely unacceptable in that this group would represent the introduction of a fifth column.[25] Finally, the Iraqi Ba'thists had the preeminent objective of preserving the party.

This last reason was the most important and may explain why Saddam Husain had not resigned by late 1983. Although many Westerners who were weighing the options for a negotiated settlement felt that such an act would be a major concession to Khomeini, this assumption may have reflected more their own hope of placating Khomeini than an understanding of the dynamics of Iraqi internal politics. Husain's resignation in 1981 or 1982 might simply have been viewed as a chink in Iraq's armor, particularly Ba'thist armor, and paved the way for another new demand by Iran. The dictates of Islamic conservatism as espoused by extreme elements influential in Tehran had narrowed the scope for accommodation, resulting, for example, in the choice Iranian leaders made when they crossed Iraq's border in July 1982. By 1983, few Ba'thists or even non-Ba'thists may have wished to replace Husain because doing so would have been politically suicidal so long as the Iranians remained intransigent. While military officers may have resented the civilian Ba'thists' conduct of the war, there is no evidence that any of them

25. In 1981 the government promulgated regulations on places of worship, appointments to the clergy, the content of Friday sermons, and other religious matters, which even Christian Iraqis have viewed as an attempt to control Shi'i activities. In 1983 the Iraqi government also executed a number of members of the prominent Shi'i religious family, al-Hakim, of al-Najaf. When Iraqi dissidents on Cyprus symbolically formed a council to overthrow Husain, the announcement was made from Tehran by the Shi'i religious leader Muhammad Baqir al-Hakim, whose father had been the leading Shi'i leader in Iraq between 1960 and 1970.

thought the Iranian threat was not real. Indeed, Iranian statements clearly indicated that Iran's goal was to set up an Islamic government in Iraq.

Another cause of frustration was that Iraqis believed all key decisions in Iranian domestic and foreign affairs were made or heavily influenced by Khomeini himself. They did not expect him to compromise his extreme Islamic conservative stance, or his distrust of Arab nationalism in general and of Iraqi Ba'thists in particular. Khomeini was, in their view, a crusader oblivious of costs and, worse still, because of ill health and jealous attendants, removed from the realities of life around him.

In a speech delivered in May 1982, Khomeini stressed the inevitability of Iran's struggle and its responsibility to Islam when he related a story he had heard about a "12 or 13 year old boy on one of the war fronts who, having lost an arm, had without hesitation picked it up and headed for the battlefront. . . . I do hope that Islam will be promoted . . . as a preamble for the reappearance of the imam mahdi [the return of the last hidden imam]."[26] Iranian Prime Minister Mir-Husain Musavi also made a statement in May 1982, after Iranian troops had retaken Khorramshahr, that left little doubt about Iranian motives and objectives:

It is certainly because of this [the victory of Khorramshahr] that we will witness a fundamental upheaval in Muslim countries. The victory of Khorramshahr is in no way a territorial victory. The effects are not limited to one country. This is not the case since this war with Saddam's regime has become very symbolic among the countries of the region and Muslim countries—a war between Islam and blasphemy. Therefore, this victory is the victory of Islam over blasphemy, and no doubt this victory will heighten Islamic liberation movements. We are very happy about this. We have always said that if there are regimes in the region which are just and popular they should rejoice in this victory and not be saddened. But this great movement will, no doubt, destroy or at least weaken all powers subservient to worldwide oppression.[27]

It was undoubtedly the frustration that Iraq's leaders felt over Iran's uncompromising position that led to a meeting in Paris between Iraq's Tariq 'Aziz and the Iranian leftist opposition leader Mas'ud Rajavi on January 9, 1983, after which both sides issued a statement of agreement on a number of issues related to the war and future relations between Iran and Iraq. This meeting was evidence of the Iraqi leaders' wish to appear conciliatory toward an Iranian political group they considered capable of establishing a mutual and binding basis of agreement.

26. FBIS, *Daily Report: SA*, May 26, 1982, p. 18.
27. FBIS, *Daily Report: SA*, June 1, 1982, p. 14.

Prospects for an end to the war thus remain constrained. As Crown Prince 'Abdullah of Saudi Arabia said in March 1983, "The war will remain limited to a border war of attrition until Iran's outlook on the nature of things changes."[28] This remains perhaps the most accurate assessment of current events.

A Time of Testing

The war presents a systemic challenge to Iraq and Iran as well as a challenge to the ideologies of their respective governments: Arab nationalism and Islamic conservatism. The challenges are complicated by the ancient differentiations between Arabs and Persians and between Shi'i and Sunni Muslims—differentiations that have never remained static, at times being negligible and at other times the source of intense hostility and armed conflict. Today, as in the past, there is a constant and evolving interplay of the factors affecting political affiliation and legitimacy, social identity, and economic exchange.

Both challenges to Iraq have immediate and long-term consequences for the Iraqi population, for the Ba'th party, and for Saddam Husain. Interviews with Iraqis both within and outside the country suggested that the Iraqi people generally felt as of 1982 that the war was justified but that its conduct had been poor. Many criticized the Iranians for their intransigence in refusing to negotiate. By May 1982 the Iraqi government was trying to portray the war as successful because the Iranian threat had been substantially reduced. Undoubtedly, however, the war has had a significant psychological impact that is less the result of economic sacrifices, from which the population at first was carefully insulated, than of knowledge that Iraq has suffered heavy losses in killed, wounded, and captured and that Iranian forces remain within striking distance of Basra, Khanaqin, and other urban centers. By early 1984 the possibility of an Iranian breakthrough that could sever Basra from Iraq and place Iran within reach of Kuwait was being seriously discussed in the West. Iraqi dead by that time were conservatively estimated to number 65,000 men.

If the Iraqi people doubted the wisdom of the war, they did not lack

---

28. FBIS, *Daily Report: MEA*, March 23, 1983, p. C5.

evidence of the Iranian threat to Iraq's internal stability. On March 28, 1982, for example, the president of Iran said:

The Iranian nation and government cannot be indifferent toward Iraq's affairs. . . . We are related by race, traditions, and religion. . . . No other government or nation in the world except Iran has the right to be concerned about Iraq's future. . . . The future government of Iraq should be an Islamic and popular one. . . . The policy of the *velayet-e faqih* [the twelfth Imam's vice regent, that is, Imam Khomeini] will be Iraq's future policy, and the leader of the Islamic nation is Imam Khomeini. There is no difference between the two nations of Iran and Iraq in accepting the Imam as the leader and following the Imam and his line. Government and state officials are limited to international borders but the Imam is not limited by geographical borders.[29]

Similar statements by Iran's religious leaders gave Iraqis little reason to suppose that Iran would refrain from invading Iraq or would cease to subvert the Iraqi population in an effort to overthrow an Arab nationalist government and replace it with an Islamic conservative one.

Prolongation of the war and the nature of its outcome undoubtedly will affect internal opposition to the Ba'th government, particularly because many of the opposition movements are religious in orientation and receive support from outside Iraq. The geographic concentration of Iraq's religious and ethnic groups makes this possibility especially worrisome for the Iraqi government. Terrorist activity by the illegal al-Da'wa movement has diminished since the start of the war, but it has not ceased. In August 1982 the explosion of a car bomb outside the Ministry of Planning in Baghdad killed more than twenty people, and other car bombings occurred in Baghdad in December 1982 and April 1983. On the whole, however, sectarian groups appeared to subsume their complaints and to identify with the larger interests of the Iraqi state, at least in the early months of the war.[30] The government encouraged this trend in a number of ways: in late 1982 it exempted Kurds from military service until mid-1983, when it rescinded the order in anticipation of an Iranian offensive in the northern Kurdish sector;[31] it advocated

29. BBC, *Summary of World Broadcasts,* ME/6992/i, March 31, 1982.

30. During visits to Karbala and al-Najaf in the summer of 1981, I saw only a few troops in the latter city outside the entrance to the main mosque, and no military equipment was visible in or around either city.

31. Despite unconfirmed rumors about a general who had mutinied in the north during 1982, foreign diplomats stationed in Baghdad have said that even the Kurds were perplexed by this order. See also BBC, *Summary of World Broadcasts,* ME/7257/A/9, February 14, 1983; and FBIS, *Daily Report: MEA,* June 27, 1983, p. E3. Anticipation of an Iranian offensive in the north may also have caused the Iraqis to approve a "limited" thrust by the Turkish military into northern Iraq to disrupt guerrilla activities on that border in late May 1983.

amnesty for men who had failed to enlist or had deserted from the military; and it excused Iraqi prisoners of war from payment of their debts and their taxes. In late 1983 and early 1984 the government began to engage the Kurdish guerrilla leader, Talabani, in a truce agreement; it allowed military officers an increasingly visible role on television and in interviews with the Western media; and it started to make overtures to political opposition groups such as the Communists.

During 1983 President Husain referred on several occasions to the Islamic character of Iraq, undoubtedly in response to domestic pressures arising from the war. It is important to recall the relationship between such statements and the basis for the legitimacy of the Ba'th party, which differs from the popularly based Islamic movements in having a structure and decisionmaking system that are highly formalized and institutionalized. Its ideology is perhaps more highly developed than that of any other party in the Middle East, and it is a party of elites in the sense of education and long-term participation in the party. One could not advance in the Ba'th hierarchy or the government bureaucracy without being literate. Hence the Ba'thists' emphasis on the Literacy Campaign, which was to make Ba'thist ideology and party membership more widely accessible, and on the "new Iraqi man," who would identify first with the state of Iraq and second with whatever other associations—religious or ethnic—he might have. Progress toward the latter goal was facilitated by intermarriage between Shi'is and Sunnis and by the loosening of local ties that accompanied migration to the cities. As one Iraqi said in expressing his frustration with war, "If only Iraq could have had another ten years of leadership under the Ba'th, then stability might be more predictable." It is uncertain to what extent the Islamic revolution in Iran will threaten the social and economic reforms achieved by the Iraqi Ba'thists during the past decade or, for that matter, those attained by other governing elites in the Middle East.

Another difficulty stemming from the war is the economic pressure it places on Iraq. Oil revenues totaled approximately $21 billion in 1979 and some $25 billion in the first nine months of 1980, but dropped to only $9 billion to $10 billion annually in 1981 and 1982. The deterioration has been manifested in several ways: the number of foreign laborers has decreased; inflation was estimated to be running at 20 percent in 1983; development projects generally have been scaled down; defense contractors are being given preferred payment status; new contractors have been asked to find their own financing or to cancel projects, while contractors expecting payment in 1984 have been asked to accept a two-year delay; and some consumer goods have been in short supply. Basra, more than Iraq's other urban centers, has suffered because "the city's raison d'être has disappeared—for three and one half years it has been a port city without a port."[32]

On the whole, however, analysts find several reasons to expect 1984 to be a better year for Iraq. European countries (especially France), Arab organizations, and the United States have begun to assist Iraq through credits and loans, refinancing of debts, and agricultural credits. The Europeans in particular see the commercial benefit of maintaining good ties with a country that imported heavily from Europe in the past and is expected to do so again. The Iraqis themselves have cut back on nonessential projects, linked oil exports to the approval of new contracts, and arranged barter deals. The fact that some projects begun in the 1970s, such as cement plants, were coming on line in 1983 and 1984 will assist in Iraqi development and reconstruction.

Moreover, Iraq has met with some success in loosening the economic stranglehold imposed by the war, especially after Syria stopped Iraqi oil shipments across its territory in 1982. By January 1984 oil shipments through Turkey had risen from no more than 650,000 bpd in 1980 to 850,000 bpd, a figure expected to increase by another 100,000 bpd or more by early 1985. During 1983 an additional 120,000 bpd were shipped by truck through Turkey and Jordan, before road damage in the latter country caused shipments through it to cease. As noted earlier, Kuwait and Saudi Arabia reportedly have also produced some 300,000 bpd on Iraq's behalf. Meanwhile, negotiations continued in 1984 on the proposed pipelines through Saudi Arabia and through Jordan. The latter pipeline has received particular attention from the U.S. government, which believes that it would help to stabilize relations among Arab moderates as well as diversify oil transportation routes away from the strategically vulnerable Gulf. The Jordanian line, however, would require fourteen to twenty months to complete.

Less clear than these signs of improvement is the extent to which Iraqis as individuals perceive the financial situation created by the war as personal deprivation, or whether interest groups can exploit it as a source of discontent to rally political opposition against the present government. If the war were to end soon and large reparations were not demanded, the inflation rate could be expected to slow and Iraqi oil production to rise according to domestic needs.

32. *Middle East Economic Digest*, March 16, 1984, p. 25.

The most serious threat to the civilian Ba'thist leadership is and will remain the military, a group that has a history of institutional development and political awareness dating from the early days of the Iraqi state. It was involved in the operation of all Iraqi governments from 1958 until the Ba'th civilians consolidated their authority in the 1970s. The fact that no political affiliations are allowed in the military except with the Ba'th party and the possibility that some officers are promoted for loyalty to the party rather than for professional competence are undoubtedly demoralizing to many otherwise loyal officers. Dissatisfaction may also rise from the fact that Saddam Husain's brother-in-law, 'Adnan Khairallah, heads the military establishment. During the war, moreover, two Iraqi generals and one commander have been executed for "treasonous actions" related mainly to the withdrawal of Iraqi forces from Khorramshahr.[33] This action by the civilian government gives rise to questions of a future rift between civilians and the military and whether the military has approved of civilian conduct of the war. Therefore, although the military is carefully watched for signs of disloyalty, its organizational ability and ready access to force make the army the likeliest threat to the Ba'th party, especially now that it has been tested and toughened in the war.

Saddam Husain himself faces opposition from political factions and coalitions within the Ba'th party itself. Neither the government nor the country is monolithic. Husain's base of political support shifted constantly in peacetime and has probably done so in war. Within the Iraqi context he represents a moderate element. His moves toward the West, his practical departures from radical rhetoric, his opposition to military involvement in government, his attempts to deemphasize sectarian differences, his efforts to continue the move toward nonalignment or diversification of dependent relationships with foreign powers, and his role in the establishment of the Kurdish Autonomous Region and in the conclusion of the Algiers Declaration of 1975 have been variously perceived as controversial by other elements in the party. Certainly the war and its high human and material costs will affect Husain's leadership, perhaps leading to his and his close associates' overthrow by other elements of the Ba'th party or by the military, or to a decrease in his maneuverability in domestic and foreign affairs. Certainly there will be future disagreements over what the goals of the war were or should have been, even if the leaders agreed initially on what was to be done.

33. This was confirmed in my interviews with Saddam Husain and Taha Yasin Ramadhan.

If Saddam Husain is not a military strategist, he is certainly a political survivor with a strong party machine backing him. Although he was the target of several assassination attempts in the summer of 1982,[34] one must recall that before the war Husain was a popular leader perceived by many Iraqis to be young, energetic, alert to the needs of his people, and a major driving force behind Iraq's economic prosperity. A non-Ba'thist in Iraq remarked that Iraqis at first had been very doubtful, even fearful of a Ba'thist government after the 1968 revolution, but that confidence in the government had increased during the 1970s because the economy improved and because the Ba'thists refrained from the excesses they had displayed during the early 1960s. It remains to be seen how well Iraqis will remember this if the war drags on.

Ironically, while protraction of the war would place greater strains on Iraqi domestic affairs, it might bring greater safety for Husain if opposition elements see him as a useful scapegoat when the war ends or simply because no one else sees a solution to the current stalemate other than Khomeini's death. Regardless of the war's conclusion, Husain will continue to confront pressures created by Syria and by his complex relationship with the Soviet Union, both of which will affect his policy decisions and perhaps his domestic political support. The postwar period thus will bring the greatest challenges not only to the political career of Saddam Husain but also to the Ba'th party.

34. Saddam Husain himself and other members of the Ba'th leadership have admitted that there have been attempts against Husain's life. It is also reported in a book recently published in Baghdad that there have been a number of plots, seven of which actually were attempted. See FBIS, *Daily Report: MEA,* May 26, 1983, p. E1.

CHAPTER SEVEN

Iraq in the Future

THE political uncertainties that will confront "Iraq the nation" and "Iraq the state" in the aftermath of the war with Iran are complex and numerous, and some are not well understood. One thing is certain: the recurring themes in Iraqi history that were discussed earlier in this study will continue to influence the policy of the Iraqi government in the near and distant future regardless of the ideological position of the ruling elite. Certain legitimate strategic concerns of the state, arising from its geographic, social, and historical context, will remain unresolved by the war. Iraqis will perceive ever more acutely the frontier role of their state as the eastern flank of the Arab world, bordering two large non-Arab neighbors: Turkey and Iran. Iraq in 1978 was a country susceptible to the export of Islamic revolutionary doctrine. Whether this in retrospect was a valid and serious concern became after the start of the war a topic on which outsiders could only speculate. What is known is that cultural, ethnic, and religious associations in Iraq will remain strong, vibrant forces in domestic politics, though it is perhaps too early to tell how much the war has fostered an Iraqi nationalism or has intensified other symbols of social and political identity that could lead to the adoption of other "isms" or to a greater fragmentation of Iraq's pluralistic groups. The state will remain economically vulnerable because it is virtually landlocked. Oil shipments and the distribution rights of the water resources of the Tigris-Euphrates system, for example, will continue to remain contingent on Iraq's good relations with its neighbors. Iraqi ruling elites will undoubtedly continue to seek means, such as nonalignment or heavy dependence on a single political bloc, to escape this dilemma.

Iraq as a Regional and Global Actor

Despite these uncertainties, Iraq will remain an important actor within the region and be of significance to the United States, Europe, and Japan for the rest of this century. Its importance stems from the size of its oil reserves and potential oil revenues, from its potential for diversifying its economy, from the coupling of its strategic position with its historical role in the region, and from the ramifications of the war with Iran.

The size of Iraq's oil resources is the most readily apparent of these factors. Iraq's proven reserves—31 billion barrels, with some Western estimates ranging above 100 billion—may be second only to those of Saudi Arabia in the Middle East and are among the largest in the world. The estimated reserves increased during the 1970s, driven by technological advances in oil exploration and political demands to intensify the search. According to an estimate made in 1981, the forty-four known oilfields in Iraq contain some 274 billion barrels of which 93 billion barrels are recoverable.[1] Iraq's minister of oil stated on February 20, 1983, that Iraq's proven reserves are 50 billion barrels and that there are an additional 46 billion barrels of estimated reserves. Before the war, Iraqi production—approximately 3.5 million bpd out of a total capacity of 4 million bpd—was 11 percent of the OPEC total for 1979, or about 5 percent of world production. Because decisions on levels of production have been linked to ambitious Ba'thist plans for social and economic development, Iraq is one of the few Arab oil producers that gradually increased productive capacity as well as production during the 1970s, guaranteeing shipments to favored Western European countries.

Iraq simultaneously experienced a steady rise in its oil revenues from $5.7 billion in 1974 to approximately $21 billion in 1979. Increased revenues supported increased expenditures. Iraq's budget for 1980 allocated about $19 billion, or half the total, to development projects. Before the outbreak of war in September 1980, oil revenues for the year had already totaled some $25 billion. Despite rising government expenditures, Iraq's current account surplus grew from $3 billion in 1977 to an

1. John Rossant, "Iraq Sets 8 Million BD-Goal, Confirms Massive Oil Reserves," *Petroleum Information International*, vol. 1 (December 7, 1981), pp. 1–2.

estimated $20 billion in 1980, and its foreign exchange reserves from $6.7 billion in 1977 to around $35 billion in 1980 prior to the war. Iraq was then thought to have invested a major portion of its foreign assets, half of them in American dollars, in countries belonging to the Organization for Economic Cooperation and Development (OECD). Until 1980 this surplus was invested conservatively, and some Western financial analysts, recognizing the country's careful and balanced investment policies, predicted that Iraq would continue to make even longer-term investments and to expand its banking facilities.

Because of the large surpluses Iraq accumulated in the latter half of the 1970s and because the government wished to diversify its economic and political relationships and obtain Western technology in order to increase the productivity of its labor force, there was a pronounced shift in Iraq's trading patterns. The Soviet Union was Iraq's largest trading partner in 1973, but by 1975 it provided less than 10 percent of Iraq's imports. In 1978 some 75 percent of Iraqi imports originated in OECD countries, primarily Japan, West Germany, France, and Italy, while 73 percent of Iraqi exports were purchased by OECD countries. The United States exported to Iraq goods worth $442 million in 1979, $724 million in 1980, and $914 million in 1981. Large though it is, the last figure accounted for less than 5 percent of Iraq's total import spending in that year. A number of American companies—among them Boeing, Lummus, John Deere, International Harvester, IBM, and Caterpillar—profited from these development expenditures. Although Iraqi purchases had declined substantially by the second year of the war, the trend toward using Western technology, expertise, and products had accelerated.

Oil wealth also affected Iraq's standing in third-world countries and other Arab states, having increased its influence within organizations such as OPEC, the Organization of Arab Petroleum Exporting Countries, and the Arab League, and among nonaligned states. Leaders of the Ba'th party have said that Iraq's increased capacity for influence and their own failures of the 1970s made them more sensitive to their domestic and foreign responsibilities. As one Iraqi expressed it, "In the late 1960s we were a ruling elite in our thirties and now we are an elite in our mid-forties. We are maturing and remain conscious of our errors." An ambitious foreign aid program begun after 1975 improved Iraq's image and its ability to "call in debts" as necessary. Jordan, for example, received over $200 million from Iraq in 1979, more than it received from either the United States or Saudi Arabia; and Syria received approximately $94 million in that year. Pursuant to these new tactics, Iraq proposed a scheme in 1979 whereby the Arab oil producers and industrialized states would provide a comprehensive program of economic assistance to third-world countries generally.

To predict the level of Iraq's future oil production or the way in which oil revenues will be used is impracticable, given the uncertainties arising from continuation of the war, the question of reparations, and the stability of the present regime. Nevertheless, if the human and material losses in the war are not catastrophic, and particularly if the present civilian faction of the Ba'th party remains in power, there is little reason to expect any substantial change in Iraq's long-term plans for internal social and economic development. Indeed, it can be argued that a certain momentum has been established that will impel future governing elites in Iraq to encourage the coherence of an Iraqi nation-state through domestic development, whatever the base of their political support or their ideology. In the short term, however, Iraq's foreign and domestic programs have been significantly reduced or entirely stopped because of the war. Payments to foreign contractors are being deferred, with some exceptions for Western European firms and firms responsible for strategic projects. Until the war ends, therefore, the Iraqi oil industry will be forced to place the highest priority on immediate problems, such as the consequences of the Syrian stoppage of Iraq's oil throughput and sabotage of oil pipelines, rather than on the development of a long-term oil strategy.

The second reason for Iraq's regional and global importance is the country's unique capacity relative to all other countries of the Middle East for long-term economic and social development based on a nonoil economy. Unlike Saudi Arabia and the Gulf shaikhdoms, which are characterized by sparse populations, arid climates, and few resources other than oil, Iraq has numerous assets. It has a larger population and thus a greater capacity to absorb oil revenues. It has a heritage of diverse economic, political, and military institutions and experience; a well-developed middle class; and strong socioeconomic links between the rural and urban communities. Most of all, Iraq possesses resources other than petroleum, not the least of which is water, offering the possibility of an expanded economic base in both agriculture and industry. Iraq therefore has been perceived by other Arab states, at least before the war, as a potentially important regional actor. The Iraqi capital of Baghdad and the urban centers of the Tigris and Euphrates river valleys at various historical times have exerted influence on the economic, military, political, and even educational life of the Middle East, while the small and competing amirates of the Gulf and the kingship of central Arabia have lacked political reach and remained virtually unknown to their external worlds until they acquired immense oil revenues in the mid-twentieth century. Also significant is the fact that the two countries—Syria and Egypt—that have social and geographic assets similar to those of Iraq lack Iraq's vast oil resources and hence its potential for development and long-term regional influence.

Another reason for Iraq's importance is its geographic position at the crossroads of current political issues. Bordering two states—Saudi Arabia and Turkey—that are currently identified with Western interests, Iraq occupies an area of strategic concern to both superpowers adjoining the so-called northern tier of Middle Eastern states and close to the Soviet frontier. It also occupies a pivotal position between Israel to the west and the Gulf to the east, where it forms the eastern flank of the Arab world.

Finally, the war itself draws attention to Iraq as an economic and political actor, for the outcome will affect not only the two combatants but also regional relations in the Middle East and the interests of outside powers. The economic stakes are readily apparent. The political stakes are less defined but hold the potential for dramatic change, in that the tension between Arab nationalism and Islamic conservatism is manifested in an extreme form by the governing elites in Iraq and Iran. The rationale for starting the war in 1980, the effectiveness with which it was conducted, and the way in which the war is justified afterward will affect not only the legitimacy of the two governments but also the content of political debate elsewhere in the Middle East. The debate already is sharpened by Soviet and American involvement in the region and by disparities of social and economic development in Middle Eastern countries. Because most of those countries have no institutionalized procedures for the voicing of legitimate opposition and 50 to 70 percent of their populations are under twenty-five years of age, politics becomes at times not only intense but also clandestine and antigovernment. The war is closely watched by ruling elites throughout the Middle East and by their opponents. Whatever its outcome, the conflict will affect the content of political dialogue in the region, perhaps even mark the onset of widespread political unrest.

The most dramatic outcome of the war would be the dismemberment of Iraq. Such a development, especially if an outside power were involved, would bring bitter recriminations from most Arab states and raise serious questions about their own stability and the value of their alliances. Dismemberment would be tantamount to opening a Pandora's box, creating a large, unstable frontier region in which the surrounding states would have conflicting claims, both to territory and to religious and ethnic groups. The encouragement of nationalist sentiment among Iraqi Kurds, as one example, would create severe problems for neighboring states having large Kurdish populations. As a strong and cohesive nation-state, however, Iraq has the potential to act as a buffer and an ally—economically, politically, militarily—for neighboring countries.

In fact, Iraq's capacity for regional influence has increased since 1975 and has been further heightened by the cumulative experience gained by the Ba'thists since 1968, which they admit has forced them to be more realistic in their expectations and pragmatic in their actions despite their radical rhetoric. Evidence of their pragmatism is found in their policy decisions relating to the Kurdish Autonomous Region in the early 1970s, their restraint in the Jordanian crisis of 1970, their caution in the October 1973 war, their increased production of oil during the 1970s, their qualified support of Palestinian groups, their signing of the Algiers Declaration and subsequent treaty of 1975, their positive intervention in the crisis between the two Yemens in 1979, their program of increased foreign aid to third-world countries since the mid-1970s, their harsh condemnation of both the Soviet invasion of Afghanistan and the Iranian seizure of American hostages in 1979, their restrained and professional diplomatic reaction at the United Nations to Israel's bombing of the nuclear reactor in 1981, their continued support for the restoration of peace in Lebanon, their reformulation of the concept of pan-Arab unity and their statement regarding Israel's right to security in 1982, their support of an arrangement for the withdrawal of foreign forces from Lebanon in May 1983, and their expulsion from Iraq of several terrorist groups that same year.

Constraints on Domestic and Foreign Policies

Three fundamental and related considerations will shape the internal and external policies of the Iraqi government regardless of the ideological inclinations of the ruling elite or the foundations of its political support within Iraq. One is that geographic features and resources unique to Iraq will continue to exert a decisive influence on patterns of settlement and human interchange within the nation-state and between Iraq and foreign countries. The second is Iraqi pluralism, embodied in distinct regional economies as well as in numerous cultural, ethnic, linguistic, and religious groups that reflect the influence of geography and the area's historical position as a frontier region. The third is that Iraq is the eastern flank of the Arab world bordering non-Arab Turkey and Iran, and as such has been considered essential to the strategic depth of the Arab nation, even by non-Iraqi Arabs.

These geographic and demographic constraints will place heavy but predictable burdens on the government. Domestically, there are at least five. First, the primary objective of any Iraqi government will be the internal consolidation of the nation-state and the establishment of a stable central governing authority that ultimately would achieve legitimacy in the perceptions of Iraq's numerous particularistic groups. Second, overlapping and at times conflicting symbols of personal identity such as religion, ethnicity, and language will remain vibrant forces in Iraq's domestic political life. Third, the availability of renewable water resources and the fact that some 30 to 40 percent of the Iraqi population remains employed in agriculture, in contrast to less than 3 percent in the oil sector, means that the government must continue to focus attention on both agriculture and irrigation. Fourth, there will be continued emphasis on coordinating and integrating the economic, political, and social interests of the three dominant Iraqi cities—Mosul, Baghdad, and Basra—and on increasing the links between rural and urban areas. Finally, and most important, Iraqis will continue to find their domestic affairs susceptible to external interference, a susceptibility arising from Iraq's geographical position as a frontier. Indeed, the frontier position has contributed to the pluralistic character of Iraqi society and continues to heighten and to multiply all Iraqi concerns.

In foreign affairs, the government must carry at least four predictable burdens. First, Iraq's frontier position and the fact that it is virtually landlocked give Iraqis an acute sense of their vulnerabilities. This sense has often led to offensive solutions, although Iraqis also recognize that good relations between them and their neighbors are valuable if not imperative. It is not coincidental that Iraq was among the first Arab countries to bring Turkey into the spheres of Arab commerce and politics; that Khomeini's talk of exporting the Islamic revolution and of the dangers of Arab nationalism was of direct and immediate concern to Iraq, the only Arab country bordering Iran and a country whose governments always have encouraged tolerance among its various ethnic and religious groups; or that, of the countries that have large Kurdish populations, Iraq is the only one that has sought to give its Kurdish population a degree of autonomy. Second, as long as oil is the mainstay of the Iraqi economy, Gulf security and Iraq's access to the Gulf will be constant sources of concern. Third, Iraq's acute sense of its vulnerabilities has resulted in an Iraqi centrism that has dominated the priorities of every Iraqi government since the revolution of 1958, regardless of the government's ideological orientation or its rhetoric. No future treaty or agreement, whether with neighbors or with the superpowers, that does not effectively quell these concerns can be expected to contribute to peaceful relations for long.

Finally, these strategic concerns will continue to make Iraq susceptible to superpower pressures, complicating its foreign relations. Therefore, unless overwhelming external pressure is placed upon Iraq, as occurred in the first half of the 1970s when the government was forced to seek a single strong alliance partner, it is probable that the trend toward nonalignment and the diversification of trading partners will continue under the present leadership. A different wing of the Ba'th party, a new military government, or even the high costs of the Iran-Iraq war under the present leadership, however, might create a situation in which nonalignment is seen as a weakness rather than a strength and lead the government to ally itself again with a single strong partner.

As is the case in other countries, Iraq's perceptions of its internal dynamics and strategic vulnerabilities undoubtedly affect the form and content of its foreign relations. A genuine understanding between Iraq and other states can occur only when areas of overlapping concern are recognized and sensitive Iraqi problems are respected as such by external powers. Therefore, let us digress briefly to consider how Soviet and American actions toward Iraq have affected Iraqi perceptions of their strategic interests.

The Soviet Union has acted toward Iraq with ambivalence and, not surprisingly, Iraq has responded in kind. On the other hand, the USSR regards Iraq as strategically important because of Iraq's geographic propinquity to its own borders and to its own sensitive Muslim population centers. Therefore, under certain conditions, the Soviets would like to realize Iraq's potential as a strong regional client. On the other hand, Iraq's adversary, Iran, has had greater strategic value since the Soviet invasion of Afghanistan. The Soviets also know that the historic Ba'thist hostility to Communist party activity in Iraq and the Ba'thist emphasis on nonalignment will make a firm state-to-state alliance troublesome as long as the present civilian wing of the Ba'th party remains in power, continues to pursue nonalignment, and can obtain assistance from other Arab states and from Western Europe. Thus, when the Iran-Iraq war began, the Soviets hoped to profit from the collapse of American influence in Iran and halted a large arms shipment for which Iraq already had paid between $1 billion and $2 billion. Only when Soviet interests in Iran began to suffer after 1981 did the USSR seek to ameliorate its position by resuming arms transfers to Iraq. Even later, it sought to appeal to both sides in the war by declaring that it was in everyone's interest to end the conflict as soon as possible, although there is no evidence that Moscow contributed to this end in any constructive way.

Political uncertainties that followed the temporary cessation of Arab assistance to Iraq in 1982 and American preoccupation with Lebanon, as well as American pressure on France in 1983 not to sell Iraq advanced weapons, led Iraqi authorities to restrain their criticism of Soviet activities. In conversation Iraqis nevertheless show their mistrust of Soviet motives. The most flagrant example of Soviet double-dealing, Iraqis say, was the cessation of Soviet arms shipments during the Kurdish dispute in the mid-1970s and again in the Iran-Iraq war despite the treaty of friendship signed in 1972. As an Iraqi official told me privately, "What we really must admire about the United States, irrespective of her Middle East policies, with which we disagree, is the steadfastness she displays toward her ally, Israel. This despite all that Israel has done to embarrass your government and president." Relations between Iraq and the Soviet Union deteriorated to such an extent that in the late 1970s the Iraqi Ba'thists began an intensive purge of Communists in the military and civilian government bureaucracy and criticized Communist party activities in other Arab countries. The Iraqi Communist leaders fled the country and the remaining members went underground. While no reasons were explicitly given for these actions, it is significant that Iraqi Ba'thists privately warned third-world governments to be careful in sending their people to the Soviet Union for military training because the Soviets "convert" military officers, return them to "subvert" the internal politics of their home countries, and as a state expect "too much in return." Relations between Iraq and the Soviet Union plummeted further in the 1970s because of Soviet involvement in the Horn of Africa and the Soviet invasion of Afghanistan, which Iraq was the first Arab country to condemn.

American attitudes toward Iraq have become increasingly ambivalent since diplomatic relations were formally severed in 1967. Although Iraq remained a relatively unknown quantity in Washington after the revolution of 1958, the prevalent impression in many American quarters was that of a state run by successive military governments and, after 1968, by radical pro-Soviet extremists. This stereotype precluded serious consideration of Iraq as a potential pro-Western ally or even as a country with which to initiate dialogue, the more so in that the U.S. position on Iraq has been viewed through the prism of American relations with Israel and, before the fall of the shah, with Iran. More recently, Israel's bombing of Iraq's nuclear reactor in 1981 and its supply of military equipment to Iran during the war were thought by many Arabs to have had American approval. Whether the United States has been involved in such activities or could make them stop is less important than the perception that American foreign policy may be designed to create internal tensions among and within Middle Eastern states, serving the interests of Israel by keeping the Arabs weak and disunited. Such Arab perceptions have undermined the stated U.S. objective of a secure and peaceful Gulf region impervious to Soviet influence and have lent credibility to left-wing and conservative Islamic movements.

Iraq and the West

After the outbreak of war, Washington perceived Iran as having greater strategic importance than Iraq; but an increasing number of terrorist attacks in the Middle East sponsored or condoned by pro-Iranian Shi'i groups, such as the bombing of the Marine headquarters in Beirut, made it less likely than ever that the United States could establish formal relations with the Islamic regime in Tehran. Iraq, on the other hand, was beginning in 1983 to be perceived more favorably by the U.S. executive branch and by some in the Pentagon, in part because expanding media coverage and diplomatic contacts since the late 1970s had begun to give the West a more rational and less biased view of Iraq. Iraq for its part sought to improve its image by curtailing its extremist rhetoric, by expelling several terrorist groups, and by supporting Egypt's readmission to the Islamic Conference Organization and to the Arab League, among other things. The trend toward a thaw in Iraqi-American relations was also encouraged by the regional political situation, which reflected increasing pressure from Islamic conservative groups and fear that an escalation of Arab-Persian hostilities could lead to a cessation of oil shipments from the Gulf.

Since 1983 the U.S. government, while ostensibly remaining neutral in the war, has begun slowly and cautiously to lean toward Iraq. Washington has ended its opposition to French arms sales to Iraq and has urged other countries, such as China and Israel, to restrict or terminate their arms sales to Iran. The United States may also have given military intelligence to Iraq or encouraged other countries to do so. In 1984 it was reported that President Reagan had authorized measures to protect other Arab Gulf states from side-effects of the war and to help prevent Iraq from collapsing under repeated Iranian offensives.[2]

It is unlikely, however, that Iraq in the near or long term will wish to be counted among the pro-Western Arab countries. Optimistically, one might predict an opening toward the West within the framework of nonalignment. Given the domestic and foreign policy concerns of Iraq, there are substantive ways in which that development could be encouraged.

All states have minimum strategic requirements, foremost of which are the security of the state, national cohesion, and access to the resources necessary to function effectively as an economic and political entity. In Iraq these requirements include distribution rights to the waters of the Tigris and Euphrates rivers, economic and political integration of the northern Kurdish and southern Shi'i areas within the state, security of oil reserves and facilities, and guaranteed safe passage for trade through the Shatt al-'Arab and the Gulf. No treaty or policy that fails to guarantee these rights can be expected to ensure for long an attitude of trust or stability in the development of relations between Iraq and its neighbors or with its foreign allies.

Thus a starting point in developing the common interests of Iraq and outside powers would be an expression of mutual commitment to the territorial integrity of nations and respect for the principle of noninterference in the domestic affairs of other countries. The manipulation by foreign powers of Iraqi interest groups such as the Kurds, who have been perpetual pawns in this region, can hardly win the trust of any Iraqi government or even opposition groups, who fully recognize their role as

2. Gerald F. Seib, "Reagan Orders Secret Plan to Shield Other Gulf States as Iran Presses War," *Wall Street Journal*, April 11, 1984.

pawns. As Kurdish leaders, the Barzani family reportedly accepted aid from all corners—the Israelis, the Soviets, the Americans, the shah, and then Khomeini—and thereby lost prestige among the Kurds for showing no discrimination in choosing patrons. Between 1975 and 1979 the Iraqi government had time to improve its standing in the north. The government must have found it ironic that, on the one hand, it was criticized by the West for its harsh repression of the political opposition while, on the other hand, the United States was involved in support of the same opposition groups, as was the Soviet Union.

If a Western country is to have a successful relationship with Iraq, no less than with any other Arab state, it must be sensitive to the powerful symbols of domestic political and social identification that are employed in the Arab world. It should also recognize that public posturing on the part of Arab governments serves many purposes. There is a wide gap between Iraqi rhetoric and the pragmatic and moderate policies of the governing elite. Iraq's extreme use of rhetoric, usually in the form of sharp and uncompromising pronouncements, has unfortunately provided its adversaries with ammunition to oppose or undermine those achievements in Iraq that are real and laudable.

Perhaps Iraqi leaders place such great emphasis on mechanical and often reiterated statements of policy because they are so intent on loyalty within the Ba'th party and on establishing the legitimacy of the government. They might find that open admissions or less dogmatic expressions of the political difficulties they confront would extend their appeal to more segments of the population. This might also lend greater flexibility to the middle ranks of the government and party bureaucracy as well as diminish their radical image in the West. Be that as it may, it is important that the West understand the function of rhetoric in countries such as Iraq, Syria, and Egypt, which have longer histories of political involvement by their populations, have more developed interest groups, and for geographic reasons have been more exposed to foreign influences than have the conservative hereditary Gulf regimes.

Another aspect of Iraqi policy that could be better appreciated, especially by the United States, is nonalignment. Genuine nonalignment is not inconsistent with Western interests. Neutralism, positive neutralism, and Ba'thist nonalignment can best be understood as Iraqi responses to pressures arising from national interests, responses that are pro-Iraqi and pro-Arab. Although the stereotype of Saddam Husain as the "butcher of Baghdad" has obscured the possible common interests of the West and Iraq, nonalignment has had consequences that are not unwelcome to the West. Iraq revealed a common concern for certain principles of international order by becoming the first Arab country to condemn publicly the Soviet invasion of Afghanistan; to agree to a boycott of the Olympic games in the Soviet Union; to oppose the right of any foreign country, including the Soviet Union, to have access to military facilities in Iraq or elsewhere in the Arab world; to criticize vociferously the Iranian capture of American hostages; to increase and reinforce its trade relations with Western Europe, including purchases of Western European military equipment; to guarantee oil supplies to Western European countries, even during the first year of the war; and to become a signatory to the Nonproliferation Treaty, agreeing to abide by its rules and to permit periodic inspections of its nuclear energy facilities by the International Atomic Energy Agency. In addition, Iraq has increased its efforts, particularly since 1975, to solidify its relations with other Arab countries such as Saudi Arabia, Jordan, Sudan, North Yemen, and Egypt.

In domestic affairs, Iraq has taken a forward position among Arab countries in stressing the role and achievements of women in both their personal and professional lives and in implementing a literacy program for the benefit of people in both rural and urban areas. Institutionalization of the Kurdish Autonomous Region, of the National Assembly, and of a civilian government represents further movement toward moderation, albeit gradual and highly regulated by the Iraqi government.

Conclusion

Much of Iraqi political behavior can be understood and anticipated because Iraq is the eastern flank of the Arab world and occupies a frontier position that has aroused strategic concerns and invited human interchange for centuries. This is reflected in the rich diversity of Iraqi social life that is found, for example, in the admixture of Turkish, Kurdish, and Farsi words in Iraq's Arabic dialect; in the similarly diverse origins of Iraqi cultures; and in the recurrent themes of Iraqi political life, particularly the attempts by all Iraqi leaders to unite the country's numerous diverse interest groups and the conflicts between Iraq and Iran.

Whether the Ba'th party's structure and policies are sufficiently strong and flexible to withstand the domestic and foreign challenges of the present difficult period probably will be known only in the aftermath of the war with Iran. Curiously enough, however, it is the social, economic, and political exigencies arising from Iraq's frontier situation that have been responsible for the wide perception among Arabs that Iraqis are tough, ruthless, strong, realistic, and pragmatic. These characteristics are subjective and not easily measured, yet they may be precisely the qualities that lend Iraq and Iraqis the ability to sustain themselves in their challenging environment.

Index

209

212